KNITTED
Cats
& Dogs

KNITTED
Cats
& Dogs

Sue Stratford

Search Press

First published in 2017

Search Press Limited
Wellwood, North Farm Road,
Tunbridge Wells, Kent TN2 3DR

This book uses material from the following
titles published by Search Press:
Knitted Cats & Kittens 2013
Knitted Dog & Puppies 2014

Reprinted 2019

Text copyright © Sue Stratford 2017
Photographs by Paul Bricknell at Search Press Studios

Photographs and design copyright © Search Press Ltd 2017

ISBN 978-1-84448-524-0

Suppliers
If you have difficulty in obtaining any of the materials and
equipment mentioned in this book, then please visit the
Search Press website for details of suppliers:
www.searchpress.com

Materials can also be obtained from the author's
own website: www.suestratford.co.uk

Patterns for the Scratching Post, Cat Bed,
Balls, Dog Bones and Dog Bowl can be
downloaded free from our website at:

https://www.searchpress.com/knittedcatsanddogs

Acknowledgements
The designs in this book would not have been
possible without extensive test knitting and critique
from lots of lovely knitty friends at The Knitting Hut.
They have also been tweaked and improved by the
skilful technical editing of Jacky Edwards.
Thanks also to everyone at Search Press who has
made this book look so fantastic.

Contents

Cats & Kittens

Kitty Kat, page 52

Super Cat, page 62

Alley Cat, page 85

Christmas Cat, page 90

Crazy Kittens, page 20

Tabby Grey, page 25

Fluff Ball, page 30

Sweet Siamese, page 32

Stripy and Tiny, page 36

Cosy Toes, page 40

Ginger Tom, page 43

Rainbow Cat, page 48

Valentino, page 68

Monster Cat, page 72

Fluffy Cat, page 76

Doorstop Cat, page 80

Happy Family, page 94

Mice, page 102

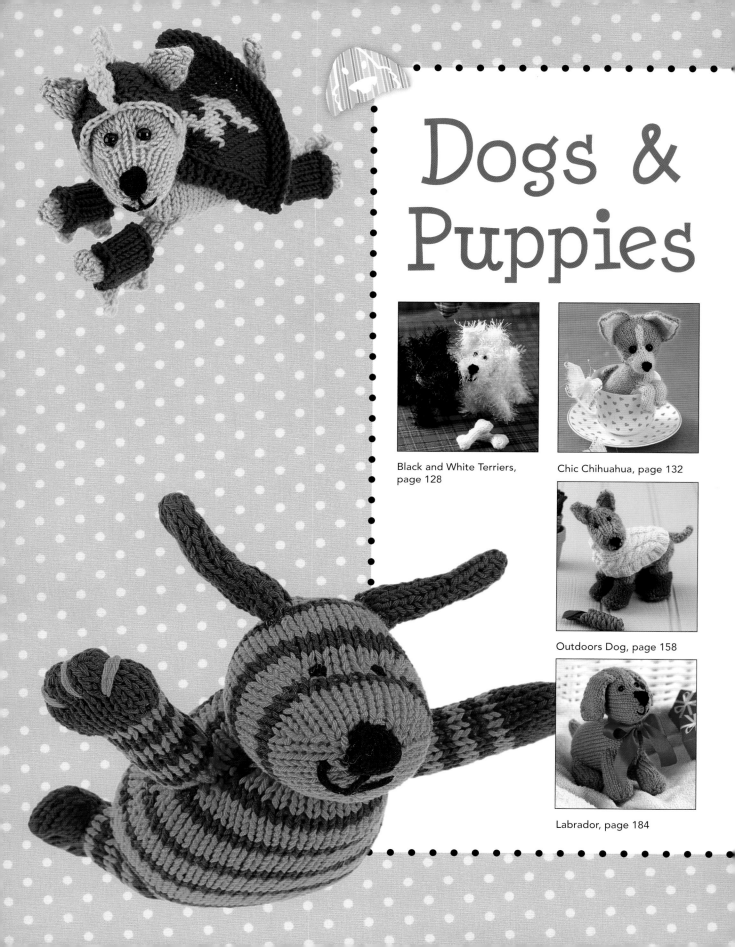

Dogs & Puppies

Black and White Terriers, page 128

Chic Chihuahua, page 132

Outdoors Dog, page 158

Labrador, page 184

Dress-up Dogs, page 106

Stripy Sausage, page 116

Fluffy Floppy Dog, page 120

Circus Dogs, page 124

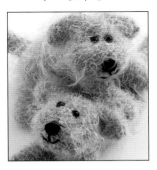
Mischief-makers, page 138

Bullseye, page 142

Stripes, page 148

Pink Poodle, page 152

Christmas Dog, page 164

Danger Dog, page 170

Best in Show, page 176

Sweetheart, page 180

Cuddle Pup, page 188

Introduction

So are you a 'dog' person or a 'cat' person? I seem to be both, which makes it great to see my favourite designs from my first two books combined here in a single volume. I love seeing people's faces when they see my designs, as they are usually chuckling and smiling – it's great to see that reaction!

As the yarns you choose can dramatically alter the look of your kitty or pup, why not use something fluffy and textured and make a real original! If you want to use yarn of a different weight than stated in the pattern, just make sure you use a needle size a couple of sizes smaller than you would usually use with that particular yarn to create a tight knit (so that it holds its shape and the toy filling doesn't show through) and remember that it will come out bigger or smaller than the dimensions on the pattern.

These cats and dogs all have their own personalities (or in the case of the cats, *purr*-sonalities). The designs have been created with both adults and children in mind so please ensure, when attaching bells, eyes, buttons and so on, that they are stitched on firmly and cannot be pulled loose, especially by small, inquisitive hands. I have used toy safety eyes for a lot of the designs, which can easily be bought online. However, you may prefer to embroider the eyes if the finished item is a gift for a child.

I'm a super cat! You'll love knitting me!

It is worth taking some time before you start knitting to look through the techniques used in the book (see page 14), as they will make your finished knit look extra special. One technique I love (and always use) is the backwards loop increase – shown as M1. This is explained on the abbreviations page (see page 192) and is a great way of increasing, which produces a virtually invisible finished result.

I have also suggested leaving a length of yarn on some pieces to enable you to sew the pieces together. This will save fastening off the end of your yarn and then joining in a new one – one less end to darn in! Talking of yarn, the amounts needed are given in grams for the cat patterns and metres (yards) for the dog patterns, as that is how they appeared in the original books.

The sewing up is what gives the creature its character and so it is worth spending some time getting the features right. I suggest using pins to check the position of the eyes before fastening them in place.

There are quite a few projects in this book that would be great for a beginner knitter to try out, such as the Black and White Terriers (page 128), Cosy Toes (page 40) and Monster Cat (page 72), not forgetting the mice (page 102)! If you are looking for a sure-fire winner, you can't beat Super Cat (page 62) and Cuddle Pup (page 188), two of the most popular designs – but which one will be yours?

Materials & tools

Here are just some of the yarns, threads, knitting needles and other materials and equipment I have used to make the cats and dogs in this book.

Yarns

The yarns used have been chosen with the character of each animal in mind. However, you can easily use different yarns to give your cat or dog a completely original look. Just look at the ply or the type of yarn used (DK, aran, laceweight and so on) and this will give you an idea of what thickness to go for. Alternatively, choose a different weight of yarn that is close to the original, but make sure you adjust the needle size used accordingly. This will prevent the shape from distorting when you stuff the cat or dog with toy filling, and the toy filling won't show through the stitches.

The materials list for each project gives the types and colours of the yarns used. In all cases, unless the pattern states how many balls are needed, just one ball or less has been used. Quantities are only provided for projects that require more than one ball.

Knitting needles

You can use any type of knitting needle to make these cuddly characters. For the smaller projects I prefer to use double-pointed needles (DPN) as they are shorter than standard needles and work well when you have relatively few stitches. Where a pattern requires stitch markers, this is stated at the beginning of the pattern.

Threads

I have used a selection of threads for embroidery and whiskers. Embroidery thread has a lovely sheen and is great for mouths and whiskers that are stitched on to the cat or dog. For whiskers that are not stitched flat but are threaded through to give the impression of real whiskers, I have used pre-waxed linen thread, but strong sewing cotton would also work well.

Scissors

These are always an essential in any knitter's kit. Try to find a small pair to keep in your knitting bag for snipping the yarn when knitting separate arms, legs and bodies. Make sure they are nice and sharp.

Filling

All of the animals are stuffed with toy filling, which is safe for children if the cat or dog is intended as a toy. Before you stuff your animal, tease the filling out to stop lumps forming and give an even result. Some of the animals have weighting beads in their bodies or arms and legs. For safety, sew a little cloth bag to put the beads in and stop them escaping, then put the bag of beads into the arm, leg or body before stuffing. Where weighting beads are used, they are listed at the start of the project.

Darning and sewing needles

You will need a blunt-ended darning needle to sew each of the animals together. The size of needle used depends on the weight of the yarn – the thicker the yarn, the larger the needle you will need. Remember to pull the sewing yarn from the base near the knitting when stitching to stop the yarn stretching and breaking.

You will also need a sewing needle for those patterns where eyes and a nose need to be embroidered on, or where a button needs to be sewn on.

Stitch holders

Stitch holders are used in a few of the patterns to 'rest' stitches on while you continue with a different part of the animals. If you have not used them before don't worry, just slide the stitches on to the holder without twisting them and leave them there until the pattern asks you to use them again, then slide them back on to your knitting needle.

Safety eyes

There is a great selection of animal safety eyes to be found online. Different sizes and colours can make a huge difference to your finished cat or dog. Where I have used clear safety eyes for the cats, I have painted the backs of the eyes with gold or silver irridescent nail polish to make the eyes stand out and 'sparkle'. Match the colour of the polish to the eyes; for example, I used gold nail polish on the amber eyes and silver on the blue and green eyes.

As an alternative to safety eyes, I have sometimes used beads, buttons or glass eyes with a metal hook at the back to secure them. These eyes are not suitable for projects intended to be used as toys; always use safety eyes for these. Make sure the eyes are attached securely and the end of the yarn or thread used is fastened properly.

Techniques

I-cord

To make an i-cord, cast on your stitches using double-pointed needles, knit them and slide them to the other end of the same needle. Pull the yarn across the back of the needle and knit the stitches again. Repeat these instructions until the cord is long enough. By pulling the yarn behind the stitches on the needle, you close the 'gap' and give the appearance of French knitting. Alternatively, you can work the stitches in stocking stitch and sew up the seam.

Mattress stitch

This is a really neat way to join two pieces of stocking stitch together. The seam is practically invisible and not at all bulky. Begin by laying the work side by side with the right side facing you. Slip your needle through the horizontal bar between the first and second stitch of the first row on one piece and then repeat this process on the opposite piece. Work back and forth up this line of stitches for about 2.5cm (1in). Gently pull the yarn in the direction of the seam (upwards) and you will see the two sets of stitches join together. Repeat this process until you reach the top of the seam.

Wrap and turn (w&t)

This technique ensures you do not end up with a 'hole' in your knitting when working short row shaping and turning your work mid-row. Slip the following stitch from the left needle to the right needle. Move the yarn from the back to the front of the work, between the needles. Slip stitch back to the left-hand needle. Turn work. After working the short row shaping on the back of the body and reaching a wrapped stitch, pick up the wrap and knit or purl with the stitch it is wrapped around. This gives a very neat result.

Fair Isle technique

Fair Isle is a method of knitting with two colours, in which only a few stitches in the contrasting colour are used. The yarn not being knitted is carried across the back of the work. It is best not to carry the contrasting yarn over more than two or three stitches without 'looping' the main colour around it. This will secure it to the back of the work and avoid large loops appearing.

Intarsia technique

Intarsia is used when knitting a block of contrasting colour. Instead of carrying the spare yarn across the back of the knitting, you work the stitches in the main colour, twist the two colours around each other (to avoid a hole forming), knit the stitches in the contrasting colour, twist again, and carry on in the main colour. This technique avoids having to carry the main colour across the back of your work.

Dress-up Dog's striking black and white sweater is knitted using the intarsia technique. See page 106.

Chain stitch

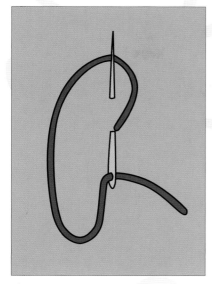
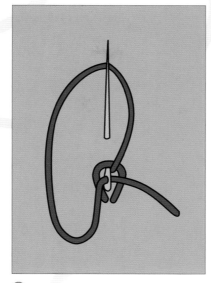
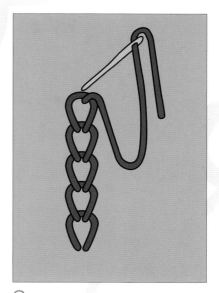

1 Bring your threaded needle from the back of the knitting to the front. Re-insert the needle from the front to the back as close as possible to the point where it first came through, forming a loop. Bring the needle point back through to the front of the knitting a short way from where it went in, so that the needle comes through inside the loop of yarn.

2 Pull the needle through the knitting and loop, remembering not to pull the loop too tightly. To continue, re-insert the needle from the front to the back and repeat the above instructions.

3 Continue in this way to create a 'chain' of stitches.

I have used chain stitches on Super Cat (page 62 and right).

French knot

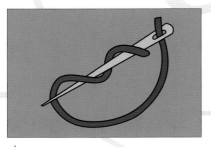 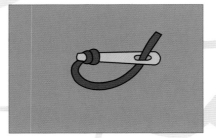 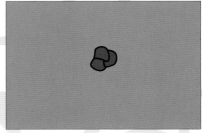

1 Bring the sewing needle through to the front of the work and wind the yarn around the needle twice.

2 Take the needle through the work, half a stitch away, holding the loops around the needle with your fingers while pulling the yarn through to the back of your work.

3 Pull the thread into a knot and fasten off.

I have used French knots on Stripes for his eyes (see right and page 148) and also for Christmas Dog's eyes and nose, and the snowflakes on his sweater (see above and page 164).

Three-needle cast off

A few of the dogs' heads are knitted from the nose towards the back of the head. The cast-off edge then forms the back of the head. By using this technique to cast off, not only do you achieve a really neat finish, but there is one less seam to sew up! You can also use this technique on some of the dogs' legs. This is noted on the patterns.

1 Divide the remaining stitches evenly between two needles. Fold the knitting so that the right sides are together.

2 Using a third needle, knit the first stitch from each needle together.

3 Knit the next stitch from each needle together. Cast off the first stitch in the usual way, by lifting it over the second stitch.

4 Repeat until all the stitches have been cast off. Turn the piece the right way out before sewing up.

Shaping the nose for the dogs

When I was making the dogs I found that sometimes the nose could end up too 'pointy'. By gathering the tip of the nose as shown below, you get a much better shape. Once the knitted nose is sewn on top, all the gathering is invisible.

1 Once you have sewn up the head seam to the point shown, run a length of yarn around the hole this leaves, two or three rows back from the edge (I have used red yarn here for clarity).

2 Tuck the two or three rows inside and gently pull the yarn to gather the wool into shape.

3 Secure the yarn and trim away the excess.

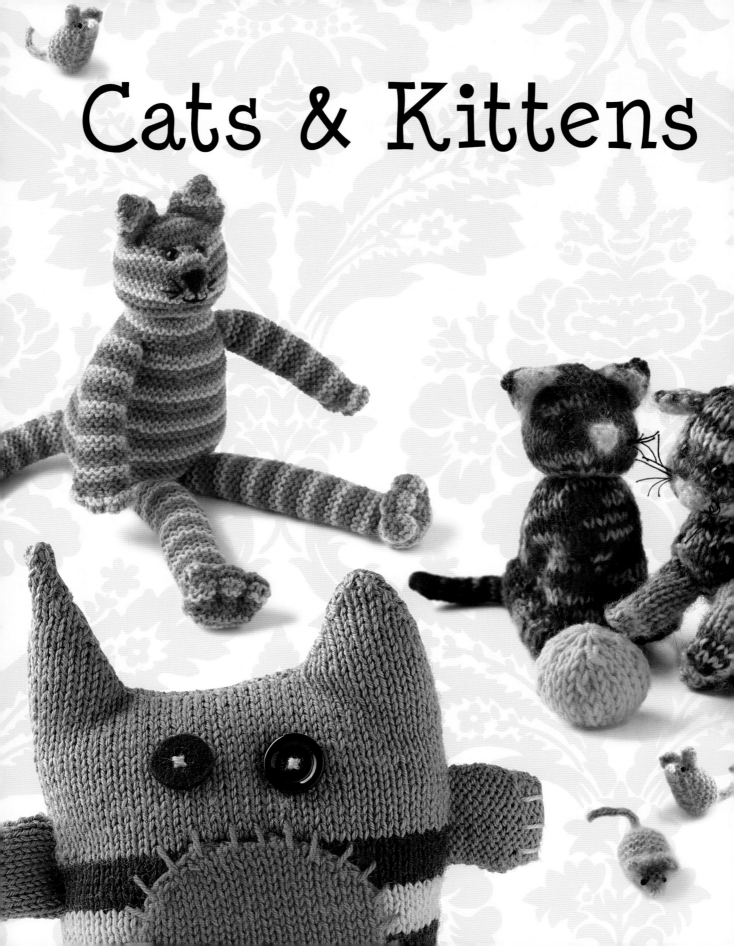

Cats & Kittens

Crazy Kittens

These three mischievous kittens are knitted in sock yarn (soft yet tough, just like them!), and using the variegated variety means that no two kittens will ever be the same! The instructions for making the mice are provided on page 102.

Materials
10g of cream 4-ply (fingering) yarn
15g of self-patterning 4-ply (fingering) sock yarn
Small amount of pale pink 2-ply (laceweight) yarn
Toy filling
Three chenille sticks
Two 4mm (1/8in) black beads
Strong white sewing cotton
Black sewing cotton

Tools
2.75mm (UK 12, US 2) and 2mm (UK 14, US 0) knitting needles
Stitch markers

Tension
7–8 sts to 2.5cm (1in) measured over SS using 4-ply (fingering) yarn and 2.75mm (UK 12, US 2) knitting needles

Size
Approximately 9cm (3½in) tall

Body and front legs
Using cream yarn and 2.75mm (UK 12, US 2) knitting needles, cast on 10 sts and knit 1 row.
Next row: P8, turn.
Next row: K3, turn.
Next row: P3, turn.
Next row: K3, turn.
Next row: Purl to end (10 sts).
Next row: K2, K3B, K5.
Change to sock yarn.
Starting with a purl row, work 5 rows in SS.
Next row: K6, M1, K3, M1, K1 (12 sts).
Starting with a purl row, work 2 rows in SS.
Next row: Cast off 1 st, purl to end (11 sts).
Next row: Cast off 5 sts, knit to end (6 sts).
Next row: Cast on 8 sts, purl to end (14 sts).
Next row: Cast on 1 st, K to last st, M1, K1 (16 sts).
Purl 1 row.
Next row: Knit to last st, M1, K1 (17 sts).
Purl 1 row.
Starting with a knit row, work 20 rows in SS, placing a marker at beg and end of the 10th row.
Next row: Knit to last 3 sts, K2tog, K1 (16 sts).
Purl 1 row.
Next row: Cast off 1 st, knit to last 3 sts, K2tog, K1 (14 sts).
Next row: Cast off 8 sts, purl to end (6 sts).
Next row: Cast on 5 sts, knit to end (11 sts).
Next row: Cast on 1 st, purl to end (12 sts).
Starting with a knit row, work 2 rows in SS.
Next row: K5, ssK, K2, K2tog, K1 (10 sts).
Starting with a purl row, work 5 rows in SS.
Change to cream yarn and knit 1 row.
Next row: P8, turn.
Next row: K3, turn.
Next row: P3, turn.
Next row: K3, turn.
Next row: Purl to end (10 sts).
Next row: K5, K3B, K2.
Cast off.

Next row: K8, **K1**, **M1**, **K3**, **M1**, **K1**, K8 (23 sts).
Next row: P1, M1, P7, **P2**, **M1**, **P3**, **M1**, **P2**, P7, M1, P1 (27 sts).
Next row: K9, **K3**, **M1**, **K3**, **M1**, **K3**, K9 (29 sts).
Next row: P9, **P11**, P9.
Next row: K9, **K11**, K9.
Next row: P9, **P11**, P9.
Next row: K9, **K2**, **ssK**, **K3**, **K2tog**, **K2**, K9 (27 sts).
Next row: P9, **P1**, **P2tog**, **P3**, **P2togtbl**, **P1**, P9 (25 sts).
Next row: K9, **ssK**, **K3**, **K2tog**, K9 (23 sts).
Next row: P8, P2tog, **P3**, P2togtbl, P8 (21 sts).
Next row: K7, ssK, **K3**, K2tog, K7 (19 sts).
Next row: P6, P2tog, **P3**, P2togtbl, P6 (17 sts).
Next row: K1, ssK, K5, **K1**, K5, K2tog, K1 (15 sts).
Break off cream yarn and continue using sock yarn only.
Next row: P1, P2tog, purl to last 3 sts, P2togtbl, P1 (13 sts).
Next row: Cast off 3 sts, K6, cast off rem 3 sts (7 sts).
With RS facing, rejoin sock yarn to rem 7 sts.
Starting with a knit row, work 12 rows in SS.
Next row: K1, ssK, K1, K2tog, K1 (5 sts).
Starting with a purl row, work 3 rows in SS.
Next row: K1, sl1, K2tog, psso, K1 (3 sts).
Purl 1 row.
Cast off.

Belly

Using cream yarn and 2.75mm (UK 12, US 2) knitting needles, cast on 3 sts.
Starting with a knit row, work 2 rows in SS.
Next row: K1, M1, knit to last st, M1, K1 (5 sts).
Starting with a purl row, work 3 rows in SS.
Rep the last 4 rows twice more (9 sts).
Starting with a knit row, work 20 rows in SS.
Next row: K1, ssK, knit to last 3 sts, K2tog, K1 (7 sts).
Starting with a purl row, work 3 rows in SS.
Rep the last 4 rows once more (5 sts).
Next row: K2tog, K1, ssK (3 sts).
Thread yarn through rem sts and fasten off.

Head

Using sock yarn and 2.75mm (UK 12, US 2) knitting needles, cast on 12 sts.
Next row: K1, M1, K5, M1, K5, M1, K1 (15 sts).
Purl 1 row.
Using the Fair Isle technique to carry the yarn (see page 14), work as follows:
Work all sts in **bold** using cream yarn and all other sts using sock yarn.
Next row: K6, M1, **K3**, M1, K6 (17 sts).
Next row: P1, M1, P6, **M1**, **P3**, **M1**, P6, M1, P1 (21 sts).

Ears (make two)
Using sock yarn and 2.75mm (UK 12, US 2) knitting needles, cast on 7 sts.

Starting with a knit row, work 2 rows in SS.

Next row: K1, ssK, K1, K2tog, K1 (5 sts).

Purl 1 row.

Next row: ssK, K1, K2tog (3 sts).

Purl 1 row.

Next row: Sl1, K2tog, psso (1 st).

Thread yarn through rem st and fasten off.

Ear linings (make two)
Using pale pink yarn and 2mm (UK 14, US 0) knitting needles, cast on 7 sts and work as for ears.

Nose
Using a double strand of pale pink yarn and 2mm (UK 14, US 0) knitting needles, cast on 3 sts.

Starting with a knit row, work 2 rows in SS.

Next row: Sl1, K2tog, psso (1 st).

Thread yarn through rem st and fasten off.

Back leg (left)
Using cream yarn and 2.75mm (UK 12, US 2) knitting needles, cast on 10 sts and knit 1 row.

Next row: P5, turn.

Next row: K3, turn.

Next row: P3, turn.

Next row: K3, turn.

Next row: Purl to end (10 sts).

Next row: K5, K3B, K2.

Break off cream yarn and continue using sock yarn only.

Starting with a purl row, work 5 rows in SS.

Next row: K4, w&t.

Next row: P3, w&t.

Next row: K3, w&t.

Next row: P3, w&t.

Next row: K3, w&t.

Next row: Purl to end (10 sts).

Next row: (K1, M1) twice, K3, M1, K1, M1, K4 (14 sts).

Purl 1 row.

Next row: K2, M1, K1, M1, K5, M1, K1, M1, K5 (18 sts).

Purl 1 row.

Next row: Cast off 3 sts, M1, knit to last st, M1, K1 (17 sts).

Next row: Cast off 6 sts, M1, purl to last st, M1, P1 (13 sts).

Starting with a knit row, work 4 rows in SS.

Next row: K1, ssK, knit to last 3 sts, K2tog, K1 (11 sts).

Next row: P1, P2tog, purl to last 3 sts, P2togtbl, P1 (9 sts).

Rep last 2 rows once more (5 sts).

Cast off.

Back leg (right)
Using cream yarn and 2.75mm (UK 12, US 2) knitting needles, cast on 10 sts and knit 1 row.

Next row: P8, turn.

Next row: K3, turn.

Next row: P3, turn.

Next row: K3, turn.

Next row: Purl to end (10 sts).

Next row: K2, K3B, K5.

Break off cream yarn and continue using sock yarn only.

Starting with a purl row, work 5 rows in SS.

Next row: K9, w&t.

Next row: P3, w&t.

Next row: K3, w&t.

Next row: P3, w&t.

Next row: K3, w&t.

Next row: Purl to end (10 sts).

Next row: K4, M1, K1, M1, K3, (M1, K1) twice (14 sts).

Purl 1 row.

Next row: K5, M1, K1, M1, K5, M1, K1, M1, K2 (18 sts).

Purl 1 row.

Next row: Cast off 6 sts, M1, knit to last st, M1, K1 (14 sts).

Next row: Cast off 3 sts, M1, purl to last st, M1, P1 (13 sts).

Starting with a knit row, work 4 rows in SS.

Next row: K1, ssK, knit to last 3 sts, K2tog, K1 (11 sts).

Next row: P1, P2tog, purl to last 3 sts, P2togtbl, P1 (9 sts).

Rep last 2 rows once more (5 sts).

Cast off.

Tail

Using sock yarn and 2.75mm (UK 12, US 2) knitting needles, cast on 7 sts.

Starting with a knit row, work 4.5cm (1¾in) in SS, ending with a purl row.

Next row: K2, K2tog, K3 (6 sts).

Starting with a purl row, work 3 rows in SS.

Change to cream yarn.

Starting with a knit row, work 3 rows in SS.

Thread yarn through rem sts and fasten off.

Making up

Pin the middle of the cast-off end of the kitten's belly to the marker at the tail end of the body and the middle of the cast-on edge to the marker between the front feet. Sew the belly to the sides of the body, being careful not to pucker the front legs when catching the stitches to the belly. Stuff with toy filling as you go.

Thread a chenille stick through the front of the body and slide the ends down inside the front legs. Run a gathering thread through the cast-on stitches of each front leg, pull tightly and secure. Sew the side seam of each front leg, stuffing with toy filling as you go. Sew the cast-off stitches of each front leg to the belly.

Sew the foot and leg seams of each back leg, as for the front legs. Slide a length of chenille stick inside each back leg and stuff lightly with toy filling. Using the photograph for guidance, sew each back leg to the body. Sew the cast-off stitches to the belly.

Sew the tail seam and slide a length of chenille stick inside. Using the photograph for guidance, sew the tail to the back of the body.

Sew the head seams and stuff the head with toy filling. Using the photograph for guidance, sew the nose to the front of the head. Sew the beads in place for eyes. Pull the thread from each eye down to the base of the head and tighten, pulling the eyes in. This gives a realistic shape to the head.

With WS together, sew one ear and one ear lining together to make one ear. Repeat for the second ear. Using the photograph for guidance, sew the ears to the head. Thread strong white sewing cotton through the face to make whiskers. Using black sewing cotton, embroider a mouth. Sew the head to the body.

Tabby Grey

This soft and cuddly tabby will be loved by its proud owner forever! Stitch it firmly, give it a name, and this knitted kitty will bring a smile to children's faces for generations to come. The instructions for the mice are provided on page 102.

Materials
2 x 50g balls of light grey 10-ply (aran) yarn
50g of of dark grey 10-ply (aran) yarn
Small amount of pale pink 4-ply (fingering) yarn
Two 10mm (⅜in) blue plastic safety eyes
Black embroidery thread
Toy filling

Needles
4mm (UK 8, US 6) and 2.75mm (UK 12, US 2) knitting needles

Tension
4–5 sts to 2.5cm (1in), measured over SS using 10-ply (aran) yarn and 4mm (UK 8, US 6) knitting needles

Size
Approximately 17cm (6¾in) long, from front to back of body excluding tail

Body, legs and tail
The body is worked from the back lower edge.
Using light grey yarn and 4mm (UK 8, US 6) knitting needles, cast on 5 sts and knit 1 row.
Next row: Cast on 3 sts, purl to end (8 sts).
Next row: Cast on 3 sts, knit to end (11 sts).
Next row: Cast on 2 sts, purl to end (13 sts).
Next row: Cast on 2 sts, knit to end (15 sts).
Purl 1 row.
Cast on 14 sts, knit to end, turn and cast on 14 sts (43 sts).
Using the Fair Isle technique to carry the yarn (see page 12), work as follows:
Work all sts in **bold** using dark grey yarn and all other sts using light grey yarn.
Next row: (P2, **P3**) three times, P13, (**P3**, P2) three times.
Next row: K1, M1, K1, (**K3**, K2) three times, K11, (**K3**, K2) twice, **K3**, K1, M1, K1 (45 sts).
Next row: P3, (**P3**, P2) three times, P11, (P3, P2) three times, P1.
Next row: (K4, **K1**) three times, K15, (**K1**, K4) three times.

Purl 1 row, carrying the dark grey yarn across the back of the work so it is in the right place for the next row.

Next row: (K4, **K1**) three times, K15, (**K1**, K4) three times.

Next row: P3, (**P3**, P2) three times, P11, (P3, P2) three times, P1.

Next row: K1, K2tog, (**K3**, K2) three times, K11, (**K3**, K2) twice, **K3**, ssK, K1 (43 sts).

Next row: (P2, **P3**) three times, P13, (**P3**, P2) three times.

Next row: Cast off 15 sts, K11, cast off rem 16 sts (12 sts).

With WS facing, rejoin light grey yarn to rem 12 sts.

Purl 1 row.

Next row: K1, M1, K2, M1, K6, M1, K2, M1, K1 (16 sts).

Starting with a purl row, work 19 rows in SS.

Next row: K6, K2tog, ssK, K6 (14 sts).

Purl 1 row.

Shape the front legs:

Next row: Cast on 14 sts, K19, K2tog, ssK, K5, turn and cast on 14 sts (40 sts).

Using the Fair Isle technique to carry the yarn (see page 14), work as follows:

Work all sts in **bold** using dark grey yarn and all other sts using light grey yarn.

Next row: (P2, **P3**) three times, P10, (**P3**, P2) three times.

Next row: K1, M1, K1, (**K3**, K2) three times, K1, K2tog, ssK, K1, (K2, **K3**) three times, K1, M1, K1 (40 sts).

Next row: P3, (**P3**, P2) three times, P6, (**P3**, P2) three times, P1.

Next row: (K4, **K1**) three times, K3, K2tog, ssK, K3, (**K1**, K4) three times (38 sts).

Purl 1 row, carrying the dark grey yarn across the back of the work so that it is in the right place for the next row.

Next row: (K4, **K1**) three times, K3, M1, K2, M1, K3, (**K1**, K4) three times (40 sts).

Next row: P3, (**P3**, P2) three times, P6, (**P3**, P2) three times, P1.

Next row: K1, K2tog, (**K3**, K2) three times, K1, M1, K2, M1, K3, (**K3**, K2) twice, **K3**, ssK, K1 (40 sts).

Next row: (P2, **P3**) three times, P10, (**P3**, P2) three times.

Next row: (K2, **K3**) three times, K4, M1, K2, M1, K4, (**K3**, K2) three times (42 sts).

Next row: P1, M1, P1, (**P3**, P2) three times, P10, (**P3**, P2) twice, **P3**, P1, M1, P1 (44 sts).

Next row: K3, (**K3**, K2) three times, K3, M1, K2, M1, K5, (**K3**, K2) three times, K1 (46 sts).

Next row: (P4, **P1**) three times, P16, (**P1**, P4) three times.

Next row: K22, M1, K2, M1, K22, carrying the dark grey yarn across the back of the work so that it is in the right place for the next row (48 sts).

Next row: (P4, **P1**) three times, P18, (**P1**, P4) three times.

Next row: K3, (**K3**, K2) three times, K5, M1, K2, M1, K7, (**K3**, K2) three times, K1 (50 sts).

Next row: P1, P2tog, (**P3**, P2) three times, P16, (**P3**, P2) twice, **P3**, P2tog, P1 (48 sts).

Next row: (K2, **K3**) three times, K8, M1, K2, M1, K8, (**K3**, K2) three times (50 sts).

Next row: Cast off 15 sts, P18, cast off rem 16 sts (19 sts).

With RS facing, rejoin light grey yarn.

Next row: K1, M1, K8, **K1**, K8, M1, K1 (21 sts).

Next row: P8, **P5**, P8 (21 sts).

Next row: K5, **K11**, K5.

Next row: P2, **P17**, P2.

Next row: K5, **K11**, K5.

Next row:: P8, **P5**, P8

Next row: K10, **K1**, K10.

Rep last 6 rows twice more.

Next row: P8, **P5**, P8 (21 sts).

Next row: Cast on 14 sts, K5, **K11**, K5, turn and cast on 14 sts (49 sts).

Next row: (P2, **P3**) three times, P7, **P5**, P7, (**P3**, P2) three times.

Next row: K1, M1, K1, (**K3**, K2) three times, K6, **K3**, K7, (**K3**, K2) twice, **K3**, K1, M1, K1 (51 sts).

Next row: P3, (**P3**, P2) three times, P7, **P1**, P9, (**P3**, P2) three times, P1.

Next row: (K4, **K1**) three times, K9, **K3**, K9, (**K1**, K4) three times.

Next row: P22, **P7**, P22, carrying dark grey yarn across the back of the work so that it is in the right place for the next row.

Next row: (K4, **K1**) three times, K9, **K3**, K9, (**K1**, K4) three times.

Next row: P3, (**P3**, P2) three times, P7, **P1**, P9, (**P3**, P2) three times, P1.

Next row: K1, K2tog, (**K3**, K2) three times, K6, **K3**, K8, (**K3**, K2) twice, **K3**, ssK, K1 (49 sts).

Next row: (P2, **P3**) three times, P6, **P7**, P6, (**P3**, P2) three times.

Next row: Cast off 22 sts, **K3**, K1, cast off 22 sts (5 sts).

With WS facing, rejoin light grey yarn.

Work the tail as follows:

Next row: Cast on 2 sts, P4, **P1**, P2, turn and cast on 2 sts (9 sts).

Next row: K3, **K3**, K3.

Next row: P1, **P7**, P1.

Next row: K3, **K3**, K3.

Next row: P4, **P1**, P4.

Rep last 4 rows four more times.

Break off dark grey yarn and continue using light grey yarn only.

Next row: (K1, K2tog) three times (6 sts).

Purl 1 row.

Next row: (K2tog) three times (3 sts).

Thread yarn through rem sts and fasten off.

Head

Made in one piece, starting at the bottom of the front of the head.

Using light grey yarn and 4mm (UK 8, US 6) knitting needles, cast on 16 sts.

Starting with a knit row, work 2 rows in SS.

Next row: K1, M1, K6, M1, K2, M1, K6, M1, K1 (20 sts).

Purl 1 row.

Next row: K1, K2tog, K6, M1, K2, M1, K6, ssK, K1 (20 sts).

Purl 1 row.

Rep last 2 rows once more.

Next row: K9, M1, K2, M1, K9 (22 sts).

Purl 1 row.

Next row: K10, M1, K2, M1, K10 (24 sts).

Purl 1 row.

Next row: K11, M1, K2, M1, K11 (26 sts).

Purl 1 row.

Next row: K10, K2tog, K2, ssK, K10 (24 sts).

Next row: P9, P2togtbl, P2, P2tog, P9 (22 sts).

Next row: K8, K2tog, K2, ssK, K8 (20 sts).

Purl 1 row.

Next row: K7, K2tog, K2, ssK, K7 (18 sts).

Purl 1 row.

Next row: K1, K2tog, knit to last 3 sts, ssK, K1 (16 sts).

Next row: P1, P2togtbl, purl to last 3 sts, P2tog, P1 (14 sts).

Rep last 2 rows once more (10 sts).

Starting with a knit row, work 2 rows in SS.

Next row: K1, M1, knit to last st, M1, K1 (12 sts).

Next row: P1, M1, purl to last st, M1, P1 (14 sts).

Rep last 2 rows once more (18 sts).

Starting with a knit row, work 2 rows in SS.

Next row: K1, M1, knit to last st, M1, K1 (20 sts).

Starting with a purl row, work 3 rows in SS.

Next row: K1, K2tog, knit to last 3 sts, ssK, K1 (18 sts).

Purl 1 row.

Rep last 2 rows three more times (12 sts).

Next row: K1, K2tog, knit to last 3 sts, ssK, K1 (10 sts).

Next row: P1, P2togtbl, purl to last 3 sts, P2tog, P1 (8 sts).

Cast off.

Markings, side of head (make six)

Using dark grey yarn and 4mm (UK 8, US 6) knitting needles, cast on 1 st.

Starting with a knit row, work 2 rows in SS.

Next row: Kfbf (3 sts).

Purl 1 row.

Next row: (K1, M1) twice, K1 (5 sts).

Purl 1 row.

Next row: ssK, K1, K2tog (3 sts).

Purl 1 row.

Next row: Sl1, K2tog, psso (1 st).

Thread yarn through rem st and fasten off.

Markings, top of head (make three)

Using dark grey yarn and 4mm (UK 8, US 6) knitting needles, cast on 1 st.

Next row: Kfbf (3 sts).

Starting with a purl row, work 3 rows in SS.

Next row: Sl1, K2tog, psso (1 st).

Thread yarn through rem st and fasten off .

Ears (make four)

Using dark grey yarn and 4mm (UK 8, US 6) knitting needles, cast on 8 sts.

Starting with a knit row, work 2 rows in SS.

Next row: K1, K2tog, knit to last 3 sts, ssK, K1 (6 sts).

Purl 1 row.

Rep last 2 rows once more (4 sts).

Next row: ssK, K2tog (2 sts).

Purl 1 row.

Next row: K2tog (1 st).

Thread yarn through rem st and fasten off.

Nose

Using pale pink yarn and 2.75mm (UK 12, US 2) knitting needles, cast on 4 sts.

Starting with a knit row, work 2 rows in SS.

Next row: ssK, K2tog (2 sts).

Next row: P2tog (1 st).

Thread yarn through rem st and fasten off.

Paw pads (make four)

Using pale pink yarn and 2.75mm (UK 12, US 2) knitting needles, cast on 3 sts and knit 1 row.

Next row: (P1, M1) twice, P1 (5 sts).

Knit 1 row.

Next row: Cast off 1 st, purl to end (4 sts).

Next row: Cast off 1 st, knit to end (3 sts).

Purl 1 row.

Next row: Sl1, K2tog, psso (1 st).

Thread yarn through rem st and fasten off.

Making up

Using the photograph for guidance, attach the safety eyes to the front of the face. Sew the side seams of the head and stuff the head with toy filling. With WS together, sew two ear pieces together to make one ear. Repeat for the second ear. Using the photograph for guidance, pin the ears to the top of the head, allowing enough space between them to attach the three markings for the top of the head. Pin the three markings for the top of the head between the ears.

Pin three side markings to each side of the head. Sew the side and top markings and the ears in place. Using pale pink yarn, sew the nose in place. Using the photograph for guidance and black embroidery thread, embroider a mouth and whiskers.

Fold the body in half from front to back and sew one side seam from the foot of the front leg, along the front leg, along the side of the body and around the back leg. Stuff the legs with toy filling. Repeat for the other side of the body, stuffing the legs and body with toy filling as you go. Sew the back seam of the body. Sew the tail seam, stuffing with toy filling as you go and sew the base of the tail to the body.

Sew a paw pad in place to the bottom of each leg, using the photograph on page 25 for guidance. Using pale pink yarn, embroider four French knots (see page 16) around the front of each paw pad for toes.

Fluff Balls

These comical cats are just about as fluffy as they get! They're quick to knit, and could be turned into brooches, keyrings or even car charms.

Materials
50g of black DK (8-ply) eyelash yarn
Small amount of black fluffy 2-ply (laceweight) yarn
Small amount of pink fluffy 2-ply (laceweight) yarn
Toy filling
Two 6mm (¼in) green glass eyes

Needles
2.75mm (UK 12, US 2) and 3.25mm (UK 10, US 3) knitting needles

Tension
Not crucial; the yarn is knitted on much smaller knitting needles than usual to give a tighter finish

Size
Approximately 6cm (2½in) tall, dependent on tension

Note: The WS will be on the outside as it has a fluffier appearance.

Body
Using black eyelash yarn and 3.25mm (UK 10, US 3) knitting needles, cast on 14 sts and purl 1 row.
Work increase rows as follows:
Next row: K1, (Kfb, K1, Kfb) to last st, K1 (22 sts).
Purl 1 row.
Next row: K1, (Kfb, K3, Kfb) to last st, K1 (30 sts).
Purl 1 row.
Next row: K1, (Kfb, K5, Kfb) to last st, K1 (38 sts).
Purl 1 row.
Next row: K1, (Kfb, K7, Kfb) to last st, K1 (46 sts).
Purl 1 row.
Starting with a knit row, work 4 rows in SS.
Next row: K1, (K2tog, K7, ssK) to last st, K1 (38 sts).
Purl 1 row.
Next row: K1, (K2tog, K5, ssK) to last st, K1 (30 sts).
Purl 1 row.
Next row: K1, (K2tog, K3, ssK) to last st, K1 (22 sts).
Purl 1 row.
Next row: K1, (K2tog, K1, ssK) to last st, K1 (14 sts).
Purl 1 row.
Thread yarn through rem sts and fasten off, leaving a length of yarn for sewing up.

Because I'm knitted in SS, the WS is 'fluffier' than the RS. This is why the WS is on the outside.

Ears (make two)

Using a double strand of black fluffy yarn and 2.75mm (UK 12, US 2) knitting needles, cast on 6 sts.

Starting with a knit row, work 2 rows in SS.

Next row: K2tog, K2, ssK (4 sts).

Purl 1 row.

Next row: K2tog, ssK (2 sts).

Purl 1 row.

Next row: K2tog (1 st).

Thread yarn through rem st and fasten off.

Ear linings (make two)

Using a single strand of pink fluffy yarn and 2.75mm (UK 12, US 2) knitting needles, work as for ears.

Nose

Using a double strand of pink fluffy yarn and 2.75mm (UK 12, US 2) knitting needles, cast on 1 st.

Next row: Kfbf (3 sts).

Starting with a purl row, work 3 rows in SS.

Next row: Sl1, K2tog, psso (1 st).

Thread yarn through rem st and fasten off.

Tail

Using black eyelash yarn and 3.25mm (UK 10, US 3) knitting needles, cast on 7 sts.

Starting with a knit row, work 4 rows in SS.

Next row: K1, M1, knit to last st, M1, K1 (9 sts).

Starting with a purl row, work 5 rows in SS.

Rep last 6 rows once more (11 sts).

Next row: K1, ssK, K1, sl1, K2tog, psso, K1, K2tog, K1 (7 sts).

Thread yarn through rem sts and fasten off.

Making up

Starting at the cast-off edge and with WS facing outwards, sew the side seam of the fluff ball and stuff with toy filling. Thread your needle and yarn through the cast-on sts, gather and secure.

With WS facing outwards, sew the side seam of the tail but do not stuff. Attach the tail to the back of the fluff ball.

With WS together, sew one ear to one ear lining to make one ear. Repeat for the second ear. Using the photograph for guidance, sew the ears to the fluff ball and sew the eyes in place.

Using pink fluffy yarn, gather around the nose to make a ball and sew in place. Trim any longer lengths of yarn around the eyes and nose so that you can see the features.

Sweet Siamese

This Siamese cat is as skinny and sleek as a knitted cat can be, but its bright blue eyes are unmistakably Siamese.

Materials
50g of light brown DK (8-ply) yarn
50g of dark brown DK (8-ply) yarn
Small amount of black 4-ply (fingering) yarn
Small amount of red 4-ply (fingering) yarn
Two 8mm (¹/₃in) blue glass eyes
Black linen thread
Toy filling
Five chenille sticks
Two 2.5cm (1in) diameter coins

Tools
3.75mm (UK 9, US 5) and 2.75mm (UK 12, US 2) knitting needles
Stitch markers

Tension
5–6 sts to 2.5cm (1in) measured over SS using DK (8-ply) yarn and 3.75mm (UK 9, US 5) knitting needles

Size
Approximately 15cm (6in) tall

Body
Using light brown yarn and 3.75mm (UK 9, US 5) knitting needles, cast on 15 sts.
Starting with a knit row, work 4 rows in SS.
Next row: K6, M1, K3, M1, K6 (17 sts).
Purl 1 row.
Next row: K7, M1, K3, M1, K7 (19 sts).
Purl 1 row.
Next row: K1, M1, K7, M1, K3, M1, K7, M1, K1 (23 sts).
Purl 1 row.
Next row: K1, M1, K9, M1, K3, M1, K9, M1, K1 (27 sts).
Purl 1 row.
Next row: K1, M1, K11, M1, K3, M1, K11, M1, K1 (31 sts).
Purl 1 row.
Next row: K1, M1, K13, M1, K3, M1, K13, M1, K1 (35 sts).
Purl 1 row.
Next row: K1, M1, K15, M1, K3, M1, K15, M1, K1 (39 sts).
Purl 1 row.
Next row: K1, K2tog, knit to last 3 sts, ssK, K1 (37 sts).
Purl 1 row.
Rep last 2 rows twice more (33 sts).
Starting with a knit row, work 2 rows in SS.
Next row: K1, ssK, K10, K2tog, K3, ssK, K10, K2tog, K1 (29 sts).
Purl 1 row.
Next row: K1, ssK, K8, K2tog, K3, ssK, K8, K2tog, K1 (25 sts).
Next row: Cast off 9 sts, purl to end (16 sts).
Next row: Cast off 9 sts, knit to end (7 sts).
Starting with a purl row, work 7 rows in SS.
Cast off.

Head
Using light brown yarn and 3.75mm (UK 9, US 5) knitting needles, cast on 8 sts.
Place markers either side of centre 2 sts.
Next row: Knit to M, M1, SM, K2, SM, M1, knit to end (10 sts).
Next row: Purl to M, M1, SM, P2, SM, M1, purl to end (12 sts).
Rep last 2 rows twice more (20 sts).

Next row: Knit to M, M1, SM, K2, SM, M1, knit to end (22 sts).

Purl 1 row, slipping markers.

Next row: Knit to 2 sts before M, ssK, SM, K2, SM, K2tog, knit to end (20 sts).

Next row: Purl to 2 sts before M, P2tog, SM, P2, SM, P2togtbl , purl to end (18 sts).

Rep last 2 rows once more (14 sts).

Remove markers.

Starting with a knit row, work 2 rows in SS.

Next row: K2, ssK, knit to last 3 sts, K2tog, K1 (12 sts).

Next row: Cast off 3 sts, purl to end (9 sts).

Next row: Cast off 3 sts, knit to end (6 sts).

Starting with a purl row, work 3 rows in SS.

Next row: K1, M1, knit to last st, M1, K1 (8 sts).

Starting with a purl row, work 5 rows in SS.

Next row: K1, ssK, knit to last 3 sts, K2tog, K1 (6 sts).

Starting with a purl row, work 3 rows in SS.

Next row: K1, ssK, K2tog, K1 (4 sts).

Purl 1 row.

Next row: K1, K2tog, K1 (3 sts).

Purl 1 row.

Cast off.

Please play with me!

Face section

Using dark brown yarn and 3.75mm (UK 9, US 5) knitting needles, cast on 6 sts.

Place markers either side of the centre 2 sts.

Next row: Knit to M, M1, SM, K2, SM, M1, knit to end (8 sts).

Next row: Purl to M, M1, SM, P2, SM, M1, purl to end (10 sts).

Next row: Rep last 2 rows once more (14 sts).

Next row: Knit to M, M1, SM, K2, SM, M1, knit to end (16 sts).

Purl 1 row, slipping markers.

Next row: Knit to 2 sts before M, ssK, SM, K2, SM, K2tog, knit to end (14 sts).

Next row: Purl to 2 sts before M, P2tog, SM, P2, SM, P2togtbl, purl to end (12 sts).

Next row: Rep last 2 rows once more (8 sts).

Next row: Knit to 2 sts before M, ssK, SM, K2, SM, K2tog, knit to end (6 sts).

Remove markers.

Next row: Cast off 2 sts, purl to end (4 sts).

Next row: Cast off 2 sts, knit to end (2 sts).

Cast off.

Ears (make two)

Using dark brown yarn and 3.75mm (UK 9, US 5) knitting needles, cast on 5 sts.

Starting with a knit row, work 2 rows in SS.

Next row: ssK, K1, K2tog (3 sts).

Purl 1 row.

Next row: Sl1, K2tog, psso (1 st).

Thread yarn through rem st and fasten off.

Ear linings (make two)

Using black yarn and 2.75mm (UK 12, US 2) knitting needles, cast on 5 sts.

Starting with a knit row, work 2 rows in SS.

Next row: ssK, K1, K2tog (3 sts).

Purl 1 row.

Next row: Sl1, K2tog, psso (1 st).

Thread yarn through rem st and fasten off.

Nose

Using black yarn and 2.75mm (UK 12, US 2) knitting needles, cast on 4 sts.

Starting with a knit row, work 2 rows in SS.

Next row: (K2tog) twice (2 sts).

Purl 1 row.

Next row: K2tog (1 st).

Thread yarn through rem st and fasten off.

Back leg (right)

*Using dark brown yarn and 3.75mm (UK 9, US 5) knitting needles, cast on 6 sts.

Starting with a knit row, work 2 rows in SS.

Next row: K1, M1, knit to last st, M1, K1 (8 sts).
Starting with a purl row, work 9 rows in SS.*
Next row: Cast off 3 sts, K1, M1, knit to last st, M1, K1 (7 sts).
Change to light brown yarn.
Next row: P1, M1, purl to last st, M1, P1 (9 sts).
Next row: K1, M1, knit to last st, M1, K1 (11 sts).
Rep last 2 rows once more (15 sts).
Starting with a purl row, work 5 rows in SS.
Next row: K1, ssK, knit to last 3 sts, K2tog, K1 (13 sts).
Purl 1 row.
Rep last 2 rows twice more (9 sts).
Next row: K1, ssK, K to last 3 sts, K2tog, K1 (7 sts).
Next row: P1, P2tog, P1, P2tog tbl, P1 (5 sts).
Cast off.

Back leg (left)
Work as for right leg from * to *.
Knit 1 row.
Next row: Cast off 3 sts, P1, M1, purl to last st, M1, P1 (7 sts).
Change to light brown yarn.
Next row: K1, M1, knit to last st, M1, K1 (9 sts).
Next row: P1, M1, purl to last st, M1, P1 (11 sts).
Rep last 2 rows once more (15 sts).
Starting with a knit row, work 5 rows in SS.
Next row: P1, P2togtbl, purl to last 3 sts, P2tog, P1 (13 sts).
Knit 1 row.
Rep last 2 rows twice more (9 sts).
Next row: K1, ssK, K to last 3 sts, K2tog, K1 (7 sts).
Next row: K1, K2tog, K1, ssK, K1 (5 sts).
Cast off.

Front legs (make two)
Using dark brown yarn and 3.75mm (UK 9, US 5) knitting needles, cast on 8 sts.
Next row: K6, turn.
Next row: P4, turn.
Next row: K4, turn.
Next row: Purl to end (8 sts).
Starting with a knit row, work 12 rows in SS.
Join in light brown yarn.
Next row: K2 using light brown yarn, K4 using dark brown yarn, K2 using light brown yarn.
Break off dark brown yarn and continue using light brown yarn only.
Next row: Cast off 2 sts, purl to end (6 sts).
Next row: Cast off 2 sts, knit to end (4 sts).
Cast off.

Tail
Using dark brown yarn and 3.75mm (UK 9, US 5) knitting needles, cast on 8 sts.

Starting with a knit row, work 4 rows in SS.
Next row: K1, ssK, K2, K2tog, K1 (6 sts).
Starting with a purl row, work 7cm (2¾in) in SS from decrease row, ending with a purl row.
Next row: K2, K2tog, K2 (5 sts).
Starting with a purl row, work 3 rows in SS.
Next row: K1, K2tog, K2 (4 sts).
Purl 1 row.
Thread yarn through rem sts and fasten off.

Collar
Using red yarn and 2.75mm (UK 12, US 2) knitting needles, cast on 4 sts.
Starting with a knit row, work in SS until collar is long enough to fit around cat's neck, ending with a purl row.
Cast off.

Making up
Sew the head seam, stuffing firmly as you go. The seam will be at the front of the head, covered by the dark brown face section.

Sew the front seam of the body and stuff with toy filling. Fold the base section up and sew it to the body, adding a little more stuffing if needed and inserting two 2.5cm (1in) diameter coins to support the cat in a sitting position.

Sew the lower part of one back leg seam and slide a length of chenille stick inside. Repeat for the other back leg. Using the photograph for guidance, pin the upper part of each back leg to either side of the body, making sure they are evenly spaced at the back and front of the cat. Sew in place, adding a little toy filling to give the thigh definition. Sew the lower leg to the side of the cat to secure.

Sew the seams of one front leg and slide a length of chenille stick inside. Repeat for the other leg. Sew the front legs to the body on either side of the front seam, making sure they are straight.

Sew the head to the body, with the cast-on edge at the neck and the shaped part of the head at the back. Using the photograph for guidance, pin the face section in place covering the seam at the front of the head and with the cast-on edge at the base of the head. The cast-off edges will form the bridge of the nose. Place a small amount of stuffing behind the face section to give definition and sew it in place.

With WS together, sew one ear piece to one ear lining to make one ear. Repeat for the second ear. Using the photograph for guidance, sew the ears to the top of the head. Using the photograph for guidance, sew the eyes in place. Sew the nose in place using black yarn and embroider a mouth using black linen thread. Thread black linen thread through the face to make whiskers.

Sew the side seam of the tail and slide a length of chenille stick inside. Sew the tail to the back of the body, between the back legs. Place the collar around the cat's neck and sew the cast-on and cast-off edges together.

Stripy and Tiny

This colourful duo are the perfect answer if you are looking for a knitting project that is fast, fun and frivolous! Self-patterning sock yarn works brilliantly, but any oddment of 4-ply (fingering) yarn will look great, too.

Materials

50g of self-patterning 4-ply (fingering) sock yarn
Black sewing cotton
Four small black beads
Toy filling

Tools

2.75mm (UK 12, US 2) double-pointed knitting needles
Stitch markers

Tension

7–8 sts to 2.5cm (1in) measured over SS using 4-ply (fingering) sock yarn and 2.75mm (UK 12, US 2) double-pointed knitting needles

Size

Stripy Cat is approximately 7cm (2¾in) tall and Tiny Cat is approximately 3.5cm (1½in) tall

Stripy Cat

Body and head

Worked in the round.

Cast on 40 sts and join to work in the round.

Knit 1 round.

Next round: K10, PM, K20, PM, K10 (40 sts).

Next round: Knit to 1 st before first M, M1, K1, SM, K1, M1, knit to 1 st before second M, M1, K1, SM, K1, M1, knit to end of round (44 sts).

Knit 2 rounds, slipping markers.

Rep last 3 rounds once more (48 sts).

Knit 6 rounds, slipping markers.

Next round: Knit to 3 sts before first M, ssK, K1, SM, K1, K2tog, knit to 3 sts before second M, ssK, K1, SM, K1, K2tog, knit to end of round (44 sts).

Knit 3 rounds, slipping markers.

Rep last 4 rounds three more times (32 sts).

Next round: K1, ssK, K2, K2tog, K1, SM, K1, ssK, K2, K2tog, K2, ssK, K2, K2tog, K1, SM, K1, ssK, K2, K2tog, K1 (24 sts).

Knit 1 round, slipping markers.

Next round: K1, ssK, K2tog, K1, SM, K1, ssK, K2tog, K2, ssK, K2tog, K1, SM, K1, K2tog, ssK, K1 (16 sts).

Knit 1 round (removing markers).

Next round: (K2tog) eight times (8 sts).

Thread yarn through rem sts and fasten off.

Our bodies are knitted in SS 'in the round' — you don't have to change to purl — you just keep knitting round and round!

Ears (make four)

Worked flat.

Cast on 6 sts.

Starting with a knit row, work 2 rows in SS.

Next row: K1, ssK, K2tog, K1 (4 sts).

Purl 1 row.

Next row: K1, K2tog, K1 (3 sts).

Next row: Sl1, P2tog, psso (1 st).

Thread yarn through rem st and fasten off.

Legs (make two)

Worked flat.

Cast on 10 sts.

Starting with a knit row, work 6 rows in SS.

Next row: (K1, K2tog) three times, K1 (7 sts).

Purl 1 row.

Thread yarn through rem sts and fasten off.

Feet (make two)

Worked flat.

Cast on 3 sts.

Next row: (Kfb) three times (6 sts).

Starting with a knit row, work 4 rows in SS.

Next row: (K2tog) three times (3 sts).

Thread yarn through rem sts and fasten off.

Toes (make six)

Worked flat.

Cast on 1 st.

Next row: Kfbf (3 sts).

Starting with a knit row, work 3 rows in SS.

Next row: Sl1, P2tog, psso (1 st).

Thread yarn through rem st and fasten off.

Tail

Worked flat.

Cast on 8 sts.

Starting with a knit row, work 4 rows in SS.

*****Next row:** K7, w&t.

Next row: P4, w&t.

Next row: Knit to end (8 sts).

Purl 1 row.*

Rep from * to * once more.

Next row: K1, M1, knit to last st, M1, K1 (10 sts).

Purl 1 row.

******Next row:** K9, w&t.

Next row: P6, w&t.

Next row: Knit to end (10 sts).

Purl 1 row.**

Next row: K1, M1, K to last st, M1, K1 (12 sts).

Purl 1 row.

*******Next row:** K11, w&t.

Next row: P8, turn.

Next row: Knit to end (12 sts).

Purl 1 row.***

Starting with a knit row, work 4 rows in SS.

Rep from *** to *** once more.

Next row: K1, ssK, knit to last 3 sts, K2tog, K1 (10 sts).

Purl 1 row.

Rep from ** to ** once more.

Next row: (K1, K2tog) three times, K1 (7 sts).

Purl 1 row.

Next row: (K1, K2tog) twice, K1 (5 sts).

Next row: ssK, K1, K2tog (3 sts).

Thread yarn through rem sts and fasten off.

Making up

Stuff the body with toy filling and sew the bottom seam. Using a running stitch, gather up each side of the body from the bottom upwards for approximately 2.5cm (1in) to give it a rounded shape.

Run a length of sock yarn around the outside edge of each foot and gather each foot into a ball. Repeat for each toe. Sew three toes to each foot, using the photograph for guidance.

Sew the side seam of one leg and sew a foot to the cast-off end of the leg. Repeat for the second leg. Attach the legs to the bottom seam of the body.

Sew the side seam of the tail, stuffing it with toy filling as you go. Attach it to the back of the body.

With WS together, sew two ear pieces together and attach them to the top of the head. Repeat for the second ear. Using a double strand of black sewing cotton, sew the beads firmly in place for the eyes.

Using the photograph for guidance and a double strand of black sewing cotton, embroider a nose and mouth. Thread a double strand of black sewing cotton through each side of the face and trim to make whiskers.

Tiny Cat

Body and head
Worked in the round.

Cast on 24 sts and join in the round.

Knit 1 round.

Next round: K4, PM, K12, PM, K8 (24 sts).

Next round: Knit to 1 st before M, M1, K1, SM, K1, M1, knit to 1 st before second M, M1, K1, SM, K1, M1, knit to end of round (28 sts).

Rep last round once more (32 sts).

Knit 3 rounds, slipping markers.

Next round: Knit to 3 sts before first M, ssK, K1, SM, K1, K2tog, knit to 3 sts before second M, ssK, K1, SM, K1, K2tog, knit to end of round (28 sts).

Work 2 rounds, slipping markers.

Rep last 3 rounds twice more (20 sts).

Knit 1 round, slipping markers.

Rep from * to * (16 sts).

Knit 1 round, slipping markers.

Rep from * to * (12 sts).

Remove markers.

Thread yarn through rem sts and fasten off.

Ears (make two)
Worked flat.

Cast on 4 sts and knit 1 row.

Next row: P1, P2tog, P1 (3 sts).

Next row: Sl1, K2tog, psso (1 st).

Thread yarn through rem st and fasten off.

Legs and feet (make two)
Worked flat.

Cast on 6 sts.

Next row: K4, turn.

Next row: P2, turn.

Next row: K2, turn.

Next row: P2, turn.

Next row: K2, turn.

Next row: P2, turn.

Next row: K4.

Purl 1 row (6 sts).

Starting with a knit row, work 4 rows in SS.

Cast off.

Tail
Worked flat.

Cast on 6 sts.

Starting with a knit row, work 4 rows in SS.

Next row: K1, M1, knit to last st, M1, K1 (8 sts).

Purl 1 row.

*Next row: K6, w&t.

Next row: P4, w&t.

Next row: Knit to end (8 sts).

Purl 1 row.*

Rep from * to * twice more.

Next row: K2, ssK, K2tog, K2 (6 sts).

Purl 1 row.

Next row: (K2tog) three times (3 sts).

Purl 1 row.

Thread yarn through rem sts and fasten off.

Making up
Stuff the body with toy filling and sew the bottom seam. Sew the side seams of each leg and foot and attach the legs to the bottom seam of the body. Sew the side seam of the tail, stuffing it with toy filling as you go. Attach to the back of the body.

Sew the ears in place at the top of the body with the right side at the back (this makes the ears curl forwards). Using black sewing cotton, sew the beads firmly in place for the eyes.

Using the photograph for guidance and a double strand of black sewing cotton, embroider a nose and mouth. Thread a double strand of black sewing cotton through each side of the face and trim to make whiskers.

I'm the tiniest cat in the book!

Cosy Toes

This cosy hot-water bottle cover is perfect for warming your toes on cold winter nights, and would make a loveable Christmas or birthday gift for a child or grandchild.

Materials

2 x 100g of super chunky fur yarn
50g of pink 5-ply (sportweight) yarn
Black embroidery thread
Two 12mm (½in) green plastic safety eyes
Safety cat nose approx. 2cm (¾in) wide
Small hot-water bottle measuring approximately 25 x 15cm (10 x 6in)
Toy filling

Needles

9mm (UK 00, US 13) and 4mm (UK 8, US 6) knitting needles

Tension

2 sts to 2.5cm (1in) measured over SS using fur yarn and 9mm (UK 00, US 13) knitting needles

Size

Approximately 30cm (11¾in) long, from base to top of the head

Note: The WS of the cat will be the outside as it is fluffier than the RS.

Body back

Using fur yarn and 9mm (UK 00, US 13) knitting needles, cast on 12 sts. Starting with a knit row, work in SS until piece is long enough to fit one side of the hot-water bottle when slightly stretched, ending with a purl row.
Cast off.

Body front

Work as for back but work an extra 8cm (3¼in) in SS. (This will overlap at the back of the hot-water bottle to hold the bottle inside.)
Cast off.

Head

The head is worked in one piece.
Using fur yarn and 9mm (UK 00, US 13) knitting needles, cast on 3 sts.
Next row: K1, M1, knit to last st, M1, K1 (5 sts).
Next row: P1, M1, purl to last st, M1, P1 (7 sts).
Rep last 2 rows once more (11 sts).
Next row: K1, M1, knit to last st, M1, K1 (13 sts).
Purl 1 row.
Starting with a knit row, work 3 rows in SS.
Next row: P1, P2tog, purl to last 3 sts, P2togtbl, P1 (11 sts).
Next row: K1, ssK, knit to last 3 sts, K2tog, K1 (9 sts).
Rep last 2 rows once more (5 sts).
Purl 1 row.
Next row: K1, M1, knit to last st, M1, K1 (7 sts).
Next row: P1, M1, purl to last st, M1, P1 (9 sts).
Rep last 2 rows once more (13 sts).
Starting with a knit row, work 3 rows in SS.
Next row: P1, P2tog, purl to last 3 sts, P2togtbl, P1 (11 sts).
Next row: K1, ssK, knit to last 3 sts, K2tog, K1 (9 sts).
Rep last 2 rows once more (5 sts).
Next row: P2tog, P1, P2togtbl (3 sts).
Cast off.

Ears (make two)

Using fur yarn and 9mm (UK 00, US 13) knitting needles, cast on 4 sts and knit 2 rows.

Next row: (K2tog) twice (2 sts).

Thread yarn through rem sts and fasten off.

Arms (make two)

Using fur yarn and 9mm (UK 00, US 13) knitting needles, cast on 4 sts. Starting with a knit row, work 2 rows in SS.

Next row: K1, K2tog, K1 (3 sts).

Purl 1 row.

Next row: K1, Kfb, K1 (4 sts).

Starting with a purl row, work 2 rows in SS.

Cast off.

Feet (make two)

Using fur yarn and 9mm (UK 00, US 13) knitting needles, cast on 4 sts and knit 1 row.

Next row: P1, M1, purl to last st, M1, P1 (6 sts).

Starting with a knit row, work 4 rows in SS.

Next row: ssK, K2, K2tog (4 sts).

Purl 1 row.

Cast off.

Tail

Using fur yarn and 9mm (UK 00, US 13) knitting needles, cast on 8 sts. Starting with a knit row, work 4 rows in SS.

Next row: K5, w&t.

Next row: P2, w&t.

Next row: K2, w&t.

Next row: P2, w&t.

Next row: Knit to end (8 sts).

Next row: Purl.

Rep last 6 rows twice more.

Starting with a knit row, work 3 rows in SS.

Next row: (P2tog) four times (4 sts).

Thread yarn through rem sts and fasten off.

Bow

Using pink yarn and 4mm (UK 8, US 6) knitting needles, cast on 10 sts and work 15cm (6in) in GS.

Cast off.

Centre of bow

Using pink yarn and 4mm (UK 8, US 6) knitting needles, cast on 5 sts and work 5cm (2in) in GS.

Cast off.

Ribbon ends (make two)

Using pink yarn and 4mm (UK 8, US 6) knitting needles, cast on 10 sts and work 3cm (1¼in) in GS.

Next row: K1, K2tog, knit to end (9 sts).

Knit 1 row.

Rep last 2 rows seven more times (2 sts).

Next row: K2tog (1 st).

Thread yarn through rem st and fasten off.

Making up

With WS facing outwards, fold the head in half. The cast-on and cast-off edges form the neck edge. Fit the safety eyes and nose in place and sew the side seams of the head. Using the photograph for guidance and black embroidery thread, embroider a mouth and whiskers. Place a small amount of toy filling inside the head to give definition. With WS facing outwards, pin the body front and back pieces together and pin the head in place.

Sew the seams of the body and sew the head to the top of the body. The top of the hot-water bottle will fit into the head. Sew the ears to the top of the head. Fold the flap from the front of the cover to the back and sew it neatly to the side seams.

With WS facing outwards, fold the tail in half lengthways and sew the seam. Attach the tail to the seam on one side of the cat.

Fold one foot in half and sew the seams. Repeat for the second foot. Sew the feet to the base of the cover. Repeat for the arms, but sew them to the side seams of the body.

Make the bow by folding the main part of the bow in half and sewing the seam. This seam will be at the back. Place the bow centre around the middle of the main bow and sew each end together, tightening it to make the bow look tied. Using the photograph for guidance, sew each short ribbon end in place behind the bow at an angle. Put the ribbon around the cat's neck, sewing each end together at the front. Sew one bow firmly to the ribbon, covering the join.

Ginger Tom

This cat's really got the cream – too much, perhaps, but although he's a little overweight he's very cuddly, and his squashy belly means he is as comfortable sitting up as he is lying down. You'll just love this gorgeous ginger tom!

Materials
50g of cream 5-ply (sportweight) yarn
50g of orange 5-ply (sportweight) yarn
Small amount of pink 4-ply (fingering) yarn
Black embroidery thread
Two 8mm (1/3in) plastic safety eyes
Toy filling

Tools
3.25mm (UK 10, US 3) and 2.75mm
(UK 12, US 2) knitting needles
Two stitch markers

Tension
6 sts to 2.5cm (1in) measured over SS using 5-ply
(sportweight) yarn and 3.25mm (UK 10, US 3)
knitting needles

Size
Approximately 19cm (7½in) tall

Body back
Note: When working the back of the body, you start by creating a triangular shape, which will be the base of the cat. You then need to pick up the stitches along the decreased edges over the next two rows to join the base to what will be the rest of the body. It is important that you pick up the stitches knitwise or purlwise as indicated, so that you don't get a line on the right side of the body.

Using cream yarn and 3.25mm (UK 10, US 3) knitting needles, cast on 12 sts.

Starting with a knit row, work 4 rows in SS.

Next row: K1, ssK, knit to last 3 sts, K2tog, K1 (10 sts).
Purl 1 row.

Next row: K1, ssK, knit to last 3 sts, K2tog, K1 (8 sts).

Next row: P1, P2togtbl, purl to last 3 sts, P2tog, P1 (6 sts).

Next row: K6, pick up 5 sts knitwise along decreased edge and knit these sts (11 sts).

Next row: P11, pick up 5 sts purlwise along decreased edge and purl these sts (16 sts).

Next row: K1, M1, knit to last st, M1, K1 (18 sts).

Next row: P1, M1, purl to last st, M1, P1 (20 sts).

Rep last 2 rows once more (24 sts).

Make two mini balls of orange yarn and use one mini ball at each side of the work.

Using the intarsia technique to carry the yarn (see page 14), work as follows:

Work all sts in **bold** using orange yarn and all other sts using cream yarn.

Next row: K2, K20, **K2**.

Next row: P4, P16, **P4**.

Next row: K7, K10, **K7**.

Next row: P4, P16, **P4**.

Next row: K2, K20, **K2**.

Purl 1 row using cream yarn.

Rep last 6 rows once more.

Next row: K2, K20, **K2**.

Next row: P4, P16, **P4**.

Next row: K7, K1, ssK, K4, K2tog, K1, **K7** (22 sts).

Next row: P4, P14, **P4**.

Next row: K2, K6, ssK, K2, K2tog, K6, **K2** (20 sts).

Break off orange yarn and continue using cream yarn only.
Purl 1 row.

Next row: K1, ssK, K5, K2tog, ssK, K5, K2tog, K1 (16 sts).
Purl 1 row.

Next row: K1, ssK, K4, K2tog, K4, K2tog, K1 (13 sts).
Purl 1 row.

Next row: K1, ssK, knit to last 3 sts, K2tog, K1 (11 sts).
Purl 1 row.

Next row: K1, ssK, knit to last 3 sts, K2tog, K1 (9 sts).
Purl 1 row.

Cast off.

Body front

Using cream yarn and 3.25mm (UK 10, US 3) knitting needles, cast on 8 sts and purl 1 row.

Next row: K1, M1, (K2, M1) three times, K1 (12 sts).
Purl 1 row.

Next row: K1, M1, K3, M1, K4, M1, K3, M1, K1 (16 sts).
Purl 1 row.

Next row: K1, M1, K4, M1, K6, M1, K4, M1, K1 (20 sts).
Purl 1 row.

Next row: K1, M1, K5, M1, K8, M1, K5, M1, K1 (24 sts).
Purl 1 row.

Next row: K1, M1, K6, M1, K10, M1, K6, M1, K1 (28 sts).

Make two mini balls of orange yarn and use one mini ball at each side of the work.

Using the intarsia technique to carry the yarn (see page 14), work as follows:

Work all sts in **bold** using orange yarn and all other sts using cream yarn.

Next row: P2, P24, **P2**.

Next row: K4, K20, **K4**.

Next row: P7, P14, **P7**.

Next row: K4, K20, **K4**.

Next row: P2, P24, **P2**.

Knit 1 row.

Rep last 6 rows once more.

Next row: P2, P24, **P2**.

Next row: K4, K4, ssK, K8, K2tog, K4, **K4** (26 sts).

Next row: P7, P12, **P7**.

Next row: K4, K4, ssK, K6, K2tog, K4, **K4** (24 sts).

Next row: P2, P20, **P2**.

Break off orange yarn and continue using cream yarn only.

Next row: K8, ssK, K4, K2tog, K8 (22 sts).
Purl 1 row.

Next row: K1, ssK, K5, K2tog, K2, ssK, K5, K2tog, K1 (18 sts).
Purl 1 row.

Next row: K1, ssK, K4, K2tog, ssK, K4, K2tog, K1 (14 sts).

Next row: P1, P2tog, purl to last 3 sts, P2togtbl, P1 (12 sts).

Next row: K1, ssK, K2, K2tog, K2, K2tog, K1 (9 sts).

Next row: P1, P2tog, P3, P2togtbl, P1 (7 sts).

Cast off.

Head

Made in one piece starting from the lower front edge.

Using cream yarn and 3.25mm (UK 10, US 3) knitting needles, cast on 9 sts and knit 1 row.

Next row: P1, M1, purl to last st, M1, P1 (11 sts).

Make two mini balls of orange yarn and use one mini ball at each side of the work.

Using the intarsia technique to carry the yarn (see page 14), work as follows:

Work all sts in **bold** using orange yarn and all other sts using cream yarn.

Next row: **K1**, M1, knit to last st, M1, **K1** (13 sts).

Next row: P1, **M1**, **P3**, P1, M1, P3, M1, P1, **P3**, **M1**, **P1** (17 sts).

Next row: K3, K4, M1, K3, M1, K4, **K3** (19 sts).

Next row: P8, M1, P3, M1, P8 (21 sts).

Next row: K2, K7, M1, K3, M1, K7, **K2** (23 sts).

Next row: P3, P17, **P3**.

Next row: K2, K19, **K2**.

Purl 1 row using cream yarn.
Next row: **K2**, K7, ssK, K1, K2tog, K7, **K2** (21 sts).
Next row: **P4**, P4, P2tog, P1, P2togtbl, P4, **P4** (19 sts).
Next row: **K2**, K5, ssK, K1, K2tog, K5, **K2** (17 sts).
Purl 1 row.
Next row: K1, ssK, K3, **K1**, K3, **K1**, K3, K2tog, K1 (15 sts).
Next row: P1, P2tog, P2, **P1**, P3, **P1**, P2, P2togtbl, P1 (13 sts).
Next row: Row 17: K1, ssK, **K3**, K1, **K3**, K2tog, K1 (11 sts).
Next row: P2, **P3**, P1, **P3**, P2.
Next row: K1, M1, K1, **K3**, K1, **K3**, K1, M1, K1 (13 sts).
Next row: P1, M1, P3, **P1**, P3, **P1**, P3, M1, P1 (15 sts).
Next row: **K2**, K3, **K1**, K3, **K1**, K3, **K2**.
Next row: **P4**, P7, **P4**.
Next row: **K2**, K11, **K2**.
Purl 1 row.
Next row: **K2**, K11, **K2**.
Next row: **P3**, P9, **P3**.
Next row: **K2**, K11, **K2**.
Purl 1 row.
Next row: **K3**, K9, **K3**.
Next row: **P4**, P7, **P4**.
Next row: **K1**, **ssK**, K9, **K2tog**, **K1** (13 sts).
Next row: **P1**, **P2tog**, P7, **P2togtbl**, **P1** (11 sts).
Break off orange yarn and continue in cream yarn only.
Knit 1 row.
Purl 1 row.
Cast off.

Ears (make four)

Using orange yarn and 3.25mm (UK 10, US 3) knitting needles, cast on 7 sts.
Starting with a knit row, work 2 rows in SS.
Next row: K2tog, knit to last 2 sts, ssK (5 sts).
Purl 1 row.
Rep last 2 rows once more (3 sts).
Next row: Sl1, K2tog, psso (1 st).
Thread yarn through rem st and fasten off.

Nose

Using pink yarn and 2.75mm (UK 12, US 2) knitting needles, cast on 5 sts.
Starting with a knit row, work 2 rows in SS.
Next row: K2tog, K1, ssK (3 sts).
Purl 1 row.
Next row: Sl1, K2tog, psso (1 st).
Thread yarn through rem st and fasten off.

Arms (make two)

Using cream yarn and 3.25mm (UK 10, US 3) knitting needles, cast on 12 sts.
Make two mini balls of orange yarn and use one mini ball at each side of the work.
Using the intarsia technique to carry the yarn (see page 14), work as follows:
Work all sts in **bold** using orange yarn and all other sts using cream yarn.
Knit 1 row.
Next row: **P2**, (P3, **P2**) twice.
Next row: **K3**, K1, **K4**, K1, **K3**.
Next row: **P2**, (P3, **P2**) twice.
Rep last 4 rows once more.
Break off orange yarn and continue using cream yarn only.
Starting with a knit row, work 2 rows in SS.
Next row: K1, M1, K4, M1, K2, M1, K4, M1, K1 (16 sts).
Starting with a purl row, work 3 rows in SS.
Next row: K1, ssK, K2, K2tog, K2, ssK, K2, K2tog, K1 (12 sts).
Cast off.

Legs (make two)

Using cream yarn and 3.25mm (UK 10, US 3) knitting needles, cast on 14 sts.
Starting with a knit row, work 2 rows in SS.
Using the intarsia technique to carry the yarn (see page 14), work as follows:
Work all sts in **bold** using orange yarn and all other sts using cream yarn.
Next row: **K2**, (K4, **K2**) twice.
Next row: **P3**, P2, **P4**, P2, **P3**.
Next row: **K2**, (K4, **K2**) twice.
Purl 1 row.
Knit 1 row.

Next row: **P2**, (P4, **P2**) twice.
Next row: **K3**, K2, **K4**, K2, **K3**.
Next row: **P2**, (P4, **P2**) twice.
Break off orange yarn and continue using cream yarn only.
Knit 1 row.
Purl 1 row.
Cast off.

Feet (make two)

Using cream yarn and 3.25mm (UK 10, US 3) knitting needles, cast on 6 sts and knit 1 row.
Next row: P1, M1, purl to last st, M1, P1 (8 sts).
Next row: K1, M1, knit to last st, M1, K1 (10 sts).
Starting with a purl row, work 5 rows in SS.
Next row: K1, ssK, knit to last 3 sts, K2tog, K1 (8 sts).
Purl 1 row.
Next row: K1, M1, knit to last st, M1, K1 (10 sts).
Starting with a purl row, work 5 rows in SS.
Next row: K1, ssK, knit to last 3 sts, K2tog, K1 (8 sts).
Next row: P1, P2tog, purl to last 3 sts, P2togtbl, P1 (6 sts).
Knit 1 row.
Cast off.

Tail

Using cream yarn and 3.25mm (UK 10, US 3) knitting needles, cast on 12 sts.
Starting with a knit row, work 4 rows in SS.
Make two mini balls of orange yarn and use one mini ball at each side of the work.
Using the Fair Isle technique to carry the yarn (see page 14), work as follows:
Work all sts in **bold** using orange yarn and all other sts using cream yarn.
Next row: **K2**, (K3, **K2**) twice.
Next row: **P3**, P1, **P4**, P1, **P3**.
Next row: **K2**, (K3, **K2**) twice.
Starting with a purl row, work 3 rows in SS, using cream yarn.
Rep last 6 rows twice more.
Break off orange yarn and continue using cream yarn only.
Next row: (K1, K2tog) four times (8 sts).
Purl 1 row.
Next row: (K2tog) four times (4 sts).
Thread yarn through rem sts and fasten off.

Making up

Sew the side seams and cast-off edges of each arm, matching the orange markings. Stuff with toy filling. Using the photograph for guidance and orange yarn, oversew the end of each arm with two long stitches to form a paw shape.

Sew the seams of each foot, stuffing with toy filling as you go. Using orange yarn, oversew the end of each foot with two long stitches to form a paw shape, as for the arms.

Sew the side seam of each leg and stuff the legs with toy filling. Sew the bottom of one leg to the top of one foot. Repeat for the second leg and foot.

Pin the body front and back pieces together, positioning the arms and legs in place between the seams of the body front and back pieces. Sew the seams of the body together, stitching the arms and legs in place as you go.

Push the safety eyes through the knitted stitches, using the photograph for guidance. Push the backs securely into place.

Sew the head seams, stuffing with toy filling as you go. With WS together, sew two ear pieces together to make one ear. Repeat for the second ear. Using the photograph for guidance, position the ears on the top of the head seam and sew in place. Sew the nose in place. Using the photograph for guidance and black embroidery thread, embroider a mouth and whiskers.

Using cream yarn, sew from the base of the head to the back of each eye, pull the thread back down to the base and tighten. This gives a realistic shape to the head. Sew the head to the body.

Sew the side seam of the tail, matching the orange markings, and stuff with toy filling. Using the photograph for guidance, sew the tail to the back of the cat.

Rainbow Cat

They say a leopard never changes its spots, but cats can definitely change their stripes! This zany cat is soaking up the sunshine, but try knitting him in blues and purples for a more dreamy night-time mood.

Materials

50g of orange 5-ply (sportweight) yarn
50g of yellow 5-ply (sportweight) yarn
50g of green 5-ply (sportweight) yarn
50g of turquoise 5-ply (sportweight) yarn
Small amount of black 4-ply (fingering) yarn
Two black 8mm (1/3in) plastic safety eyes
Toy filling
Small piece of heavyweight interfacing or card cut to fit inside the base

Needles

3.25mm (UK 10, US 3) and 2.75mm (UK 12, US 2) knitting needles

Tension

6 sts to 2.5cm (1in) measured over GS using 5-ply (sportweight) yarn and 3.25mm (UK 10, US 3) knitting needles

Size

Approximately 32cm (12½in) tall

Stripe pattern

Each piece of the cat is knitted in a two-row garter stitch stripe pattern using 5-ply (sportweight) yarn as follows:
knit 2 rows in orange;
knit 2 rows in yellow;
knit 2 rows in green;
knit 2 rows in turquoise.

Body

Work in two-row garter stitch stripe pattern throughout.
NB: the cast-on row is counted as the first row of the stripe pattern.
Using orange yarn and 3.25mm (UK 10, US 3) knitting needles, cast on 14 sts.
Knit 3 rows.
Next row: K1, M1, knit to last st, M1, K1 (16 sts).
Knit 1 row.
Rep last 2 rows twice more (20 sts).
Knit 14 rows.
Next row: K1, ssK, knit to last 3 sts, K2tog, K1 (18 sts).
Knit 1 row.
Rep last 2 rows twice more (14 sts).
Knit 2 rows.
Next row: Cast on 21 sts, knit to end (35 sts).
Next row: Cast on 21 sts, knit to end (56 sts).
Knit 23 rows.
Next row: K2, K2tog, (K5, K2tog) seven times, K3 (48 sts).
Knit 1 row.
Next row: K2, K2tog, (K4, K2tog) seven times, K2 (40 sts).
Knit 7 rows.
Next row: K1, K2tog, (K3, K2tog) seven times, K2 (32 sts).
Knit 5 rows.
Next row: K1, K2tog, (K2, K2tog) seven times, K1 (24 sts).
Knit 3 rows.
Next row: (K1, K2tog) eight times (16 sts).
Thread yarn through rem sts and fasten off.

Head

Work in two-row garter stitch stripe pattern throughout.
NB: the cast-on row is counted as the first row of the stripe pattern.
Using orange yarn and 3.25mm (UK 10, US 3) knitting needles, cast on 30 sts.
Next row: K7, M1, K1, M1, K6, M1, K2, M1, K6, M1, K1, M1, K7 (36 sts).
Knit 1 row.
Next row: K8, M1, K1, ssK, K6, M1, K2, M1, K6, K2tog, K1, M1, K8 (38 sts).
Knit 1 row.
Next row: K9, M1, K1, ssK, K6, M1, K2, M1, K6, K2tog, K1, M1, K9 (40 sts).
Knit 1 row.
Next row: K10, M1, K1, ssK, K6, M1, K2, M1, K6, K2tog, K1, M1, K10 (42 sts).
Knit 1 row.
Next row: K20, M1, K2, M1, K20 (44 sts).
Knit 1 row.
Next row: K21, M1, K2, M1, K21 (46 sts).
Knit 1 row.
Next row: K22, M1, K2, M1, K22 (48 sts).
Knit 1 row.
Next row: K21, ssK, K2, K2tog, K21 (46 sts).
Knit 1 row.
Next row: K20, ssK, K2, K2tog, K20 (44 sts).
Knit 1 row.
Next row: K19, ssK, K2, K2tog, K19 (42 sts).
Knit 1 row.
Next row: K18, ssK, K2, K2tog, K18 (40 sts).
Knit 1 row.
Next row: K17, ssK, K2, K2tog, K17 (38 sts).
Knit 1 row.
Next row: K1, ssK, knit to last 3 sts, K2tog, K1 (36 sts).
Rep last row twice more (32 sts).

Next row: K6, ssK, K2tog, K12, ssK, K2tog, K6 (28 sts).
Next row: K5, ssK, K2tog, K10, ssK, K2tog, K5 (24 sts).
Next row: K4, ssK, K2tog, K8, ssK, K2tog, K4 (20 sts).
Next row: K3, ssK, K2tog, K6, ssK, K2tog, K3 (16 sts).
Cast off.

Ears (make four)

Work in two-row garter stitch stripe pattern throughout.
NB: the cast-on row is counted as the first row of the stripe pattern.
Using orange yarn and 3.25mm (UK 10, US 3) knitting needles, cast on 8 sts.
Knit 2 rows.
Next row: K1, ssK, knit to last 3 sts, K2tog, K1 (6 sts).
Knit 1 row.
Next row: K1, ssK, K2tog, K1 (4 sts).
Knit 1 row.
Next row: (K2tog) twice (2 sts).
Next row: K2tog (1 st).
Thread yarn through rem st and fasten off.

Nose

Using black yarn and 2.75mm (UK 12, US 2) knitting needles, cast on 5 sts.
Starting with a knit row, work 2 rows in SS.
Next row: K2tog, K1, ssK (3 sts).
Purl 1 row.
Next row: Sl1, K2tog, psso (1 st).
Thread yarn through rem st and fasten off.

Arms (make two)

Work in two-row garter stitch stripe pattern throughout.
NB: the cast-on row is counted as the first row of the stripe pattern.
Using orange yarn and 3.25mm (UK 10, US 3) knitting needles, cast on 14 sts and work 5 repeats of the two-row stripe pattern. Work paw in stripe pattern as follows:
Next row: K1, M1, K5, M1, K2, M1, K5, M1, K1 (18 sts).
Knit 1 row.
Next row: K1, M1, K7, M1, K2, M1, K7, M1, K1 (22 sts).
Knit 3 rows.
Next row: K1, ssK, K5, K2tog, K2, K2tog, K5, ssK, K1 (18 sts).
Next row: K1, ssK, K3, K2tog, K2, K2tog, K3, ssK, K1 (14 sts).
Cast off.

Legs (make two)

Work in two-row garter stitch stripe pattern throughout.
NB: the cast-on row is counted as the first row of the stripe pattern.
Using orange yarn and 3.25mm (UK 10, US 3) knitting needles, cast on 16 sts and work 7 repeats of the two-row stripe pattern.
Cast off.

Feet (make two)

Work in two-row garter stitch stripe pattern throughout.
NB: the cast-on row is counted as the first row of the stripe pattern.
Using orange yarn and 3.25mm (UK 10, US 3) knitting needles, cast on 7 sts.
Knit 1 row.
Next row: K1, M1, knit to last st, M1, K1 (9 sts).
Next row: K1, M1, knit to last st, M1, K1 (11 sts).
Knit 5 rows.
Next row: K1, M1, knit to last st, M1, K1 (13 sts).
Knit 1 row.
Rep last 2 rows once more (15 sts).
Knit 2 rows.
Next row: K1, ssK, knit to last 3 sts, K2tog, K1 (13 sts).
Rep last row once more (11 sts).
Knit 2 rows.
Next row: K1, M1, knit to last st, M1, K1 (13 sts).
Rep last row once more (15 sts).
Knit 2 rows.
Next row: K1, ssK, knit to last 3 sts, K2tog, K1 (13 sts).
Knit 1 row.
Rep last 2 rows once more (11 sts).
Knit 4 rows.
Next row: K1, ssK, knit to last 3 sts, K2tog, K1 (9 sts).
Next row: K1, ssK, knit to last 3 sts, K2tog, K1 (7 sts).
Cast off.

Tail

Work in two-row garter stitch stripe pattern throughout.
NB: the cast-on row is counted as the first row of the stripe pattern.
Using orange yarn and 3.25mm (UK 10, US 3) knitting needles, cast on 14 sts and work 9 repeats of the two-row stripe pattern.
Next row: (K2, K2tog) three times, K2 (11 sts).
Knit 1 row.
Next row: K1, (K2tog) five times (6 sts).
Thread yarn through rem sts and fasten off.

Making up

Use the orange yarn to sew the cat together as each part of the cat starts with orange yarn. You can then use the cast-on ends of yarn to sew up the cat.

Sew the back seam and cast-off edge of the head. Using the photograph for guidance, attach the black safety eyes to the head. Stuff the head. Gather the cast-on edge of the head and secure. Place two ears together and carefully sew them together. Repeat for the second ear. Attach the ears to the head. Using the photograph for guidance and black yarn, sew the nose in place and embroider a mouth and whiskers.

Sew the back seam of the body, fold up the base and sew it in place. Place a piece of heavyweight interfacing or card in the base to make it firm and flat. Stuff the body with toy filling. Gather the neck edge and secure. Sew the head to the body.

Sew the seams of each arm, stuffing with toy filling as you go. Using orange yarn, oversew the end of each arm with two long stitches to form a paw shape. Sew the arms to the side of the body.

Sew the seams of each foot, stuffing with toy filling as you go. Using orange yarn, oversew the end of each foot with two long stitches to form a paw shape, as for the arms. Sew the seams of each leg, stuffing with toy filling as you go.

Sew the bottom of one leg to the top of one foot. Repeat for the second leg and foot. Using the photograph for guidance, attach the legs to the body. Sew the tail seam, stuffing with toy filling as you go. Sew the tail to the back of the body.

Kitty Kat

A girl just can't have too many clothes – and that goes for cats, too. This fabulous feline has an outfit for bedtime and one for daytime, and just loves to dress up.

Materials
50g of grey DK (8-ply) yarn
50g of cream DK (8-ply) yarn
Small amount of pink 2-ply (laceweight) yarn
Two 9mm (1/3in) plastic safety eyes
Black embroidery thread
Toy filling

Needles
3.75mm (UK 9, US 5) knitting needles
Two stitch markers

Tension
4–5 sts to 2.5cm (1in) measured over SS using DK (8-ply) yarn and 3.75mm (UK 9, US 5) knitting needles

Size
Approximately 25cm (9¾in) tall

Body back
Using grey yarn and 3.75mm (UK 9, US 5) knitting needles, cast on 10 sts.
Starting with a knit row, work 2 rows in SS.
Next row: K1, M1, knit to last st, M1, K1 (12 sts).
Next row: P1, M1, purl to last st, M1, P1 (14 sts).
Rep last 2 rows once more (18 sts).
Next row: K1, M1, knit to last st, M1, K1 (20 sts).
Starting with a purl row, work 9 rows in SS.
Next row: K1, ssK, knit to last 3 sts, K2tog, K1 (18 sts).
Purl 1 row.
Rep last 2 rows twice more (14 sts).
Next row: K1, ssK, knit to last 3 sts, K2tog, K1 (12 sts).
Starting with a purl row, work 3 rows in SS.
Rep last 4 rows twice more (8 sts).
Cast off.

Head

Using grey yarn and 3.75mm (UK 9, US 5) knitting needles, cast on 12 sts.

Next row: K1, M1, K5, M1, K5, M1, K1 (15 sts).

Purl 1 row.

Using the Fair Isle technique to carry the yarn (see page 14), work as follows:

Work all sts in **bold** using cream yarn and all other sts using grey yarn.

Next row: K6, M1, **K3**, M1, K6 (17 sts).

Next row: P1, M1, P6, **M1**, **P3**, **M1**, P6, M1, P1 (21 sts).

Next row: K8, **K1**, **M1**, **K3**, **M1**, **K1**, K8 (23 sts).

Next row: P1, M1, P7, **P2**, **M1**, **P3**, **M1**, **P2**, P7, M1, P1 (27 sts).

Next row: K9, **K3**, **M1**, **K3**, **M1**, **K3**, K9 (29 sts).

Next row: P9, **P11**, P9.

Next row: K9, **K11**, K9.

Next row: P9, **P11**, P9.

Next row: K9, **K2**, **ssK**, **K3**, **K2tog**, **K2**, K9 (27 sts).

Next row: P9, **P1**, **P2tog**, **P3**, **P2togtbl**, **P1**, P9 (25 sts).

Next row: K9, **ssK**, K9, **K3**, **K2tog** (23 sts).

Next row: P8, P2tog, **P3**, P2togtbl, P8 (21 sts).

Next row: K7, K7, **K3**, ssK, K2tog (19 sts).

Next row: P6, P2tog, **P3**, P2togtbl, P6 (17 sts).

Next row: K1, ssK, K5, **K1**, K5, K2tog, K1 (15 sts).

Break off cream yarn and continue using grey yarn only.

Next row: P1, P2tog, purl to last 3 sts, P2togtbl, P1 (13 sts).

Next row: Cast off 3 sts, K6, cast off rem 3 sts (7 sts).

With WS facing, rejoin grey yarn to rem 7 sts.

Starting with a purl row, work 10 rows in SS.

Next row: P1, P2tog, K1, P2togtbl, P1 (5 sts).

Starting with a knit row, work 2 rows in SS.

Next row: K1, sl1, K2tog, psso, K1 (3 sts).

Purl 1 row.

Cast off.

Ears (make four)

Using grey yarn and 3.75mm (UK 9, US 5) knitting needles, cast on 7 sts.

Starting with a knit row, work 2 rows in SS.

Next row: ssK, knit to last 2 sts, K2tog (5 sts).

Purl 1 row.

Rep last 2 rows once more (3 sts).

Next row: Sl1, K2tog, psso (1 st).

Thread yarn through rem st and fasten off.

Nose

Using a double strand of pink yarn and 3.75mm (UK 9, US 5) knitting needles, cast on 5 sts.

Starting with a knit row, work 2 rows in SS.

Next row: ssK, K1, K2tog (3 sts).

Purl 1 row.

Next row: Sl1, K2tog, psso (1 st).

Thread yarn through rem st and fasten off.

Body front

Using grey yarn and 3.75mm (UK 9, US 5) knitting needles, cast on 10 sts.

Starting with a knit row, work 2 rows in SS.

Place markers 4 sts in from each end of the last row.

Next row: K1, M1, knit to M, SM, M1, knit to M, M1, SM, knit to last st, M1, K1 (14 sts).

Next row: P1, M1, purl to last st, M1, P1, slipping markers (16 sts).

Rep last 2 rows twice more (28 sts).

Next row: K1, M1, knit to M, SM, M1, knit to M, M1, SM, knit to last st, M1, K1 (32 sts).

Starting with a purl row work 7 rows in SS, slipping markers.

Next row: K1, ssK, knit to M, SM, K2tog, knit to 2 sts before M, ssK, SM, knit to last 3 sts, K2tog, K1 (28 sts).

Purl 1 row, slipping markers.

Rep last 2 rows three more times (16 sts).

Remove markers.

Next row: K1, ssK, knit to last 3 sts, K2tog, K1 (14 sts).

Starting with a purl row, work 3 rows in SS.

Rep last 4 rows once more (12 sts).

Next row: K1, ssK, knit to last 3 sts, K2tog, K1 (10 sts).

Purl 1 row.

Cast off.

Arms (make two)

Using grey yarn and 3.75mm (UK 9, US 5) knitting needles, cast on 10 sts.

Starting with a knit row, work 10 rows in SS.

Change to cream yarn.

Starting with a knit row, work 2 rows in SS.

Next row: K1, M1, K3, M1, K2, M1, K3, M1, K1 (14 sts).

Purl 1 row.

Next row: K1, M1, K5, M1, K2, M1, K5, M1, K1 (18 sts).

Purl 1 row.

Next row: K1, ssK, K3, K2tog, K2, ssK, K3, K2tog, K1 (14 sts).

Cast off.

Legs (make two)

Using grey yarn and 3.75mm (UK 9, US 5) knitting needles, cast on 10 sts.

Starting with a knit row, work 12 rows in SS.

Cast off.

Feet (make two)

Using cream yarn and 3.75mm (UK 9, US 5) knitting needles, cast on 6 sts and knit 1 row.

Next row: P1, M1, purl to last st, M1, P1 (8 sts).

Next row: K1, M1, knit to last st, M1, K1 (10 sts).

Starting with a purl row, work 5 rows in SS.

Next row: K1, K2tog, knit to last 3 sts, ssK, K1 (8 sts).

Purl 1 row.

Next row: K1, M1, knit to last st, M1, K1 (10 sts).

Starting with a purl row, work 5 rows in SS.

Next row: K1, ssK, knit to last 3 sts, K2tog, K1 (8 sts).

Next row: P1, P2tog, purl to last 3 sts, P2togtbl, P1 (6 sts).

Knit 1 row.

Cast off.

Tail

Using grey yarn and 3.75mm (UK 9, US 5) knitting needles, cast on 9 sts.

Starting with a knit row, work 10 rows in SS.

*****Next row:** K6, w&t.

Next row: P3, w&t.

Next row: Knit to end (9 sts).

Purl 1 row.

Rep from * twice more.

Starting with a knit row, work 11 rows in SS.

Change to cream yarn.

Purl 1 row.

Next row: (K1, K2tog) three times (6 sts).

Purl 1 row.

Next row: (K2tog) three times (3 sts).

Thread yarn through rem sts and fasten off.

Making up

Place the body back and body front pieces together and sew the seams, stuffing with toy filling as you go.

Sew the head seams in place at the back of the head. Push the safety eyes through the knitting using the photograph for guidance and secure. Stuff with toy filling and gather the bottom seam to secure. With WS together, sew two ear pieces together to make one ear. Repeat for the second ear. Using the photograph for guidance, sew the ears to the top of the head. Using the photograph for guidance, sew the nose in place. Using black embroidery thread, embroider a mouth and whiskers.

Using a needle and grey yarn, sew from the base of the head to the back of each eye, pull the thread back down to the base and tighten. This gives a realistic shape to the head. Sew the head to the body.

Sew the side seam and the cast-off edges of each arm and stuff with toy filling. Using cream yarn, oversew the end of each arm with two long stitches to form a paw shape. Sew the seams of each foot, stuffing with toy filling as you go. Using cream yarn, oversew the end of each foot with two long stitches to form a paw shape, as for the arms. Sew the side seam of each leg and stuff with toy filling. Sew the bottom of one leg to the top of one foot. Repeat for the second leg and foot. Attach the legs to the bottom seam of the body.

Sew the side seam of the tail and stuff with toy filling. Using the photograph for guidance, sew the tail to the back of the cat.

Kitty Kat's Daytime Clothes

Materials

50g of orange 5-ply (sportweight) yarn
50g of blue 5-ply (sportweight) yarn
Two 16mm (¾in) buttons for dress with fish motifs
Two 10mm buttons for shoes
Blue ribbon approximately 56cm (22in) long x ¾cm (¼in) wide

Needles

3.25mm (UK 10, US 3) and 2.75mm
(UK 12, US 2) knitting needles

Tension

Approximately 6 sts to 2.5cm (1in) measured over
SS using 5-ply (sportweight) yarn and 3.25mm (UK
10, US 3) knitting needles

Size

To fit Kitty Kat

Bloomers (make two pieces)

Using orange yarn and 2.75mm (UK 12, US 2) knitting
needles, cast on a picot edge as follows:
(Cast on 5 sts, cast off 2 sts, pass st on right knitting
needle to left knitting needle) eight times, cast on 2 sts
(26 sts).
Next row: (K3, M1) eight times, K2 (34 sts).
Purl 1 row.
Next row: (K2tog) seventeen times (17 sts).
Purl 1 row.
Change to 3.25mm (UK 10, US 3) knitting needles.
Next row: (Kfb) seventeen times (34 sts).
Purl 1 row.
Next row: Cast off 3 sts, M1, (K2, M1) thirteen times, K4
(45 sts).
Next row: Cast off 3 sts, purl to end (42 sts).
Next row: K1, ssK, K6, (M1, K5) to last 8 sts, M1, K5,
K2tog, K1 (46 sts).
Next row: P1, P2tog, purl to last 3 sts, P2togtbl, P1
(44 sts).
Starting with a knit row, work 14 rows in SS.
Next row: (K2, K2tog) eleven times (33 sts).
Purl 1 row.
Work 3 rows in (K1, P1) rib.
Keeping rib correct throughout as set, work as follows:
Next row: (rib 4 sts, P2tog, YO) five times, rib 3 sts.
This row creates eyelet holes to thread ribbon through.
Work 3 rows in rib.
Cast off.

Dress back

Using blue yarn and 2.75mm (UK 12, US 2) knitting
needles, cast on a picot edge as follows:
(Cast on 5 sts, cast off 2 sts, pass st on right knitting
needle to left knitting needle) thirteen times, cast on 2 sts
(41 sts).
Knit 4 rows.
Next row: (K8, M1) four times, K9 (45 sts).
Change to 3.25mm (UK 10, US 3) knitting needles.
Starting with a knit row, work 3 rows in SS.
Using the Fair Isle technique to carry the yarn, work fish
design as follows (see page 14).
Work all sts marked in bold using orange yarn and all
other sts using blue yarn.
Next row: (K5, **K1**, **K1**, K3) four times, K5.
Next row: (P4, **P6**) four times, P5.
Next row: (K5, **K1**, **K1**, K3) four times, K5.
Break off orange yarn and continue using blue yarn only.
Starting with a purl row, work 13 rows in SS.
Next row: K2, (K2tog, K1) to last 4 sts, K2tog, K2 (31 sts).
Work 5 rows in (K1, P1) rib.*
Work in rib as follows:
Next row: Cast off 5 sts, rib to end (26 sts).
Next row: Cast off 5 sts, rib to end (21 sts).

Work 8 rows in (K1, P1) rib.

Next row: Rib 7 sts, cast off 7 sts, rib to end.

Working on first 7 sts only, continue in rib until work measures 3cm (1¼in).

Next row: K1, P1, K2tog, YO, K1, P1, K1 (7 sts).

Work 1 row in rib.

Next row: ssK, K1, P1, K1, K2tog (5 sts).

Cast off.

Rejoin blue yarn to rem 7 sts and complete to match first side.

Dress front

Work as for back of dress to *.

Cast off.

Fish

Using orange yarn and 2.75mm (UK 12, US 2) knitting needles, cast on 2 sts.

Next row: K1, M1, K1 (3 sts).

Purl 1 row.

Next row: (K1, M1) twice, K1 (5 sts).

Purl 1 row.

Next row: ssK, K1, K2tog (3 sts).

Purl 1 row.

Next row: Sl1, K2tog, psso (1 st).

Next row: Kfbf (3 sts).

Next row: (K1, M1) twice, K1 (5 sts).

Purl 2 rows (the second row forms a fold line).

Next row: P2tog, P1, P2tog (3 sts).

Next row: Sl1, K2tog, psso (1 st).

Next row: Kfbf (3 sts).

Next row: (K1, M1) twice, K1 (5 sts).

Purl 1 row.

Next row: ssK, K1, K2tog (3 sts).

Purl 1 row.

Next row: Sl1, K2tog, psso (1 st).

Thread yarn through rem st and fasten off.

Shoes (make two)

Using blue yarn and 3.25mm (UK 10, US 3) knitting needles, cast on 5 sts and knit 1 row.

Next row: K1, M1, knit to last st, M1, K1 (7 sts).

Knit 2 rows.

Rep last 3 rows twice more (11 sts).

Knit 2 rows.

Next row: Cast on 13 sts, knit to end (24 sts).

Next row: Cast on 13 sts, knit to end (37 sts).

Shape base of shoe.

Next row: K13, ssK, K7, K2tog, K13 (35 sts).

Next row: K12, ssK, K7, K2tog, K12 (33 sts).

Next row: K11, ssK, K7, K2tog, K11 (31 sts).

Next row: K10, ssK, K7, K2tog, K10 (29 sts).

Next row: K9, (ssK) twice, K3, (K2tog) twice, K9 (25 sts).

Cast off.

Strap for left shoe

Using blue yarn and 3.25mm (UK 10, US 3) knitting needles, cast on 10 sts and knit 1 row.

Next row: K1, K2tog, YO, K7 (10 sts).

Knit 1 row.

Cast off.

Strap for right shoe

Using blue yarn and 3.25mm (UK 10, US 3) knitting needles, cast on 10 sts and knit 1 row.

Next row: K7, YO, K2tog, K1 (10 sts).

Knit 1 row.

Cast off.

Making up

Place the two pieces of the bloomers together and sew the front seam. Sew the back seam, leaving a gap of approximately 2.5cm (1in) for the cat's tail to fit through.

Sew the short seams for the legs. Thread blue ribbon through the eyelet holes in the ribbed top edge of the bloomers, making sure the ribbon is long enough to tie in a bow.

Place the back and front of the dress together and join the side seams. Using the photograph for guidance, sew the buttons to the top of the ribbed bib of the dress.

Fold the fish in half along the fold line and sew the seam around the outside, stuffing it with toy filling as you go.

Using the photograph for guidance and blue ribbon, make a small bow with a long tail and sew it to the bottom of the ribbed bib of the dress.

Sew the fish to the bottom of the tail of the ribbon.

Sew the back seam of one shoe and sew the base in place. Repeat for the second shoe. Using the photograph for guidance, sew a strap and a button to each shoe.

Kitty Kat's Night-time Clothes

Materials
50g of pink 5-ply (sportweight) yarn
10g of white 4-ply (fingering) angora yarn
Three 10mm ($^3/_8$in) heart-shaped buttons
Black embroidery thread
Pink sewing cotton
Small amount of toy filling

Tools
3.25mm (UK 10, US 3) and 2.75mm (UK 12, US 2) knitting needles
Stitch holder

Tension
6 sts to 2.5cm (1in) measured over SS using 5-ply (sportweight) yarn and 3.25mm (UK 10, US 3) knitting needles

Size
To fit Kitty Kat

Pyjamas (left side)
Using pink yarn and 2.75mm (UK 12, US 2) knitting needles, cast on 26 sts and work 2 rows in (K1, P1) rib.
Join in white angora yarn without breaking off pink yarn.
Starting with a knit row, work 2 rows in SS. Break off white yarn.
Change to pink yarn and 3.25mm (UK 10, US 3) knitting needles.
Starting with a knit row, work 8 rows in SS.
Next row: K1, M1, K11, M1, K2, M1, K11, M1, K1 (30 sts).
Purl 1 row.
Next row: K1, M1, K13, M1, K2, M1, K13, M1, K1 (34 sts).
Purl 1 row.
Next row: K1, M1, K15, M1, K2, M1, K15, M1, K1 (38 sts).
Purl 1 row.
Next row: Cast off 3 sts, K14, M1, K2, M1, K18 (37 sts).
Next row: Cast off 3 sts, purl to end (34 sts).
Next row: K1, ssK, K13, M1, K2, M1, K13, K2tog, K1 (34 sts).
Next row: P1, P2tog, purl to last 3 sts, P2togtbl, P1 (32 sts).
Next row: K15, M1, K2, M1, K15 (34 sts).
Starting with a purl row, work 15 rows in SS.
Next row: K14, ssK, K2, K2tog, K14 (32 sts).
Purl 1 row.
Next row: K13, ssK, K2, K2tog, K13 (30 sts).
Purl 1 row.**

Next row: K12, ssK, K2, K2tog, K12 (28 sts).
Next row: Cast on 3 sts, (P1, K1) three times, purl to end (31 sts).
Next row: K11, ssK, K2, K2tog, K8, (P1, K1) three times (29 sts).
Keeping the rib correct as set and starting with a purl row, work 3 rows in SS.
Next row: K12, cast off 2 sts, K8, rib 6 sts (27 sts).
Keeping the rib correct as set, work on the first 15 sts only.
Next row: Rib 6 sts, P9.
Next row: K1, K2tog, K6, rib 6 sts (14 sts).
Next row: Rib 6 sts, P8.
Next row: K1, K2tog, K5, rib 6 sts (13 sts).
Next row: Rib 6 sts, P7.
Keeping the rib correct as set and starting with a knit row, work 2 rows in SS.
Next row: K7, place next 6 sts on a stitch holder.
Work on the 7 sts on the needle only.
Starting with a purl row, work 2 rows in SS.
Next row: Cast off 3 sts, purl to end (4 sts).

Knit 1 row.

Cast off.

With WS facing, rejoin pink yarn to rem 12 sts and purl 1 row.

Next row: K9, ssK, K1 (11 sts).

Purl 1 row.

Next row: K8, ssK, K1 (10 sts).

Purl 1 row.

Starting with a knit row, work 6 rows in SS.

Next row: Cast off 6 sts, knit to end (4 sts).

Purl 1 row.

Cast off.

Pyjamas (right side)

Work as for left side to ** (30 sts).

Next row: Cast on 3 sts, (K1, P1) three times, K9, K2tog, K2, ssK, K12 (31 sts).

Next row: Purl to last 6 sts, rib 6 sts as set.

Next row: (K1, P1) three times, K8, K2tog, K2, ssK, K11 (29 sts).

Next row: Purl to last 6 sts, rib 6 sts as set.

Next row: K1, P1, K2tog, YO, K1, P1, knit to end.

Next row: Purl to last 6 sts, rib 6 sts as set.

Keeping rib correct as set, work as follows:

Next row: Rib 6 sts, K9, cast off 2 sts, K11 (27 sts).

Work on the first 12 sts only.

Purl 1 row.

Next row: K1, K2tog, K9 (11 sts).

Purl 1 row.

Next row: K1, K2tog, K8 (10 sts).

Purl 1 row.

Starting with a knit row, work 7 rows in SS.

Next row: Cast off 6 sts, purl to end (4 sts).

Knit 1 row.

Cast off.

With WS facing, rejoin pink yarn to rem 15 sts.

Next row: P9, rib 6 sts (15 sts).

Next row: Rib 6 sts, K6, ssK, K1 (14 sts).

Next row: Purl 8 sts, rib 6 sts.

Next row: K1, P1, ssK, YO, K1, P1, K5, K2tog, K1 (13 sts).

Keeping rib correct as set and starting with a purl row, work 3 rows in SS.

Next row: Rib 6 sts and place these sts on a stitch holder, K7.

Work on the 7 sts on the needle only.

Purl 1 row.

Next row: Cast off 3 sts, knit to end (4 sts).

Purl 1 row.

Cast off.

Sleeves (make two)

Using pink yarn and 2.75mm (UK 12, US 2) knitting needles, cast on 24 sts and work 2 rows in (K1, P1) rib.

Change to white yarn.

Starting with a knit row, work 2 rows in SS.

Change to pink yarn and 3.25mm (UK 10, US 3) knitting needles.

Starting with a knit row, work 12 rows in SS.

Cast off.

Bunny's face (on front of pyjamas)

Using white yarn and 2.75mm (UK 12, US 2) knitting needles, cast on 5 sts.

Next row: K1, M1, knit to last st, M1, K1 (7 sts).

Purl 1 row.

Rep last 2 rows twice more (11 sts).

Starting with a knit row, work 4 rows in SS.

Next row: ssK, knit to last 2 sts, K2tog (9 sts).

Purl 1 row.

Rep last 2 rows twice more (5 sts).

Cast off.

Bunny's ears (make two)

Using white yarn and 2.75mm (UK 12, US 2) knitting needles, cast on 5 sts.

Starting with a knit row, work 8 rows in SS.

Next row: ssK, K1, K2tog (3 sts).

Purl 1 row.

Cast off.

Slippers (make two)

Using pink yarn and 3.25mm (UK 10, US 3) knitting needles, cast on 5 sts and knit 1 row.

Next row: K1, M1, knit to last st, M1, K1 (7 sts).

Knit 2 rows.

Rep last 3 rows twice more (11 sts).

Knit 2 rows.

Next row: Cast on 13 sts, knit to end (24 sts).

Next row: Cast on 13 sts, knit to end (37 sts).

Shape base of slipper as follows:

Next row: K13, ssK, K7, K2tog, K13 (35 sts).

Next row: K12, ssK, K7, K2tog, K12 (33 sts).

Next row: K11, ssK, K7, K2tog, K11 (31 sts).

Next row: K10, ssK, K7, K2tog, K10 (29 sts).

Next row: K9, (ssK) twice, K3, (K2tog) twice, K9 (25 sts).

Next row: K8, (ssK) twice, K1, (K2tog) twice, K8 (21 sts).

Cast off.

Bunny ears on slippers (make four)

Using white yarn and 2.75mm (UK 12, US 2) knitting needles, cast on 5 sts.

Starting with a knit row, work 8 rows in SS.

Next row: ssK, K1, K2tog (3 sts).

Purl 1 row.

Next row: K1, M1, K1, M1, K1 (5 sts).
Purl 1 row.
Starting with a knit row, work 8 rows in SS.
Cast off.

Bunny tails on slippers (make two)

Using white yarn and 2.75mm (UK 12, US 2) knitting needles, cast on 5 sts.
Next row: K1, M1, knit to last st, M1, K1 (7 sts).
Purl 1 row.
Rep last 2 rows twice more (11 sts).
Starting with a knit row, work 6 rows in SS.
Next row: ssK, knit to last 3 sts, K2tog (9 sts).
Purl 1 row.
Rep last 2 rows twice more (5 sts).
Thread yarn through rem sts.

Making up

With RS together, place the right and left pyjama pieces together and sew the shoulder seams. Sew the back seam, leaving a gap of approximately 2.5cm (1in) for the cat's tail to fit through.

With right side of pyjamas facing, using pink yarn and 2.75mm (UK 12, US 2) knitting needles, and keeping rib correct as set, rib the 6 sts from the first stitch holder, pick up and knit 6 sts up the front collar edge, 12 sts across the back of the neck, 6 sts down the front collar edge and, keeping rib correct as set, rib the 6 sts from the second stitch holder (36 sts).
Change to white yarn and rib 2 rows.
Change to pink yarn.
Next row: Rib to last 4 sts, yo, P2tog, K1, P1.
Next row: Rib.
Cast off loosely and evenly in rib.
Sew sleeve seams and attach sleeves to the pyjama armholes, sew front seam and leg seams, sew button band and buttonhole bands in place.

Pin the bunny face to the front of the pyjamas, stuffing very lightly with toy filling to give it definition. Using the photograph for guidance, position the bunny ears behind the top edge of the face. Sew the head and ears in place. Using black embroidery thread, embroider the bunny's eyes and nose.

Using pink sewing cotton and a sewing needle, sew the buttons in place to match the buttonhole positions.

Sew the back seam of one slipper and sew the base in place. Repeat for the second slipper.

Run a gathering thread around the edge of the tail and pull into a 'ball', stuffing lightly.

Fold one bunny ear in half lengthways and sew the side seam. Repeat for the other three bunny ears. Using the photograph for guidance, sew two bunny ears to the front of each slipper. Sew a bunny tail to the back seam of each slipper.

Super Cat

Is it a bird? Is it a plane? No, it's Super Cat! Tough on the outside but soft in the middle, this has got to be the cuddliest superhero of all time.

Materials

50g of dark grey 5-ply (sportweight) yarn
50g of light grey 5-ply (sportweight) yarn
Small amount of blue DK (8-ply) yarn
Small amount of black 4-ply (fingering) yarn
Two 10mm (³⁄₈in) green glass eyes
Toy filling
Five chenille sticks for arms, legs and tail

Needles

3.25mm (UK 10, US 3) and 2.75mm (UK 12, US 2) knitting needles
Two stitch markers

Tension

6 sts to 2.5cm (1in) measured over SS using 5-ply (sportweight) and 3.25mm (UK 10, US 3) knitting needles

Size

Approximately 18cm (7in) tall

Body front

Using dark grey yarn and 3.25mm (UK 10, US 3) knitting needles, cast on 8 sts.
Starting with a knit row, work 2 rows in SS.
Place markers 3 sts in from each end of last row.
Next row: K1, M1, knit to M, SM, M1, knit to M, M1, SM, knit to last st, M1, K1 (12 sts).
Next row: P1, M1, purl to last st, M1, P1, slipping markers (14 sts).
Rep last 2 rows twice more (26 sts).
Starting with a knit row, work 10 rows in SS, slipping markers.
Next row: K1, ssK, knit to M, SM, K2tog, knit to 2 sts before M, ssK, SM, knit to last 3 sts, K2tog, K1 (22 sts).
Purl 1 row.
Rep last 2 rows once more (18 sts).
Remove markers.
Next row: K1, ssK, knit to last 3 sts, K2tog, K1 (16 sts).
Starting with a purl row, work 3 rows in SS.
Rep last 4 rows three more times (10 sts).
Next row: K1, ssK, knit to last 3 sts, K2tog, K1 (8 sts).
Purl 1 row.
Cast off.

Help us, Super Cat, help us!

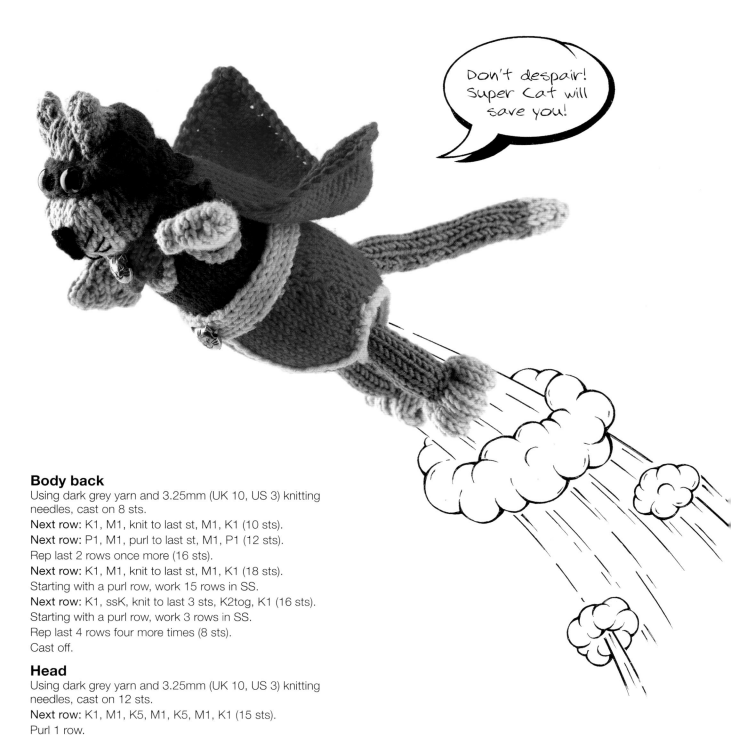

Don't despair! Super Cat will save you!

Body back

Using dark grey yarn and 3.25mm (UK 10, US 3) knitting needles, cast on 8 sts.

Next row: K1, M1, knit to last st, M1, K1 (10 sts).

Next row: P1, M1, purl to last st, M1, P1 (12 sts).

Rep last 2 rows once more (16 sts).

Next row: K1, M1, knit to last st, M1, K1 (18 sts).

Starting with a purl row, work 15 rows in SS.

Next row: K1, ssK, knit to last 3 sts, K2tog, K1 (16 sts).

Starting with a purl row, work 3 rows in SS.

Rep last 4 rows four more times (8 sts).

Cast off.

Head

Using dark grey yarn and 3.25mm (UK 10, US 3) knitting needles, cast on 12 sts.

Next row: K1, M1, K5, M1, K5, M1, K1 (15 sts).

Purl 1 row.

Using the Fair Isle technique to carry the yarn (see page 14), work as follows:

Work all sts in **bold** using light grey yarn and all other sts using dark grey yarn.

Next row: K6, M1, **K3**, M1, K6 (17 sts).
Next row: P1, M1, P6, **M1**, **P3**, **M1**, P6, M1, P1 (21 sts).
Next row: K8, **K1**, **M1**, **K3**, **M1**, **K1**, K8 (23 sts).
Next row: P1, M1, P7, **P2**, **M1**, **P3**, **M1**, **P2**, P7, M1, P1 (27 sts).
Next row: K9, **K3**, **M1**, **K3**, **M1**, **K3**, K9 (29 sts).
Next row: P9, **P11**, P9.
Next row: K9, **K11**, K9.
Next row: P9, **P11**, P9.
Next row: K9, **K2**, **ssK**, **K3**, **K2tog**, **K2**, K9 (27 sts).
Next row: P9, **P1**, **P2tog**, **P3**, **P2togtbl**, **P1**, P9 (25 sts).
Next row: K9, **ssK**, **K3**, **K2tog**, K9 (23 sts).
Next row: P8, P2tog, **P3**, P2togtbl, P8 (21 sts).
Next row: K7, ssK, **K3**, K2tog, K7 (19 sts).
Next row: P6, P2tog, **P3**, P2togtbl, P6 (17 sts).
Next row: K1, ssK, K5, **K1**, K5, K2tog, K1 (15 sts).
Break off light grey yarn and continue using dark grey yarn only.
Next row: P1, P2tog, purl to last 3 sts, P2togtbl, P1 (13 sts).
Next row: Cast off 3 sts, K6, cast off rem 3 sts (7 sts).
With WS facing, rejoin dark grey yarn to rem 7 sts. Starting with a purl row, work 11 rows in SS.
Next row: K1, ssK, K1, K2tog, K1 (5 sts).
Starting with a purl row, work 3 rows in SS.
Next row: ssK, K1, K2tog (3 sts).
Purl 1 row.
Cast off.

Ears (make four)
Using dark grey yarn and 3.25mm (UK 10, US 3) knitting needles, cast on 7 sts.
Starting with a knit row, work 2 rows in SS.
Next row: ssK, knit to last 2 sts, K2tog (5 sts).
Purl 1 row.
Rep last 2 rows once more (3 sts).
Next row: Sl1, K2tog, psso (1 st).
Thread yarn through rem st and fasten off.

Nose
Using black yarn and 2.75mm (UK 12, US 2) knitting needles, cast on 5 sts.
Starting with a knit row, work 2 rows in SS.
Next row: ssK, K1, K2tog (3 sts).
Purl 1 row.
Next row: Sl1, K2tog, psso (1 st).
Thread yarn through rem st and fasten off.

Arms (make two)
Using dark grey yarn and 3.25mm (UK 10, US 3) knitting needles, cast on 10 sts.
Starting with a knit row, work 12 rows in SS.
Change to light grey yarn.
Starting with a knit row, work 2 rows in SS.
Next row: K1, M1, K3, M1, K2, M1, K3, M1, K1 (14 sts).
Purl 1 row.
Next row: K1, M1, K5, M1, K2, M1, K5, M1, K1 (18 sts).
Purl 1 row.
Next row: K1, ssK, K3, K2tog, K2, ssK, K3, K2tog, K1 (14 sts).
Cast off.

Legs (make two)
Using dark grey yarn and 3.25mm (UK 10, US 3) knitting needles, cast on 10 sts.
Starting with a knit row, work 14 rows in SS.
Cast off.

Feet (make two)
Using light grey yarn and 3.25mm (UK 10, US 3) knitting needles, cast on 6 sts and knit 1 row.
Next row: P1, M1, purl to last st, M1, P1 (8 sts).
Next row: K1, M1, knit to last st, M1, K1 (10 sts).
Starting with a purl row, work 5 rows in SS.
Next row: K1, ssK, knit to last 3 sts, K2tog, K1 (8 sts).
Purl 1 row.
Next row: K1, M1, knit to last st, M1, K1 (10 sts).
Starting with a purl row, work 5 rows in SS.
Next row: K1, ssK, knit to last 3 sts, K2tog, K1 (8 sts).
Next row: P1, P2tog, purl to last 3 sts, P2togtbl, P1 (6 sts).
Knit 1 row.
Cast off.

Tail
Using dark grey yarn and 3.25mm (UK 10, US 3) knitting needles, cast on 9 sts.
Starting with a knit row, work 7cm (2¾in) in SS, ending with a purl row.
Change to light grey yarn.
Starting with a knit row, work 2 rows in SS.
Next row: (K1, K2tog) three times (6 sts).
Purl 1 row.
Next row: (K2tog) three times (3 sts).
Thread yarn through rem sts and fasten off.

Eye mask
Using blue yarn and 3.25mm (UK 10, US 3) knitting needles, cast on 56 sts and knit 1 row.
Next row: P1, P2tog, purl to last 3 sts, P2togtbl, P1 (54 sts).
Next row: K1, ssK, knit to last 3 sts, K2tog, K1 (52 sts).
Rep last 2 rows once more (48 sts).
Cast off loosely and evenly.

Making up

Sew the head seams together, stuffing with toy filling as
you go. With WS together, sew two ear pieces together
to make one ear. Repeat for the second ear. Using the
photograph for guidance, sew the ears to the top of the
head. Place the eye mask around the head at eye level
and pin to secure. Using the photograph for guidance,
sew the eyes in place on top of the eye mask and then
sew the eye mask in place, folding the ends of the
eye mask over each other to form a 'knot'. Using the
photograph for guidance and black yarn, sew the nose in
place and embroider a mouth and whiskers.

Using a needle and dark grey yarn, sew from the base
of the head to the back of each eye, pull the thread back
down to the base and tighten. This gives a realistic shape
to the head.

Sew the side seam and the cast-off edges of each arm.
Place a chenille stick inside each arm. Stuff with toy filling.
Using the photograph for guidance and light grey yarn,
oversew the end of each arm with two long stitches to
form a paw shape.

Sew the seams of each foot, stuffing with toy filling as
you go. Using light grey yarn, oversew the end of each
foot with two long stitches to form a paw shape, as for
the arms.

Sew the side seam of each leg. Place a chenille stick
inside each leg. Stuff with toy filling. Sew the bottom of
one leg to the top of one foot. Repeat with the second leg
and foot.

Pin the side seams of the body front and body back
pieces together. Pin the arms into the side seams
approximately 1.5cm (½in) from the top and pin the legs
into the bottom seam, making sure you leave a 4–5 stitch
gap between the legs to allow for fitting the outfit.

Sew the side seams of the body together, stitching the
arms and legs in place and stuffing with toy filling as you
go. Sew the head to the top of the body.

Sew the side seam of the tail and slide a chenille stick
inside. Stuff with toy filling. Using the photograph for
guidance, sew the tail to the back of the cat approximately
2cm (¾in) up from the bottom seam.

Super Cat's Outfit

Materials
50g of red DK (8-ply) yarn
50g of blue DK (8-ply) yarn
50g of yellow DK (8-ply) yarn
Two small metal buttons with cat motif

Needles
3.25mm (UK 10, US 3) knitting needles

Tension
6–7 sts to 2.5cm (1in) measured over SS using DK
(8-ply) yarn and 3.25mm (UK 10, US 3) knitting needles

Size
To fit Super Cat

Front

Using red yarn and 3.25mm (UK 10, US 3) knitting
needles, cast on 4 sts.

Starting with a knit row, work 2 rows in SS.

Next row: K1, M1, knit to last st, M1, K1 (6 sts).
Purl 1 row.
Rep last 2 rows once more (8 sts).
Next row: K1, M1, knit to last st, M1, K1 (10 sts).
Next row: P1, M1, purl to last st, M1, P1 (12 sts).
Rep last 2 rows three more times (24 sts).
Next row: K1, M1, knit to last st, M1, K1 (26 sts).
Starting with a purl row, work 5 rows in SS.
Next row: K1, ssk, knit to last 3 sts, K2tog, K1 (24 sts).
Purl 1 row.
Rep last 2 rows once more (22 sts).
Change to blue yarn.
Next row: K1, ssK, knit to last 3 sts, K2tog, K1 (20 sts).
Purl 1 row.
Rep last 2 rows once more (18 sts).
Starting with a knit row, work 4 rows in SS.
**Next row: Cast off 2 sts, K4, cast off 4 sts, K4, cast off 2
sts (leaving two sets of 5 sts).
With WS facing, rejoin blue yarn to first set of 5 sts and
*purl 1 row.
Next row: ssK, K1, K2tog (3 sts).
Starting with a purl row, work 4 rows in SS.
Cast off.*
With WS facing, rejoin blue yarn to the second set of 5 sts
and work from * to * to match first side.

Back

Using red yarn and 3.25mm (UK 10, US 3) knitting
needles, cast on 4 sts.

Starting with a knit row, work 2 rows in SS.

Next row: K1, M1, knit to last st, M1, K1 (6 sts).
Purl 1 row.
Rep last 2 rows once more (8 sts).
Next row: K1, M1, knit to last st, M1, K1 (10 sts).
Next row: P1, M1, purl to last st, M1, P1 (12 sts).
Next row: K1, M1, K4, cast off 2 sts, K3, M1, K1 (12 sts).
Next row: P1, M1, P5, cast on 2 sts, P5, M1, P1 (16 sts).
Next row: K1, M1, knit to last st, M1, K1 (18 sts).
Next row: P1, M1, purl to last st, M1, P1 (20 sts).
Rep last 2 rows once more (24 sts).
Next row: K1, M1, knit to last st, M1, K1 (26 sts).
Starting with a purl row, work 5 rows in SS.
Next row: K1, ssK, knit to last 3 sts, K2tog, K1 (24 sts).
Purl 1 row.
Rep last 2 rows once more (22 sts).
Change to blue yarn.
Next row: K1, ssK, knit to last 3 sts, K2tog, K1 (20 sts).
Purl 1 row.
Rep last 2 rows once more (18 sts).
Starting with a knit row, work 4 rows in SS.
Complete back by working as for front from ** to end.

Cape

Using red yarn and 3.25mm (UK 10, US 3) knitting needles, cast on 40 sts.

Starting with a knit row, work 2 rows in SS.

Next row: K1, ssK, knit to last 3 sts, K2tog, K1 (38 sts).

Purl 1 row.

Rep last 2 rows twelve more times (14 sts).

Next row: K4, cast off 6 sts, K3 (leaving 2 sets of 4 sts, which will make the collar).

Turn and work on first set of 4 sts only.

Starting with a purl row, work 9 rows in SS.

Next row: ssK, turn and cast on 2 sts, turn, K2tog (4 sts).

Purl 1 row.

Next row: K1, K2tog, K1 (3 sts).

Cast off.

With RS facing, rejoin red yarn to second set of 4 sts.

Starting with a knit row, work 10 rows in SS.

Next row: K1, K2tog, K1 (3 sts).

Cast off.

Cape edgings

With RS facing, using red yarn and 3.25mm (UK 10, US 3) knitting needles, pick up and knit 30 sts along bottom edge of cape. Cast off knitwise.

With RS facing, using red yarn and 3.25mm (UK 10, US 3) knitting needles, pick up and knit 31 sts along right side edge of cape and 3 sts across top of collar. Cast off knitwise.

With RS facing, using red yarn and 3.25mm (UK 10, US 3) knitting needles, pick up and knit 3 sts across top of collar and 31 sts along left front edge. Cast off knitwise.

With RS facing, using red yarn and 3.25mm (UK 10, US 3) knitting needles, pick up and knit 28 sts around inside neck edge of cape.

Cast off knitwise.

Belt

Using yellow yarn and 3.25mm (UK 10, US 3) knitting needles, cast on 4 sts.

Starting with a knit row, work in SS until belt fits around middle of outfit, covering the colour change and ending with a purl row.

Cast off.

Making up

Press all outfit pieces lightly to make them easier to sew together. Sew the front and back cast-on edges of the outfit together.

With RS facing and yellow yarn, pick up and knit 24 sts evenly around one leg edge. Cast off knitwise. Repeat for the second leg edge.

Using the photograph for guidance, start at the middle front of the outfit, where the red and blue yarns join, and using yellow yarn and chain stitch (see page 15), embroider an upside-down 'Y' on the front of the red pants.

Join the side seams of the outfit. With RS facing and yellow yarn, pick up and knit 14 sts evenly around one armhole edge. Cast off knitwise. Repeat this for the second armhole.

With RS facing and yellow yarn, pick up and knit 18 sts around the front neck edge. Cast off knitwise. With RS facing and yellow yarn, pick up and knit 15 sts around the back neck edge. Cast off knitwise. Sew all yarn ends in.

Join one shoulder seam. Put the outfit on the cat. Insert the tail into the hole at the back of the outfit. Join the second shoulder seam.

Join the cast-on and cast-off edges of the belt and sew the belt in place, on the outfit, covering the red and blue colour change. Sew a button onto the front of the belt. Sew a button onto the cape tie opposite the cape tie with the buttonhole on. Place the cape on the cat and button it up.

Valentino

Romance is in the air for Valentino. He's got a big heart (and a belly to match), and his irresistible charm means you will fall head over heels in love with him. A perfect gift for your Valentine! Instructions for the mice are provided on page 102.

Materials

25g of black sparkly 2-ply (laceweight) yarn (use double throughout)
Small amount of pale pink 2-ply (laceweight) yarn
Small amount of red 4-ply (fingering) yarn
Small amount of green 4-ply (fingering) yarn
Toy filling
Two 6mm (¼in) green glass eyes
Chenille stick

Needles

2.75mm (UK 12, US 2) and 2mm (UK 14, US 0) knitting needles

Tension

8 sts to 2.5cm (1in) measured over SS using a double strand of 2-ply (laceweight) yarn and 2.75mm (UK 12, US 2) knitting needles

Size

Approximately 13cm (5in) tall

Body and head (make two)

Using a double strand of black sparkly yarn and 2.75mm (UK 12, US 2) knitting needles, cast on 28 sts.
Starting with a knit row, work 2 rows in SS.
Next row: K1, M1, knit to last st, M1, K1 (30 sts).
Purl 1 row.
Rep the last 2 rows three more times (36 sts).
Starting with a knit row, work 16 rows in SS.
Next row: K1, ssK, knit to last 3 sts, K2tog, K1 (34 sts).
Purl 1 row.
Rep the last 2 rows four more times (26 sts).
Next row: K1, ssK, knit to last 3 sts, K2tog, K1 (24 sts).
Next row: P1, P2tog, purl to last 3 sts, P2togtbl, P1 (22 sts).
Rep the last 2 rows twice more (14 sts).
Starting with a knit row, work 8 rows in SS.
Next row: K1, ssK, knit to last 3 sts, K2tog, K1 (12 sts).

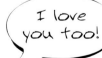

I love you too!

I love you!

Purl 1 row.

Rep the last 2 rows once more (10 sts).

Next row: K1, ssK, knit to last 3 sts, K2tog, K1 (8 sts).

Next row: P1, P2tog, purl to last 3 sts, P2togtbl, P1 (6 sts).

Cast off.

Base

Using a double strand of black sparkly yarn and 2.75mm (UK 12, US 2) knitting needles, cast on 20 sts.

Starting with a knit row, work 2 rows in SS.

Next row: K1, M1, knit to last st, M1, K1 (22 sts).

Next row: P1, M1, purl to last st, M1, P1 (24 sts).

Rep last 2 rows once more (28 sts).

Starting with a knit row, work 4 rows in SS.

Next row: K1, ssK, knit to last 3 sts, K2tog, K1 (26 sts).

Next row: P1, P2tog, purl to last 3 sts, P2togtbl, P1 (24 sts).

Rep last 2 rows once more (20 sts).

Starting with a knit row, work 2 rows in SS.

Cast off.

Ears (make two)

Using a double strand of black sparkly yarn and 2.75mm (UK 12, US 2) knitting needles, cast on 5 sts.

Starting with a knit row, work 2 rows in SS.

Next row: K1, sl1, K2tog, psso, K1 (3 sts).

Purl 1 row.

Next row: Sl1, K2tog, psso (1 st).

Thread yarn through rem st and fasten off.

Ear linings (make two)

Using a single strand of pale pink yarn and 2mm (UK 14, US 0) knitting needles, cast on 5 sts.

Starting with a knit row, work 2 rows in SS.

Next row: K1, sl1, K2tog, psso, K1 (3 sts).

Purl 1 row.

Next row: Sl1, K2tog, psso (1 st).

Thread yarn through rem st and fasten off.

Arms (make two)

Using a double strand of black sparkly yarn and 2.75mm (UK 12, US 2) knitting needles, cast on 10 sts.

Starting with a knit row, work 8 rows in SS.

Next row: K1, ssK, K4, K2tog, K1 (8 sts).

Purl 1 row.

Cast off.

Fingers and toes (make four)

Using a double strand of black sparkly yarn and 2.75mm (UK 12, US 2) knitting needles, cast on 2 sts.

Next row: (Kfb) twice (4 sts).

Next row: (Kfb) four times (8 sts).

Next row: Knit.

Next row: (P2tog) four times (4 sts).

Next row: (K2tog) twice (2 sts).

Next row: Purl.

Rep last 6 rows twice more to make three toes.

Cast off.

Tail

Using a double strand of black sparkly yarn and 2.75mm (UK 12, US 2) knitting needles, cast on 8 sts.

Starting with a knit row, work 8 rows in SS.

*****Next row:** K6, w&t.

Next row: P4, w&t.

Next row: Knit to end (8 sts).

Purl 1 row.*

Rep from * to * three more times.

Starting with a knit row, work 12 rows in SS.

Next row: K1, ssK, K2, K2tog, K1 (6 sts).

Purl 1 row.

Next row: K1, ssK, K2tog, K1 (4 sts).

Thread yarn through rem sts and fasten off.

Heart

Using red yarn and 2.75mm (UK 12, US 2) knitting needles, cast on 2 sts.

Next row: (Kfb) twice (4 sts).

Purl 1 row.

Next row: K1, M1, knit to last st, M1, K1 (6 sts).

Purl 1 row.

Rep last 2 rows seven more times (20 sts), working one side of the top of the heart and leaving the rem 10 sts on the other needle.

*****Next row:** K1, ssk, K4, K2tog, K1 (8 sts).

Turn and work over these 8 sts only.

Purl 1 row.

Next row: K1, ssK, K2, K2tog, K1 (6 sts).

Purl 1 row.

Next row: K1, ssK, K2tog, K1 (4 sts).

Next row: P2tog, P2togtbl (2 sts).

Cast off.*

With RS facing, rejoin red yarn to rem 10 sts.

Work as for other side of heart from * to *.

Rosebud

Using green yarn and 2.75mm (UK 12, US 2) knitting needles, cast on 16 sts and knit 1 row.

Change to red yarn.

Starting with a purl row, work 3 rows in SS.

Next row: K13, w&t.

Purl 1 row.

Next row: K10, w&t.

Purl 1 row.

Next row: K6, w&t.

Purl 1 row (16 sts).

Cast off, picking up 'wraps' and knitting them together with sts on needle.

Roll the rose petal sideways from the smallest side to the largest side to form the bud and stitch to hold in place.

Rosebud stem

Using green yarn and 2.75mm (UK 12, US 2) knitting needles, cast on 3 sts.

Starting with a knit row, work in SS until stem measures 5cm (2in) long, ending with a purl row.

Thread yarn through sts and fasten off.

Sew the side seam of the stem and sew to the base of the rosebud. Alternatively, work the stem as an i-cord (see page 14).

Leaves (make two)

Using green yarn and 2.75mm (UK 12, US 2) knitting needles, cast on 2 sts.

Next row: K1, M1, K1 (3 sts).

Knit 1 row.

Next row: K1, M1, K1, M1, K1 (5 sts).

Knit 3 rows.

Next row: ssK, K1, K2tog (3 sts).

Knit 1 row.

Next row: Sl1, K2tog, psso (1 st).

Thread yarn through rem st and fasten off.

Sew the leaves to the stem of the rosebud.

Making up

Using the photograph for guidance, sew the cat's eyes in place. Join the side seams of the body and head, stuffing with toy filling as you go. Sew the base in place. Sew the seams of each arm.

Using black sparkly yarn, take one set of fingers and toes and run a thread around each of the three fingers and toes and gather to make a paw. Repeat for the other three sets of fingers and toes. Stitch a paw to the end of each arm, and two paws to the base of the cat where the front cast-on seam and the base join. Stuff the arms lightly and sew them to the sides of the body.

With WS together sew one ear to one ear lining to make one ear. Repeat for the second ear. Using the photograph for guidance, sew the ears to the top of the head.

Sew the side seam of the tail. Slide a chenille stick inside the tail and sew it to one side of the body.

Using green yarn, sew the stem of the rosebud to the paw on the opposite side to the side with the tail.

Using the photograph for guidance and a double strand of pink yarn, embroider a French knot (see page 16) for the nose and embroider a mouth with straight stitches. Sew the heart to the belly, stuffing it slightly with toy filling to give definition.

Will you marry me?

Monster Cat

A freak of nature he might be, but for those of us with a quirky sense of humour he's the perfect pet. Let your imagination run wild and design your own cat-like creature that's not quite as cute as the real thing, but definitely just as cuddly.

Materials

50g of blue 5-ply (sportweight) yarn
50g of brown 5-ply (sportweight) yarn
50g of yellow 5-ply (sportweight) yarn
50g of orange 5-ply (sportweight) yarn
Toy filling
One 2.5cm (1in) button with four holes
Brown felt circle 2.5cm (1in) across

Needles

3.25mm (UK 10, US 3) knitting needles

Tension

6 sts to 2.5cm (1in) measured over SS using
5-ply (sportweight) yarn and 3.25mm (UK 10, US 3)
knitting needles

Size

Approximately 16cm (6¼in) tall

Body front, head and ears

Using blue yarn, cast on 40 sts.
Starting with a knit row, work 16 rows.
Carrying blue yarn up the side of the work, change to brown yarn.
Starting with a knit row, work 6 rows.
Change to yellow yarn.
Starting with a knit row, work 6 rows.
Change to brown yarn.
Starting with a knit row, work 6 rows.
Change to blue yarn.
Starting with a knit row, work 22 rows.*
Next row: K14, cast off 15, K10 (25 sts).
Turn and, working over first 11 sts only, purl 1 row.
Next row: K1, K2tog, knit to end (10 sts).
Purl 1 row.
Rep last 2 rows six more times (3 sts).
Cast off.
With WS facing, rejoin blue yarn to rem 14 sts and purl 1 row.
Starting with a knit row, work 2 rows in SS.
Next row: K1, ssK, knit to last 3 sts, K2tog, K1 (12 sts).
Purl 1 row.
Rep last 2 rows four more times (4 sts).
Next row: K1, K2tog, K1 (3 sts).
Cast off.

Body back, head and ears

Work as for body front, head and ears front to *.

Next row: K11, cast off 15, K13 (25 sts).

Turn and, working over first 14 sts only, purl 1 row.

Starting with a knit row, work 2 rows in SS.

Next row: K1, ssK, knit to last 3 sts, K2tog, K1 (12 sts).

Purl 1 row.

Rep last 2 rows four more times (4 sts).

Next row: K1, K2tog, K1 (3 sts).

Cast off.

With WS facing, rejoin blue yarn to rem 11 sts and purl 1 row.

Next row: Knit to last 3 sts, K2tog, K1 (10 sts).

Purl 1 row.

Rep last 2 rows six more times (3 sts).

Cast off.

Base

Using blue yarn, cast on 30 sts.

Starting with a knit row, work 2 rows in SS.

Next row: K1, M1, knit to last st, M1, K1 (32 sts).

Purl 1 row.

Rep last 2 rows three more times (38 sts).

Starting with a knit row, work 4 rows in SS.

Next row: K1, ssK, knit to last 3 sts, K2tog, K1 (36 sts).

Purl 1 row.

Rep last 2 rows three more times (30 sts).

Cast off.

Belly

Using orange yarn, cast on 10 sts.

Purl 1 row.

Next row: K1, M1, knit to last st, M1, K1 (12 sts).

Next row: P1, M1, purl to last st, M1, P1 (14 sts).

Rep last 2 rows once more (18 sts).

Next row: K1, M1, knit to last st, M1, K1 (20 sts).

Purl 1 row.

Rep last 2 rows once more (22 sts).

Starting with a knit row, work 10 rows in SS.

Next row: K1, ssK, knit to last 3 sts, K2tog, K1 (20 sts).

Purl 1 row.

Rep last 2 rows once more (18 sts).

Next row: K1, ssK, knit to last 3 sts, K2tog, K1 (16 sts).

Next row: P1, P2tog, purl to last 3 sts, P2togtbl, P1 (14 sts).

Rep last 2 rows once more (10 sts).

Cast off.

Arms (make two)

Using blue yarn, cast on 12 sts.

Starting with a knit row, work 10 rows in SS.

Next row: K1, ssK, knit to last 3 sts, K2tog, K1 (10 sts).

Purl 1 row.

Rep last 2 rows once more (8 sts).

Next row: K1, M1, knit to last st, M1, K1 (10 sts).

Purl 1 row.

Rep last 2 rows once more (12 sts).

Starting with a knit row, work 10 rows in SS.

Cast off.

Feet (make two)

Using brown yarn, cast on 12 sts.

Starting with a knit row, work 8 rows in SS.

Next row: K1, ssK, knit to last 3 sts, K2tog, K1 (10 sts).

Purl 1 row.

Rep last 2 rows once more (8 sts).

Next row: K1, M1, knit to last st, M1, K1 (10 sts).

Purl 1 row.

Rep last 2 rows once more (12 sts).

Starting with a knit row, work 8 rows in SS.

Cast off.

Tail

Using blue yarn, cast on 22 sts.

Starting with a knit row, work 10 rows in SS.

Change to brown yarn.

Starting with a knit row, work 4 rows.

Change to yellow yarn.

Starting with a knit row, work 4 rows.

Change to brown yarn.

Starting with a knit row, work 4 rows.

Change to blue yarn.

Starting with a knit row, continue in SS until work measures 12cm (4¾in) from end of last brown stripe, ending with a purl row.

Next row: K1, ssK, K5, ssK, K2, K2tog, K5, K2tog, K1 (18 sts).

Purl 1 row.

Next row: K1, ssK, K3, ssK, K2, K2tog, K3, K2tog, K1 (14 sts).

Purl 1 row.

Cast off.

Making up

Fold each arm in half; one arm with WS on the outside and the other with RS on the outside to provide contrast. Sew the side seams and stuff each arm with toy filling. Repeat for the feet.

Sew the tail seam and gently stuff the end of the tail. Using the photograph for guidance, tie a knot in the tail. Lightly stuff the rest of the tail with toy filling.

Pin the side seams of the body front, head and ears and the body back, head and ears together. Using the photograph for guidance, position the arms and tail into the side seams. Sew the side seams together, stitching the arms and tail in place and stuffing with toy filling as you go.

Pin the base to the bottom of the body. Using the photograph for guidance, position the feet into the seam between the bottom of the body front and the base. Sew the base to the bottom of the body, stitching the feet in place and lightly topping up with toy filling as you go.

Using the button as a template, cut out one brown felt eye. This will ensure both eyes are the same size. Using contrast-coloured yarn, sew on both eyes, forming an 'X' in the centre of each.

Using the photograph for guidance, sew the belly to the front of the cat using orange yarn and long stitches to add detail. Using yellow yarn, oversew the end of each arm with three long stitches to form claws. Repeat for each foot, using orange yarn.

Fluffy Cat

Small, sweet and very, very fluffy, this cute kitten is quick to knit and won't ever grow up! Instructions for the mice are provided on page 102.

Materials

50g of white 4-ply (fingering) angora yarn
Small amount of pale pink 2-ply (laceweight) yarn
Two 8mm (1/3in) plastic safety eyes, painted on the backs with silver nail polish
Toy filling
Pink ribbon
Chenille stick
Strong sewing thread

Tools

2.75mm (UK 12, US 2) and 2mm (UK 14, US 0) knitting needles
Stitch holder

Tension

7–8 sts to 2.5cm (1in) measured over SS using 4-ply (fingering) angora yarn and 2.75mm (UK 12, US 2) knitting needles

Size

Approximately 18cm (7in) long

Tail, body and front legs

Using white angora yarn and 2.75mm (UK 12, US 2) knitting needles, cast on 4 sts.
Starting with a knit row, work 2 rows in SS.
Next row: K1, M1, K2, M1, K1 (6 sts).
Starting with a purl row, work 2 rows in SS.
*Next row: P5, w&t.
Next row: K4, w&t.
Next row: Purl to end (6 sts).
Knit 1 row.*
Work from * to * ten more times.
Next row: Cast off 1 st, purl to end (5 sts).
Next row: Cast off 1 st, knit to end (4 sts).
Next row: Cast on 8 sts, purl across 12 sts on needle, turn and cast on 8 sts (20 sts).
Starting with a knit row, work 2 rows in SS.
Next row: K1, M1, knit to last st, M1, K1 (22 sts).
Next row: P1, M1, purl to last st, M1, P1 (24 sts).
Next row: K19, w&t.
Next row: P14, w&t.
Next row: Knit to end (24 sts).
Purl 1 row.
Next row: K1, M1, knit to last st, M1, K1 (26 sts).
Next row: P1, M1, purl to last st, M1, P1 (28 sts).
**Next row: K23, w&t.
Next row: P18, w&t.
Next row: Knit to end (28 sts).
Purl 1 row.**
Rep from ** to ** twice more.
Next row: K1, M1, knit to last st, M1, K1 (30 sts).
Starting with a purl row, work 11 rows in SS.
The stitches are now divided for the two front legs and the body.
Next row: K4, cast off 6, K9, cast off 6, K3.
Turn and, working on the first 4 sts only (which will form the first leg), purl 1 row.
Leave rem sts on a holder.
Next row: Cast on 6 sts, knit to end (10 sts).
***Starting with a purl row, work 9 rows in SS.

Next row: K3, (K2tog) twice, K3 (8 sts).
Next row: P2, (P2tog) twice, P2 (6 sts).
Thread yarn through rem sts and fasten off.***
With RS facing, rejoin white yarn to the 4 sts at other end of knitting on holder and knit 1 row.
Next row: Cast on 6 sts, purl to end (10 sts).
Knit 1 row.
Work from *** to *** as for first leg .
With RS facing, rejoin white yarn to centre 10 sts on holder and work as follows:
Next row: K2, ssK, K2, K2tog, K2 (8 sts).
Starting with a purl row, work 5 rows in SS.
Next row: K1, M1, knit to last st, M1, K1 (10 sts).
Purl 1 row.
Rep last 2 rows once more (12 sts).
Starting with a knit row, work 12 rows in SS.
Next row: K1, M1, knit to last st, M1, K1 (14 sts).
Purl 1 row.
Rep last 2 rows once more (16 sts).
Starting with a knit row, work 4 rows in SS.
Next row: K1, ssK, knit to last 3 sts, K2tog, K1 (14 sts).
Purl 1 row.
Rep last 2 rows once more (12 sts).
Starting with a knit row, work 4 rows in SS.
Next row: K1, ssK, knit to last 3 sts, K2tog, K1 (10 sts).
Starting with a purl row, work 5 rows in SS.
Next row: K1, ssK, knit to last 3 sts, K2tog, K1 (8 sts).
Purl 1 row.
Next row: K1, ssK, knit to last 3 sts, K2tog, K1 (6 sts).
Next row: P1, P2tog, P2togtbl, P1 (4 sts).
Cast off.

Head
Using white yarn and 2.75mm (UK 12, US 2) knitting needles, cast on 20 sts and purl 1 row.
Next row: K4, M1, K1, M1, K4, M1, K2, M1, K4, M1, K1, M1, K4 (26 sts).
Purl 1 row.
Next row: K5, M1, K1, K2tog, K4, M1, K2, M1, K4, ssK, K1, M1, K5 (28 sts).
Purl 1 row.
Next row: K6, M1, K1, K2tog, K4, M1, K2, M1, K4, ssK, K1, M1, K6 (30 sts).
Purl 1 row.
Next row: K14, M1, K2, M1, K14 (32 sts).
Purl 1 row.
Next row: K15, M1, K2, M1, K15 (34 sts).
Purl 1 row.
Next row: K16, M1, K2, M1, K16 (36 sts).
Purl 1 row.

Next row: K15, ssK, K2, K2tog, K15 (34 sts).
Next row: P14, P2tog, P2, P2togtbl, P14 (32 sts).
Next row: K13, ssK, K2, K2tog, K13 (30 sts).
Purl 1 row.
Next row: K11, ssK, K4, K2tog, K11 (28 sts).
Purl 1 row.
Next row: K1, ssK, knit to last 3 sts, K2tog, K1 (26 sts).
Next row: P1, P2tog, purl to last 3 sts, P2togtbl, P1 (24 sts).
Next row: K4, K2tog, ssK, K8, ssK, K2tog, K4 (20 sts).
Next row: P3, P2togtbl, P2tog, P6, P2togtbl, P2tog, P3 (16 sts).
Next row: K2, ssK, K2tog, K4, ssK, K2tog, K2 (12 sts).
Cast off (WS).

Ears (make two)
Using white yarn and 2.75mm (UK 12, US 2) knitting needles, cast on 8 sts.
Starting with a knit row, work 2 rows in SS.
Next row: K1, K2tog, K2, ssK, K1 (6 sts).
Purl 1 row.
Next row: K1, ssK, K2tog, K1 (4 sts).
Purl 1 row.
Next row: ssK, K2tog (2 sts).
Next row: P2tog (1 st).
Thread yarn through rem st and fasten off.

Ear linings (make two)
Using pale pink yarn and 2mm (UK 14, US 0) knitting needles, cast on 7 sts.
Starting with a knit row, work 2 rows in SS.
Next row: K1, K2tog, K1, ssK, K1 (5 sts).
Purl 1 row.
Next row: ssK, K1, K2tog (3 sts).
Purl 1 row.
Next row: Sl1, K2tog, psso (1 st).
Thread yarn through rem st and fasten off.

Nose
Using pale pink yarn and 2mm (UK 14, US 0) knitting needles, cast on 3 sts.
Starting with a knit row, work 2 rows in SS.
Next row: Sl1, K2tog, psso (1 st).
Thread yarn through rem st and fasten off.

Back leg (right)
****Using white yarn and 2.75mm (UK 12, US 2) knitting needles, cast on 6 sts and knit 1 row.
Next row: K1, M1, knit to last st, M1, K1 (10 sts).
Starting with a purl row, work 7 rows in SS.****
Next row: Cast off 4 sts, K1, M1, knit to last st, M1, K1 (8 sts).

Next row: P1, M1, purl to last st, M1, P1 (10 sts).
Next row: K1, M1, knit to last st, M1, K1 (12 sts).
Next row: P1, M1, purl to last st, M1, P1 (14 sts).
Starting with a knit row, work 4 rows in SS.
Next row: K1, ssK, knit to last 3 sts, K2tog, K1 (12 sts).
Next row: Purl.
Rep last 2 rows once more.
Next row: K1, ssK, knit to last 3 sts, K2tog, K1 (8 sts).
Next row: P1, P2togtbl, purl to last 3 sts, P2tog , P1 (6 sts).
Cast off.

Back leg (left)
Follow instructions for right back leg from **** to ****.
Next row: Knit.
Next row: Cast off 4 sts, P1, M1, purl to last st, M1, P1 (8 sts).
Next row: K1, M1, knit to last st, M1, K1 (10 sts).
Next row: P1, M1, purl to last st, M1, P1 (12 sts).
Next row: K1, M1, knit to last st, M1, K1 (14 sts).
Starting with a purl row, work 4 rows in SS.
Next row: P1, P2tog, purl to last 3 sts, P2togtbl, P1 (12 sts).
Next row: Knit.
Rep last 2 rows once more (10 sts).
Next row: P1, P2tog, purl to last 3 sts, P2togtbl (8 sts).
Next row: K1, ssK, knit to last 3 sts, K2tog, K1 (6 sts).
Cast off.

Making up
Sew the side seams of each front leg and stuff each front leg with toy filling. Fold the narrow middle front section of the cat downwards. Sew the edge of the middle section to the cast-off edge down towards the front legs. Continue sewing under the legs to the side of the body then towards the tail, stuffing with toy filling as you go. Using the photograph for guidance, sew the cast-on stitches of each front leg to the front of the body. Sew the tail seam, sliding a piece of chenille stick inside. Sew the tail to the body.

Using the photograph for guidance, attach the safety eyes to the head and sew the back seam of the head. Stuff the head with toy filling.

With WS together and using pale pink yarn, sew one ear to one ear lining to make one ear. Repeat for the second ear. Using the photograph for guidance, sew the ears to the top of the head. Using pale pink yarn, sew the nose in place. Thread strong white sewing thread through the face to make whiskers. Sew the head to the body.

Sew the lower part of each back leg together and stuff gently. Using the photograph for guidance, pin the back legs in place, with the lower leg pointing downwards. Fold the lower leg up to lie along the side seam of the body and sew in place, stitching the inside of the lower leg to the side of the body.

I only want to play!

Doorstop Cat

Cats can be useful, and this one proves it! Big, heavy and full of character, he makes a wonderful doorstop (though he sometimes dreams of escaping and playing in the garden).

Body back, head and ears

Use light brown yarn for the body of the cat and dark brown yarn for the markings.

Make two mini balls of dark brown yarn and use one mini ball at each side of the work.

Using the intarsia technique (see page 14), twist the yarns together at the back, where they join, to avoid holes.

Work all sts in **bold** using dark brown yarn and all other sts using light brown yarn.

Using light brown yarn and 4mm (UK 8, US 6) knitting needles, cast on 35 sts and knit 1 row.

Next row: P1, M1, P33, M1, P1 (37 sts).

Next row: K1, M1, K35, M1, K1 (39 sts).

Next row: P1, M1, P37, M1, P1 (41 sts).

Next row: K40, M1, K1 (42 sts).

Next row: **P6**, P35, M1, P1 (43 sts).

Next row: **K5**, K30, **K8**.

Next row: **P10**, P26, **P7**.

Next row: **K8**, K24, **K11**.

Next row: **P12**, P22, **P9**.

Next row: **K10**, K23, **K10**.

Next row: **P6**, P26, **P11**.

Next row: **K12**, K27, **K4**.

Next row: **P2**, P28, **P13**.

Next row: **K8**, K34, **K1**.

Next row: P38, **P5**.

Next row: **K3**, K36, **K4**.

Next row: **P8**, P33, **P2**.

Next row: K33, **K10**.

Next row: **P13**, P26, **P4**.

Next row: **K7**, K25, **K11**.

Next row: **P9**, P25, **P9**.

Next row: **K10**, K26, **K7**.

Next row: **P5**, P27, **P11**.

Next row: **K12**, K27, **K4**.

Next row: **P2**, P34, **P7**.

Next row: **K5**, K23, **K3**, K11, **K1**.

Next row: P9, **P5**, P25, **P4**.

Next row: **K2**, K28, **K8**, K5.

Next row: P3, **P9**, P31.

Next row: **K3**, K29, **K10**, K1.

Next row: **P1**, **P2togtbl**, **P7**, P26, **P7** (42 sts).

Next row: **K10**, K24, **K8**.

Next row: **P7**, P24, **P11**.

Next row: **K8**, K17, **K3**, K7, **K4**, **K2tog**, **K1** (41 sts).

Next row: **P5**, P6, **P4**, P20, **P6**.

Next row: **K4**, K22, **K6**, K5, **K1**, **K2tog**, **K1** (40 sts).

Next row: **P1**, P2togtbl, P4, **P6**, P24, **P3** (39 sts).

Next row: **K1**, K2tog, K24, **K8**, K1, K2tog, **K1** (37 sts).

Next row: **Cast off 2 sts**, **P8**, P26 (35 sts).

Next row: **K5**, K22, **K5**, **K2tog**, K1 (34 sts).

Next row: **Cast off 2 sts**, **P4**, P20, **P7** (32 sts).

Next row: **K1**, **K2tog**, **K5**, K12, **K5**, K3, **K1**, **K2tog**, **K1** (30 sts).

Next row: Cast off 2 sts, P2, **P7**, P10, **P8** (28 sts).

Next row: **K6**, K13, **K6**, K2tog, K1 (27 sts).

Materials

100g of light brown marbled DK (8-ply) yarn

100g of dark brown marbled DK (8-ply) yarn

Small amount of black 4-ply (fingering) yarn

Two 12mm (½in) plastic safety eyes, painted on the backs with gold nail polish

Toy filling

Sock

Rice (enough to weight the doorstop)

Needles

2.75mm (UK 12, US 2) and 4mm (UK 8, US 6) knitting needles

Tension

5–6 sts to 2.5cm (1in) measured over SS using DK (8-ply) yarn and 4mm (UK 8, US 6) knitting needles

Size

Approximately 23cm (9in) tall from base to top of head

Next row: **P1**, **P2tog**, **P4**, P16, **P4** (26 sts).
Next row: **K3**, K17, **K3**, **K2tog**, **K1** (25 sts).
Next row: **P1**, **P2tog**, **P1**, P19, **P2** (24 sts).
Next row: **K1**, K21, **K2**.
Next row: **P1**, P23.
Next row: **K1**, K20, K2tog, K1 (23 sts).
Next row: **P3**, P17, **P3**.
Next row: **K5**, K13, **K5**.
Next row: **P4**, P13, **P6**.
Next row: **K4**, K16, **K3**.
Next row: **P2**, P19, **P2**.
Next row: **K1**, K10, **K1**, K10, **K1**.
Next row: P11, **P1**, P11.
Next row: K8, **K1**, K1, **K3**, K1, **K1**, K8.
Next row: P8, **P1**, P1, **P3**, P1, **P1**, P8.
Next row: K7, **cast off 9 sts**, K6 (14 sts).
Break off dark brown yarn and continue using light brown yarn only.
Work on first set of 7 sts only.
Purl 1 row.

Next row: K1, K2tog, K4 (6 sts).
Purl 1 row.
Next row: K1, K2tog, K3 (5 sts).
Purl 1 row.
Next row: K1, K2tog, K2 (4 sts).
Next row: P2tog, P2togtbl (2 sts).
Next row: K2tog (1 st).
Thread yarn through rem st and fasten off.
With WS facing, rejoin light brown yarn to rem 7 sts.
Purl 1 row.
Next row: K4, ssK, K1 (6 sts).
Purl 1 row.
Next row: K3, ssK, K1 (5 sts).
Purl 1 row.
Next row: K2, ssK, K1 (4 sts).
Next row: P2tog, P2togtbl (2 sts).
Next row: K2tog (1 st).
Thread yarn through rem st and fasten off.

Body front, head and ears

Use light brown yarn for the body of the cat and dark brown yarn for the markings.

Make two mini balls of dark brown yarn and use one mini ball at each side of the work.

Using the intarsia technique (see page 14), twist the yarns together at the back, where they join, to avoid holes.

Work all sts in **bold** using dark brown yarn and all other sts using light brown yarn.

Using light brown yarn and 4mm (UK 8, US 6) knitting needles, cast on 36 sts and knit 1 row.

Next row: P1, M1, P34, M1, P1 (38 sts).
Next row: K1, M1, K36, M1, K1 (40 sts).
Next row: P39, M1, P1 (41 sts).
Next row: **K5**, K35, M1, K1 (42 sts).
Next row: **P1**, **M1**, **P3**, P31, **P7** (43 sts).
Next row: **K9**, K27, **K7**.
Next row: **P8**, P24, **P11**.
Next row: **K12**, K22, **K9**.
Next row: **P10**, P23, **P10**.
Next row: **K6**, K26, **K11**.
Next row: **P12**, P27, **K4**.
Next row: **K2**, K28, **K13**.
Next row: **P8**, P34, **P1**.
Next row: K38, **K5**.
Next row: **P3**, P36, **P4**.
Next row: **K8**, K33, **K2**.
Next row: P33, **P10**.
Next row: **K13**, K26, **K4**.
Next row: **P7**, P25, **P11**.
Next row: **K9**, K25, **K9**.
Next row: **P10**, P26, **P7**.
Next row: **K5**, K27, **K11**.
Next row: **P12**, P27, **P4**.
Next row: **K2**, K34, **K7**.
Next row: **P7**, P34, **P2**.
Next row: **K1**, K11, **K3**, K23, **K5**.
Next row: **P4**, P25, **P5**, P9.
Next row: K5, **K8**, K28, **K2**.
Next row: P31, **P9**, P3.
Next row: **K11**, K29, **K3**.
Next row: **P7**, P26, **P7**, **P2togtbl**, **P1** (42 sts).
Next row: **K8**, K24, **K10**.
Next row: **P11**, P24, **P7**.
Next row: **K1**, **K2tog**, **K4**, K7, **K3**, K17, **K8** (41 sts).
Next row: **P6**, P20, **P4**, P6, **P5**.
Next row: **K1**, **k2tog**, **K1**, K5, **K6**, K22, **K4** (40 sts).
Next row: **P3**, P24, **P6**, P4, **P2togtbl**, **P1** (39 sts).
Next row: Cast off 2 sts, K2, **K8**, K25, **K1** (37 sts).
Next row: P27, **P7**, **P2togtbl**, P1 (36 sts).
Next row: Cast off 2 sts, **K2tog**, **K4**, K22, **K5** (33 sts).
Next row: **P7**, P22, **P4**.

Next row: **Cast off 2 sts**, K2, K3, **K5**, K13, **K7** (31 sts).
Next row: **P8**, P10, **P7**, P3, **P2togtbl**, P1 (30 sts).
Next row: **Cast off 2 sts**, K6, K14, **K4**, **K2tog**, **K1** (27 sts).
Next row: **P4**, P17, **P6**.
Next row: **K1**, **K2tog**, **K3**, K18, **K3** (26 sts).
Next row: **P2**, P20, **P1**, **P2togtbl**, **P1** (25 sts).
Next row: **K1**, **K2tog**, K21, **K1** (24 sts).
Next row: P23, **P1**.
Next row: K1, K2tog, K20, **K1** (23 sts).
Next row: **P3**, P17, **P3**.
Next row: **K5**, K13, **K5**.
Next row: **P6**, P13, **P4**.
Next row: **K4**, K16, **K3**.
Next row: **P2**, P19, **P2**.
Next row: **K1**, K10, **K1**, K10, **K1**.
Next row: P11, **P1**, P11.
Next row: K8, **K1**, K1, **K3**, K1, **K1**, K8.
Next row: P8, **P1**, P1, **P3**, P1, **P1**, P8.
Next row: K7, **cast off 9 sts**, K6 (14 sts).

Break off dark brown yarn and continue using light brown yarn only.

Work on first set of 7 sts only.

Purl 1 row.

Knit 1 row.

Next row: P4, P2togtbl, P1 (6 sts).

Knit 1 row.

Next row: P3, P2togtbl, P1 (5 sts).

Knit 1 row.

Next row: P2, P2togtbl, P1 (4 sts).

Next row: ssK, K2tog (2 sts).

Next row: P2tog (1 st).

Thread yarn through rem st and fasten off.

With WS facing, rejoin light brown yarn to rem 7 sts.

Purl 1 row.

Knit 1 row.

Next row: P1, P2tog, P4 (6 sts).

Knit 1 row.

Next row: P1, P2tog, P3 (5 sts).

Knit 1 row.

Next row: P1, P2tog, P2 (4 sts).

Next row: ssK, K2tog (2 sts).

Next row: P2tog (1 st).

Thread yarn through rem st and fasten off.

Base

Using light brown yarn and 4mm (UK 8, US 6) knitting needles, cast on 18 sts.

Starting with a knit row, work 2 rows in SS.

Next row: K1, M1, knit to last st, M1, K1 (20 sts).

Next row: P1, M1, purl to last st, M1, P1 (22 sts).

Rep last 2 rows twice more (30 sts).

Starting with a knit row, work 4 rows in SS.

Next row: K1, K2tog, knit to last 3 sts, ssK, K1 (28 sts).

Next row: P1, P2togtbl, purl to last 3 sts, P2tog, P1 (26 sts).

Rep last 2 rows twice more (18 sts).

Starting with a knit row, work 2 rows in SS.

Cast off.

Nose

Using black yarn and 2.75mm (UK 12, US 2) knitting needles, cast on 4 sts and knit 1 row.

Next row: P2tog, P2togtbl (2 sts).

Next row: K2tog (1 st).

Thread yarn through rem st and fasten off.

Toes (make two sets of three toes)

Using light brown yarn and 4mm (UK 8, US 6) knitting needles, cast on 2 sts.

Next row: **(Kfb) twice (4 sts).

Next row: (Kfb) four times (8 sts).

Knit 1 row.

Next row: (P2tog) four times (4 sts).

Next row: ssK, K2tog (2 sts).

Purl 1 row.**

Work from ** to ** twice more.

Cast off.

Tail

Using dark brown yarn and 4mm (UK 8, US 6) knitting needles, cast on 10 sts.

Starting with a knit row, work 11cm (4^1/$_3$in) in SS, ending with a knit row.

*****Next row:** P4, w&t.

Next row: K4, turn.

Next row: P6, w&t.

Next row: K6, turn.

Next row: P8, w&t.

Next row: K8, turn.

Rep from * four more times.

Purl 1 row (10 sts).

Next row: K1, K2tog, knit to last 3 sts, ssK, K1 (8 sts).

Purl 1 row.

Rep last 2 rows twice more (4 sts).

Cast off.

Making up

Place the body front, head and ears and the body back, head and ears together and sew the side seams, matching the markings. Using the photograph for guidance, attach the eyes.

Stuff two-thirds of the cat with toy filling. Fill the foot of the sock with rice so that it fits inside the cat. Firmly tie a piece of yarn around the heel to secure the rice in the sock, and fold the leg of the sock over the foot. Place the sock inside the cat and stuff with more toy filling until you are happy with the shape. Pin the base in place and sew the seam. Using the photograph for guidance, pin the tail in place, stuff lightly to make it look three dimensional and sew on securely.

Using the photograph for guidance and black yarn, sew the nose in place and embroider a mouth and whiskers.

Gather around the edges of each toe to give definition. Sew each set of three toes to the seam between the base of the cat and the front of the body.

Alley Cat

This artful alley cat is full of mischief, but he's just a big softy at heart.
With his cheeky grin and gentle nature, you will find him irresistible!

Materials

100g of ginger DK (8-ply) yarn
50g of cream DK (8-ply) yarn
Small amount of black 4-ply (fingering) yarn
Toy filling
Two 12mm (½in) plastic safety eyes, painted on the backs with gold nail polish

Needles

2.5mm (UK 13, US 1) and 4mm (UK 8, US 6) knitting needles

Tension

5 sts to 2.5cm (1in) measured over SS using DK (8-ply) yarn and 4mm (UK 8, US 6) knitting needles

Size

Approximately 31cm (12¼in) tall

Note: When knitting with the ginger yarn you are working in reverse stocking stitch, which means the 'wrong' side of the work becomes the 'right' side. This gives texture to the cat. When working with the cream yarn you are working in stocking stitch.

Body front

Using ginger yarn and 4mm (UK 8, US 6) knitting needles, cast on 20 sts.
Starting with a knit row, work 2 rows in SS.
Next row: K1, M1, knit to last st, M1, K1 (22 sts).
Next row: P1, M1, purl to last st, M1, P1 (24 sts).
Rep last 2 rows three more times (36 sts).
Next row: K26, w&t.
Next row: P16, w&t.
Next row: K19, w&t.
Next row: P22, w&t.
Next row: Knit to end (36 sts).

Starting with a purl row, work 5 rows in SS.

Next row: K1, ssK, knit to last 3 sts, K2tog, K1 (34 sts).

Starting with a purl row, work 3 rows in SS.

Rep last 4 rows seven more times (20 sts).

Next row: K1, ssK, knit to last 3 sts, K2tog, K1 (18 sts).

Purl 1 row.

Rep last 2 rows twice more (14 sts).

Cast off.

Body back

NB: when working the back of the body you start by creating a triangular shape which will be the base of the cat. You then need to pick up the stitches along the decreased edges over the next two rows to join the base to what will be the rest of the body. It is important that you pick up the stitches knitwise or purlwise as indicated so that you don't get a line on the right side of the body.

Using ginger yarn and 4mm (UK 8, US 6) knitting needles, cast on 20 sts.

Starting with a knit row, work 2 rows in SS.

Next row: K1, ssK, knit to last 3 sts, K2tog, K1 (18 sts).

Purl 1 row.

Rep last 2 rows four more times (10 sts).

Next row: K10, pick up 7 sts purlwise along decreased edge and purl these sts (17 sts).

Next row: P17, pick up 7 sts knitwise along decreased edge and knit these sts (24 sts).

Next row: K1, M1, knit to last st, M1, K1 (26 sts).

Next row: P1, M1, purl to last st, M1, P1 (28 sts).

Rep last 2 rows three more times (40 sts).

Starting with a knit row, work 6 rows in SS.

Next row: K1, ssK, knit to last 3 sts, K2tog, K1 (38 sts).

Starting with a purl row, work 3 rows in SS.

Rep last 4 rows once more (36 sts).

Next row: K1, ssK, K14, K2tog, K14, K2tog, K1 (33 sts).

Starting with a purl row, work 3 rows in SS.

Next row: K1, ssK, K27, K2tog, K1 (31 sts).

Starting with a purl row, work 3 rows in SS.

Next row: K1, ssK, K11, sl1, K2tog, psso, K11, K2tog, K1 (27 sts).

Starting with a purl row, work 3 rows in SS.

Next row: K1, ssK, K9, K2tog, K10, K2tog, K1 (24 sts).

Starting with a purl row, work 3 rows in SS.

Next row: K1, ssK, knit to last 3 sts, K2tog, K1 (22 sts).

Starting with a purl row, work 3 rows in SS.

Rep last 4 rows once more (20 sts).

Next row: K1, ssK, knit to last 3 sts, K2tog, K1 (18 sts).

Purl 1 row.

Rep last 2 rows twice more (14 sts).

Cast off.

Bib

Using cream yarn and 4mm (UK 8, US 6) knitting needles, cast on 12 sts and knit 1 row.

Next row: P1, M1, purl to last st, M1, P1 (14 sts).

Next row: K1, M1, knit to last st, M1, K1 (16 sts).

Rep last 2 rows once more (20 sts).

Next row: P1, M1, purl to last st, M1, P1 (22 sts).

Starting with a knit row, work 6 rows in SS.

Next row: K1, ssK, knit to last 3 sts, K2tog, K1 (20 sts).

Starting with a purl row, work 3 rows in SS.

Rep last 4 rows six more times (8 sts).

Cast off.

Head

Using ginger yarn and 4mm (UK 8, US 6) knitting needles, cast on 16 sts.

Purl 1 row.

*****Next row:** K1, M1, knit to last st, M1, K1 (18 sts).

Next row: P1, M1, purl to last st, M1, P1 (20 sts).

Rep last 2 rows once more (24 sts).

Next row: K1, M1, knit to last st, M1, K1 (26 sts).

Starting with a purl row, work 13 rows in SS.*

Next row: K1, ssK, knit to last 3 sts, K2tog, K1 (24 sts).

Next row: P1, P2tog, purl to last 3 sts, P2togtbl, P1 (22 sts).

Rep last 2 rows once more (18 sts).

Next row: K1, ssK, knit to last 3 sts, K2tog, K1 (16 sts).

Purl 1 row.

Rep from * to * (26 sts).

Next row: K1, ssK, knit to last 3 sts, K2tog, K1 (24 sts).

Next row: P1, P2tog, purl to last 3 sts, P2togtbl, P1 (22 sts).

Rep last 2 rows once more (18 sts).

Next row: K1, ssK, knit to last 3 sts, K2tog, K1 (16 sts).

Cast off.

Face

Using cream yarn and 4mm (UK 8, US 6) knitting needles, cast on 18 sts.

Next row: K1, M1, K7, M1, K2, M1, K7, M1, K1 (22 sts).

Purl 1 row.

Next row: K1, ssK, K7, M1, K2, M1, K7, K2tog, K1 (22 sts).

Purl 1 row.

Rep last 2 rows four more times.

Next row: K1, ssK, knit to last 3 sts, K2tog, K1 (20 sts).

Purl 1 row.

Next row: K1, ssK, K4, K2tog, K2, ssK, K4, K2tog, K1 (16 sts).

Purl 1 row.

Next row: K1, ssK, K2, K2tog, K2, ssK, K2, K2tog, K1 (12 sts).

Arms (make two)

Using ginger yarn and 4mm (UK 8, US 6) knitting needles, cast on 18 sts.

Starting with a knit row, work 7cm (2¾in) in SS, ending with a knit row.

Change to cream DK (8-ply) yarn.

Starting with a knit row, work 4 rows in SS.

Next row: K1, M1, K7, M1, K2, M1, K7, M1, K1 (22 sts).

Purl 1 row.

Next row: K1, M1, K9, M1, K2, M1, K9, M1, K1 (26 sts).

Purl 1 row.

Starting with a knit row, work 2 rows in SS.

Next row: K1, ssK, K7, ssK, K2, K2tog, K7, K2tog, K1 (22 sts).

Next row: P1, P2tog, P5, P2togtbl, P2, P2tog, P5, P2togtbl, P1 (18 sts).

Cast off.

Legs (make two)

Using ginger yarn and 4mm (UK 8, US 6) knitting needles, cast on 18 sts and work 8cm (3⅛in) in SS.

Cast off.

Feet (make two)

Using cream yarn and 4mm (UK 8, US 6) knitting needles, cast on 7 sts and knit 1 row.

Next row: P1, M1, purl to last st, M1, P1 (9 sts).

Next row: K1, M1, knit to last st, M1, K1 (11 sts).

Starting with a purl row, work 5 rows in SS.

Next row: K1, M1, knit to last st, M1, K1 (13 sts).

Purl 1 row.

Rep last 2 rows once more (15 sts).

Starting with a knit row, work 2 rows in SS.

Next row: K1, ssK, knit to last 3 sts, K2tog, K1 (13 sts).

Next row: P1, P2tog, purl to last 3 sts, P2togtbl, P1 (11 sts).

Starting with a knit row, work 3 rows in SS.

Next row: P1, M1, purl to last st, M1, P1 (13 sts).

Next row: K1, M1, knit to last st, M1, K1 (15 sts).

Starting with a purl row, work 3 rows in SS.

Next row: K1, ssK, knit to last 3 sts, K2tog, K1 (13 sts).

Purl 1 row.

Rep last 2 rows once more (11 sts).

Starting with a K row, work 4 rows in SS.

Next row: K1, ssK, knit to last 3 sts, K2tog, K1 (9 sts).

Next row: P1, P2tog, purl to last 3 sts, P2togtbl, P1 (7 sts).

Cast off.

Purl 1 row.

Next row: K1, ssK, knit to last 3 sts, K2tog, K1 (10 sts).

Purl 1 row.

Rep last 2 rows three more times (4 sts).

Next row: ssK, K2tog (2 sts).

Cast off.

Ears (make two)

The ears are worked in GS.

Using ginger yarn and 4mm (UK 8, US 6) knitting needles, cast on 12 sts and knit 2 rows.

Next row: K1, ssK, knit to last 3 sts, K2tog, K1 (10 sts).

Knit 2 rows.

Rep last 3 rows three more times (4 sts).

Next row: ssK, K2tog (2 sts).

Next row: K2tog (1 st).

Thread yarn through rem st and fasten off.

Nose

Using black yarn and 2.5mm (UK 13, US 1) knitting needles, cast on 5 sts.

Starting with a knit row, work 2 rows in SS.

Next row: ssK, K1, K2tog (3 sts).

Purl 1 row.

Next row: Sl1, K2tog, psso (1 st).

Thread yarn through rem st and fasten off.

Tail

Using ginger yarn and 4mm (UK 8, US 6) knitting needles, cast on 16 sts, and work 14cm (5½in) in SS, ending with a K row.

Change to cream yarn.

Starting with a knit row (RS), work 8 rows in SS.

Next row: (K2, K2tog) four times (12 sts).

Purl 1 row.

Next row: (K2, K2tog) three times (9 sts).

Purl 1 row.

Next row: (K2tog) four times, K1 (5 sts).

Thread yarn through rem sts and fasten off.

Making up

Sew the side seam and the end of each arm and stuff with toy filling, remembering that the 'wrong' side of the ginger yarn knitting will be on the outside. Using the photograph for guidance and cream yarn, oversew the end of each arm with two long stitches to form a paw shape. With the reverse stocking stitch facing outwards, sew the seams of each leg. With WS together, sew the seams of each foot, stuffing with toy filling as you go. Using cream yarn, oversew the end of each foot with two long stitches to form a paw shape, as for the arms.

Sew the bottom of one leg to the top of one foot, and stuff with toy filling. Repeat for the second leg and foot.

Sew the side seam of the tail, remembering that the 'wrong' side of the ginger yarn knitting will be on the outside. Stuff with toy filling.

With the reverse stocking stitch facing outwards, pin the body front and back pieces together, positioning the arms and legs in place between the seams.

Sew the side seams of the body together, stitching the arms and legs in place as you go. Stuff with toy filling.

Using the photograph for guidance, sew the tail to the back of the body, remembering that the 'wrong' side of the ginger yarn knitting is the 'right' side.

With the reverse stocking stitch facing outwards, sew the side seams of the head and stuff lightly with toy filling. Sew the face to the front of the head with the right side of the face facing outwards and stuff lightly to give definition as you go. Paint the back of the safety eyes with gold nail polish and attach them to the face, using the photograph for guidance.

Place more toy filling inside the head. Using the photograph for guidance and black yarn, sew the nose to the front of the face and embroider a mouth and whiskers. Sew the ears to the top of the head. Sew the head to the body. Sew the bib to the front of the body, matching the top of the bib to the cream bottom edge of the face.

Christmas Cat

What a lovely surprise to find in your Christmas stocking! This cute kitten makes a great tree decoration or stocking filler for the festive season. The pattern for the little white mouse is also provided.

Materials

50g of red 5-ply (sportweight) yarn
50g of green 5-ply (sportweight) yarn
50g of grey DK (8-ply) yarn
Small amount of pale pink 2-ply (laceweight) yarn
Small amount of white 4-ply (fingering) angora yarn
Two 8mm (1/3in) plastic safety eyes, painted on the backs with gold nail polish
Toy filling
Two tiny blue beads
Strong black sewing cotton
White sewing cotton

Needles

2.75mm (UK 12, US 2) and 3.25mm (UK 10, US 3) knitting needles

Tension

6 sts to 2.5cm (1in) measured over GS using 5-ply (sportweight) yarn and 3.25mm (UK 10, US 3) knitting needles

Size

Approximately 20cm (7¾in) long, from top of cat's head to toe of stocking

Happy Christmas!

Stocking

Note: The heel and toe of the Christmas stocking are knitted in garter stitch using short row shaping. Start by working one less stitch on each row to create the heel/toe shape. Once you have reached the middle of the heel/toe, work outwards again, working one extra stitch on every row to get back to the top of the heel/toe. The heel and toe are worked over half the row (17 sts).

Using red yarn and 3.25mm (UK 10, US 3) knitting needles, cast on a picot edging as follows:

(Cast on 5 sts, cast off 2 sts, pass st on right knitting needle to left knitting needle) eleven times, cast on 1 st (34 sts).

Work 12 rows in GS.

Starting with a knit row, work 4 rows in SS.

Change to green yarn.

Starting with a knit row, work 2 rows in SS.

Change to red yarn.

Starting with a knit row, work 2 rows in SS.

Rep the last 4 rows six more times.

Change to green yarn.

Starting with a knit row, work 2 rows in SS.

Change to red yarn.

Knit 1 row.

Begin heel shaping.

NB: all slipped stitches are slipped knitwise.

*Next row: (WS) K17, turn.
Next row: Sl1, K15, turn.
Next row: Sl1, K14, turn.
Next row: Sl1, K13, turn.
Next row: Sl1, K12, turn.
Next row: Sl1, K11, turn.
Next row: Sl1, K10, turn.
Next row: Sl1, K9, turn.
Next row: Sl1, K8, turn.
Next row: Sl1, K7, turn.
Next row: Sl1, K6, turn.
Next row: Sl1, K5, turn.
Next row: Sl1, K4, turn.
Next row: Sl1, K3, turn.

You will now start working outwards again, working one extra stitch on each row.
Next row: Sl1, K4, turn.
Next row: Sl1, K5, turn.
Next row: Sl1, K6, turn.
Next row: Sl1, K7, turn.
Next row: Sl1, K8, turn.
Next row: Sl1, K9, turn.
Next row: Sl1, K10, turn.
Next row: Sl1, K11, turn.
Next row: Sl1, K12, turn.
Next row: Sl1, K13, turn.
Next row: Sl1, K14, turn.
Next row: Sl1, K15, turn.
Next row: Sl1, K16, turn.
Next row: Sl1, K17, turn.
Next row: Purl across all sts (34 sts).*
Change to green yarn.
Starting with a knit row, work 2 rows in SS.
Change to red yarn.
Starting with a knit row, work 2 rows in SS.
Rep the last 4 rows twice more.
Change to green yarn.
Starting with a knit row, work 2 rows in SS.

Change to red yarn.
Knit 1 row.
Rep from * to * as for heel shaping.
With RS together, cast off rem 34 sts using the three-needle cast-off technique (see page 17) and red yarn.

Hanging loop
Using red yarn and 3.25mm (UK 10, US 3) knitting needles, cast on 18 sts and knit 1 row.
Cast off.

Cat

Head
Using grey yarn and 3.25mm (UK 10, US 3) knitting needles, cast on 12 sts.
Next row: K1, M1, K5, M1, K5, M1, K1 (15 sts).
Purl 1 row.
Next row: K6, M1, K3, M1, K6 (17 sts).
Next row: P1, M1, P6, M1, P3, M1, P6, M1, P1 (21 sts).
Next row: K9, M1, K3, M1, K9 (23 sts).
Next row: P1, M1, P9, M1, P3, M1, P9, M1, P1 (27 sts).
Next row: K12, M1, K3, M1, K12 (29 sts).
Starting with a purl row, work 3 rows in SS.
Next row: K11, ssK, K3, K2tog, K11 (27 sts).
Next row: P10, P2tog, P3, P2togtbl, P10 (25 sts).
Next row: K9, ssK, K3, K2tog, K9 (23 sts).
Next row: P8, P2tog, P3, P2togtbl, P8 (21 sts).
Next row: K7, ssK, K3, K2tog, K7 (19 sts).
Next row: P6, P2tog, P3, P2togtbl, P6 (17 sts).
Next row: K1, ssK, K11, K2tog, K1 (15 sts).
Next row: P1, P2tog, purl to last 3 sts, P2togtbl, P1 (13 sts).
Next row: Cast off 3 sts, K6, cast off rem 3 sts (7 sts).
With WS facing, rejoin grey yarn to rem 7 sts.
Starting with a purl row, work 11 rows in SS.
Next row: K1, ssK, K1, K2tog, K1 (5 sts).
Starting with a purl row, work 3 rows in SS.
Next row: K1, sl1, K2tog, psso, K1 (3 sts).
Purl 1 row.
Cast off.

Ears (make two)
Using grey yarn and 3.25mm (UK 10, US 3) knitting needles, cast on 6 sts.
Starting with a knit row, work 2 rows in SS.
Next row: ssK, K2, K2tog (4 sts).
Purl 1 row.
Next row: ssK, K2tog (2 sts).
Next row: P2tog (1 st).
Thread yarn through rem st and fasten off.

Ear linings (make two)
Using a double strand of pink yarn and 2.75mm (UK 12, US 2) knitting needles, cast on 7 sts.
Starting with a knit row, work 2 rows in SS.

Next row: ssK, knit to last 2 sts, K2tog (5 sts).
Purl 1 row.
Rep the last 2 rows once more (3 sts).
Next row: Sl1, K2tog, psso (1 st).
Thread yarn through rem st and fasten off.

Nose

Using a double strand of pink yarn and 2.75mm (UK 12, US 2) knitting needles, cast on 3 sts.
Starting with a knit row, work 2 rows in SS.
Next row: Sl1, K2tog, psso (1 st).
Thread yarn through rem st and fasten off

Feet (make two)

Using grey yarn and 3.25mm (UK 10, US 3) knitting needles, cast on 2 sts.
Next row: (Kfb) twice (4 sts).
Next row: (Kfb) four times (8 sts).
Knit 1 row.
Next row: (P2tog) four times (4 sts).
Next row: (K2tog) twice (2 sts).
Purl 1 row.
Rep last 6 rows twice more to make three toes.
Cast off.

Mouse

Body and head

Using white angora yarn and 2.75mm (UK 12, US 2) knitting needles, cast on 3 sts and knit 1 row.
Next row: K1, M1, knit to last st, M1, K1 (5 sts).
Rep last row six more times (17 sts).
Next row: (K2tog) four times, K1, (K2tog) four times (9 sts).
Next row: (K2tog) twice, K1, (K2tog) twice (5 sts).
Thread yarn through rem sts and fasten off.

Ears (make two)

Using white angora yarn and 2.75mm (UK 12, US 2) knitting needles, cast on 4 sts and knit 4 rows.
Next row: (K2tog) twice (2 sts).
Next row: K2tog (1 st).
Thread yarn through rem st and fasten off.

Tail

Using white angora yarn and 2.75mm (UK 12, US 2) knitting needles, cast on 3 sts.
Starting with a knit row, work in SS until tail measures 4cm (1½in), ending with a purl row.
Thread yarn through sts to fasten off.
Alternatively, work the mouse's tail as an i-cord (see page 14).

Making up (for Stocking, Cat and Mouse)

Join the side seam of the stocking, carefully lining up the stripes. Fold over the red cuff at the top of the stocking and lightly stuff the stocking with toy filling. Fold the

hanging loop in half and sew it to the side seam on the inside of the stocking.

Attach the safety eyes to the cat's head and sew the head seams in place at the back of the head. Stuff with toy filling. With WS together, sew one ear to one ear lining to make one ear. Repeat for the second ear. Using the photograph for guidance, sew the ears to the top of the cat's head. Sew the nose in place. Thread strong black sewing cotton through each side of the face and trim to make whiskers.

Using a sewing needle and grey yarn, sew from the base of the head through to the back of each eye, pull the yarn back down to the base and tighten. This gives a realistic shape to the head. Place the cat's head inside the stocking and sew the head to the inside edge of the stocking all the way round, so that the head is peeping out of the stocking.

Sew around each of the cat's 'toes' and gather to form each one into a bobble. Attach the feet to the front of the stocking just under the head, where the head and the stocking meet.

Sew the seam of the mouse's body and head, stuffing with toy filling as you go. Using the photograph for guidance, sew the mouse's ears in place. Using white sewing cotton and a sewing needle, sew two tiny blue beads to the head for eyes. Thread a strand of white sewing cotton though each side of the face and trim to make whiskers. Using pale pink yarn, embroider the nose.

Sew the side seam of the tail to the base of the body and attach the mouse to the stocking.

Happy Family

This mother and her two playful kittens make a delightful family group. Knit as many kittens as you like and in whatever colours you choose – a gorgeous gift for cat lovers everywhere!

Mother Cat

Materials
50g of white 10-ply (aran) yarn
50g of black 10-ply (aran) yarn
Small amount of pale pink 4-ply (fingering) yarn
Small amount of red 4-ply (fingering) yarn
Toy filling
Three chenille sticks
Two 10mm (³/₈in) blue eyes
Black embroidery thread
10mm (³/₈in) brass bell

Tools
2.75mm (UK 12, US 2) and 4mm (UK 8, US 6) knitting needles
Stitch markers

Tension
4 sts to 2.5cm (1in) measured over SS using 10-ply (Aran) yarn and 4mm (UK 8, US 6) knitting needles

Size
Approximately 15cm (6in) tall

Body and front legs
Using white yarn and 4mm (UK 8, US 6) knitting needles, cast on 10 sts.
Knit 1 row.
Next row: P8, turn.
Next row: K3, turn,
Next row: P3, turn,
Next row: K3, turn.
Next row: Purl to end (10 sts).

Next row: Purl to end (10 sts).
Next row: K2, K3B, K5.
Starting with a purl row, work 5 rows in SS.
Next row: K6, M1, K3, M1, K1 (12 sts).
Purl 1 row.
Change to black yarn.
Starting with a knit row, work 3 rows in SS.
Next row: Cast off 1 st, purl to end (11 sts).
Next row: Cast off 5 sts, knit to end (6 sts).
Next row: Cast on 8 sts, purl to end (14 sts).
Next row: K1, M1, knit to last st, M1, K1 (16 sts).
Next row: P1, M1, purl to end (17 sts).
Next row: Knit to last st, M1, K1 (18 sts).
Next row: P1, M1, purl to end (19 sts).
Starting with a purl row, work 24 rows in SS, placing a marker at beg and end of the 12th row.
Next row: Knit to last 3 sts, K2tog, K1 (18 sts).
Next row: P1, P2tog, purl to end (17 sts).
Next row: K1, ssK, knit to last 3 sts, K2tog, K1 (15 sts).
Next row: Cast off 8 sts, P3, P2tog, P1 (6 sts).
Next row: Cast on 5 sts, knit to end (11 sts).
Next row: Cast on 1 st, purl to end (12 sts).
Starting with a knit row, work 3 rows in SS.
Change to white yarn.
Starting with a purl row, work 3 rows in SS.
Next row: K5, ssK, K2, K2tog, K1 (10 sts).

Starting with a purl row, work 5 rows in SS.
Next row: K5, turn.
Next row: P3, turn.
Next row: K3, turn.
Next row: P3, turn.
Next row: Knit to end (10 sts).
Next row: P5, P3B, P2.
Cast off.

Belly
Using white yarn and 4mm (UK 8, US 6) knitting needles, cast on 3 sts.
Starting with a knit row, work 2 rows in SS.
Next row: K1, M1, knit to last st, M1, K1 (5 sts).
Starting with a purl row, work 3 rows in SS.
Rep the last 4 rows three more times (11 sts).
Starting with a knit row, work 14 rows in SS.
Next row: K1, ssK, knit to last 3 sts, K2tog, K1 (9 sts).
Starting with a purl row, work 3 rows in SS.
Rep the last 4 rows once more (7 sts).
Next row: K2tog, K3, ssK (5 sts).
Purl 1 row.
Cast off.

Head
Using black yarn and 4mm (UK 8, US 6) knitting needles, cast on 12 sts.
Next row: K1, M1, K5, M1, K5, M1, K1 (15 sts).
Purl 1 row.

Let's play cat and mouse!

Using the Fair Isle technique to carry the yarn (see page 14), work as follows:

Work all sts in **bold** using black yarn and all other sts using white yarn.

Next row: **K6**, **M1**, K3, **M1**, **K6** (17 sts).
Next row: **P1**, **M1**, **P6**, M1, P3, M1, **P6**, **M1**, **P1** (21 sts).
Next row: **K8**, K1, M1, K3, M1, K1, **K8** (23 sts).
Next row: **P1**, **M1**, **P7**, P2, M1, P3, M1, P2, **P7**, **M1**, **P1** (27 sts).
Next row: **K9**, K3, M1, K3, M1, K3, **K9** (29 sts).
Next row: **P9**, P11, **P9**.
Next row: **K9**, K11, **K9**.
Next row: **P9**, P11, **P9**.
Next row: **K9**, K2, ssK, K3, K2tog, K2, **K9** (27 sts).
Next row: **P9**, P1, P2tog, P3, P2togtbl, P1, **P9** (25 sts).
Next row: **K9**, ssK, K3, K2tog, **K9** (23 sts).
Next row: **P8**, **P2togtbl**, P3, **P2tog**, **P8** (21 sts).
Next row: **K7**, **ssK**, K3, **K2tog**, **K7** (19 sts).
Next row: **P6**, **P2togtbl**, P3, **P2tog**, **P6** (17 sts).
Next row: **K1**, **ssK**, **K5**, K1, **K5**, **K2tog**, **K1** (15 sts).
Break off white yarn and continue using black yarn only.
Next row: P1, P2tog, purl to last 3 sts, P2togtbl, P1 (13 sts).
Next row: Cast off 3 sts, K6, cast off rem 3 sts (7 sts).
With RS facing, rejoin black yarn to rem 7 sts.
Starting with a knit row, work 12 rows in SS.
Next row: K1, ssK, K1, K2tog, K1 (5 sts).
Starting with a purl row, work 3 rows in SS.
Next row: K1, sl1, K2tog, psso, K1 (3 sts).
Purl 1 row.
Cast off.

Ears (make two)
Using black yarn and 4mm (UK 8, US 6) knitting needles, cast on 7 sts.
Starting with a knit row, work 2 rows in SS.
Next row: K1, ssK, K1, K2tog, K1 (5 sts).
Purl 1 row.
Next row: ssK, K1, K2tog (3 sts).
Purl 1 row.
Next row: Sl1, K2tog, psso (1 st).
Thread yarn through rem st and fasten off.

Ear linings (make two)
Using pale pink yarn and 2.75mm (UK 12, US 2) knitting needles, work as for ears.

Nose
Using pale pink yarn and 2.75mm (UK 12, US 2) knitting needles, cast on 4 sts.
Starting with a knit row, work 2 rows in SS.
Next row: ssK, K2tog (2 sts).
Next row: P2tog (1 st).
Thread yarn through rem st and fasten off.

Back leg (left)
Using white yarn and 4mm (UK 8, US 6) knitting needles, cast on 10 sts and knit 1 row.
Next row: P5, turn.
Next row: K3, turn.
Next row: P3, turn.
Next row: K3, turn.
Next row: Purl to end (10 sts).
Next row: K5, K3B, K2.
Starting with a purl row, work 7 rows in SS.
Next row: K4, w&t.
Next row: P3, w&t.
Next row: K3, w&t.
Next row: P3, w&t.
Next row: K3, w&t.
Next row: Purl to end (10 sts).
Next row: (K1, M1) twice, K3, M1, K1, M1, K4 (14 sts).
Using the Fair Isle technique to carry the yarn (see page 14), work as follows:
Work all sts in **bold** using black yarn and all other sts using white yarn.
Next row: P8, **P6**.
Next row: **K2**, **M1**, **K1**, **M1**, **K4**, K1, M1, K1, M1, K5 (18 sts).
Next row: P8, **P10**.
Next row: **Cast off 3 sts**, **M1**, **K7**, K6, M1, K1 (17 sts).
Next row: Cast off 6 sts, M1, **purl to last st**, **M1**, **P1** (13 sts).
Break off white yarn and continue using black yarn only.
Starting with a knit row, work 4 rows in SS.
Next row: K1, ssK, knit to last 3 sts, K2tog, K1 (11 sts).
Next row: P1, P2tog, purl to last 3 sts, P2togtbl, P1 (9 sts).
Rep last 2 rows once more (5 sts).
Cast off.

Back leg (right)
Using white yarn and 4mm (UK 8, US 6) knitting needles, cast on 10 sts and knit 1 row.
Next row: P8, turn.
Next row: K3, turn.
Next row: P3, turn.
Next row: K3, turn.
Next row: Purl to end (10 sts).
Next row: K2, K3B, K5.
Starting with a purl row, work 7 rows in SS.
Next row: K9, w&t.
Next row: P3, w&t.
Next row: K3, w&t.
Next row: P3, w&t.
Next row: K3, w&t.
Next row: Purl to end (10 sts).
Next row: K4, M1, K1, M1, K3, (M1, K1) twice (14 sts).

Using the Fair Isle technique to carry the yarn (see page 14), work as follows:

Work all sts in **bold** using black yarn and all other sts using white yarn.

Next row: P6, P8.

Next row: K5, M1, K1, M1, K1, K4, M1, K1, M1, K2 (18 sts).

Next row: P10, P8.

Next row: Cast off 6 sts, M1, knit to last st, M1, K1 (14 sts).

Next row: Cast off 3 sts, M1, purl to last st, M1, P1 (13 sts).

Break off white yarn and continue using black yarn only.

Starting with a knit row, work 4 rows in SS.

Next row: K1, K2tog, knit to last 3 sts, ssK, K1 (11 sts).

Next row: P1, P2togtbl, purl to last 3 sts, P2tog, P1 (9 sts).

Rep last 2 rows once more (5 sts).

Cast off.

Tail

Using black yarn and 4mm (UK 8, US 6) knitting needles, cast on 7 sts.

Starting with a knit row, work 8cm (3¼in) in SS, ending with a purl row.

Change to white yarn.

Starting with a knit row, work 2 rows in SS.

Next row: (K1, K2tog) twice, K1 (5 sts).

Purl 1 row.

Thread yarn through rem sts and fasten off.

Collar

Using red yarn and 2.75mm (UK 12, US 2) knitting needles, cast on 5 sts.

Starting with a knit row, work in SS until collar is long enough to go around the cat's neck, ending with a purl row.

Cast off.

Making up

Pin the middle of the cast-off end of the cat's belly to the marker at the tail end of the body, and the middle of the cast-on edge to the marker between the front paws. Sew the belly to the sides of the body, being careful not to pucker the front legs when catching the stitches to the belly. Stuff with toy filling as you go.

Thread a chenille stick through the front of the body and slide the ends down inside the front legs. Run a gathering thread through the cast-on stitches of each front leg, pull tightly and secure. Sew the side seam of each front leg, stuffing with toy filling as you go. Sew the cast-off stitches of each front leg to the belly. Sew the foot and leg seams of each back leg, as for the front legs.

Slide a length of chenille stick inside each back leg and stuff lightly with toy filling. Using the photograph for guidance, sew each back leg to the body. Sew the cast-off stitches to the belly.

Sew the tail seam and slide a length of chenille stick inside. Using the photograph for guidance, sew the tail to the back of the body.

Sew the head seams and stuff the head with toy filling. Using the photograph for guidance, attach the eyes to the head. Fold the head piece in half and sew the back seams, stuffing with toy filling as you go. Using a needle and black yarn, sew from the base of the head to the back of each eye, pull the thread back down to the base and tighten. This gives a realistic shape to the head. With WS together, sew one ear and one ear lining together to make one ear. Repeat for the second ear. Using the photograph for guidance, sew the ears to the top of the head.

Using the photograph for guidance and pale pink yarn, sew the nose in place. Using black embroidery thread, embroider a mouth and whiskers.

Sew the head to the body. Place the collar around the cat's neck and sew the cast-on and cast-off edges together. Sew the bell in place.

Happy Family Kitten

Materials
10g of white 4-ply (fingering) yarn
15g of black 4-ply (fingering) yarn
Small amount of pale pink 4-ply (fingering) yarn
Small amount of red 4-ply (fingering) yarn
Toy filling
Three chenille sticks
Two 6mm (¼in) blue eyes
Black embroidery thread
Small brass bell

Tools
2.75mm (UK 12, US 2) knitting needles
Stitch markers

Tension
7–8 sts to 2.5cm (1in) measured over SS using
4-ply (fingering) yarn and 2.75mm (UK 12, US 2)
knitting needles

Size
Approximately 8cm (3¼in) tall

Body and front legs
Using white yarn and 2.75mm (UK 12, US 2) knitting
needles, cast on 8 sts and knit 1 row.
Next row: P6, turn.
Next row: K3, turn.
Next row: P3, turn.
Next row: K3, turn.
Next row: Purl to end (8 sts).
Next row: K2, K3B, K3.
Starting with a purl row, work 5 rows in SS.
Next row: K4, M1, K3, M1, K1 (10 sts).
Purl 1 row.
Change to black yarn.
Knit 1 row.
Next row: Cast off 1 st, purl to end (9 sts).
Next row: Cast off 4 sts, knit to end (5 sts).
Next row: Cast on 8 sts, purl to end (13 sts).
Next row: K1, M1, knit to last st, M1, K1 (15 sts).
Next row: P1, M1, purl to end (16 sts).
Next row: Knit to last st, M1, K1 (17 sts).
Purl 1 row.
Starting with a knit row, work 16 rows in SS, placing a
marker at beg and end of the 8th row.
Next row: Knit to last 3 sts, ssK, K1 (16 sts).

Next row: P1, P2tog, purl to end (15 sts).
Next row: K1, K2tog, knit to last 3 sts, ssK, K1 (13 sts).
Next row: Cast off 8 sts, purl to end (5 sts).
Next row: Cast on 4 sts, knit to end (9 sts).
Next row: Cast on 1 st, purl to end (10 sts).
Change to white yarn.
Starting with a knit row, work 2 rows in SS.
Next row: K4, ssK, K1, K2tog, K1 (8 sts).
Starting with a purl row, work 6 rows in SS.
Next row: P6, turn.
Next row: K3, turn.
Next row: P3, turn.
Next row: K3, turn.
Next row: Purl to end (8 sts).
Next row: K2, K3B, K3.
Cast off.

Belly
Using white yarn and 2.75mm (UK 12, US 2) knitting
needles, cast on 3 sts.
Starting with a knit row, work 2 rows in SS.
Next row: K1, M1, knit to last st, M1, K1 (5 sts).

Starting with a purl row, work 3 rows in SS.

Rep last 4 rows twice more (9 sts).

Starting with a knit row, work 10 rows in SS.

Next row: K1, ssK, knit to last 3 sts, K2tog, K1 (7 sts).

Starting with a purl row, work 3 rows in SS.

Rep last 4 rows once more (5 sts).

Next row: ssK, K1, K2tog (3 sts).

Purl 1 row.

Cast off.

Head

Using black yarn and 2.75mm (UK 12, US 2) knitting needles, cast on 8 sts.

Next row: K1, M1, K3, M1, K3, M1, K1 (11 sts).

Purl 1 row.

Using the Fair Isle technique (see page 14), work as follows:

Work all sts in **bold** using black yarn and all other sts using white yarn.

Next row: **K4**, **M1**, K3, **M1**, **K4** (13 sts).

Next row: **P1**, **M1**, **P4**, M1, P3, M1, **P4**, **M1**, **P1** (17 sts).

Next row: **K6**, K1, M1, K3, M1, K1, **K6** (19 sts).

Next row: **P1**, **M1**, **P5**, P2, M1, P3, M1, P2, **P5**, **M1**, **P1** (23 sts).

Next row: **K7**, K3, M1, K3, M1, K3, **K7** (25 sts).

Next row: **P7**, P11, **P7**.

Next row: **K7**, K2, K2tog, K3, ssK, K2, **K7** (23 sts).

Next row: **P7**, P1, P2tog, P3, P2togtbl, P1, **P7** (21 sts).

Next row: **K7**, K2tog, K3, ssK, **K7** (19 sts).

Next row: **P6**, **P2tog**, P3, **P2togtbl**, **P6** (17 sts).

Next row: **K5**, **ssK**, K3, **K2tog**, **K5** (15 sts).

Next row: P4, **P2togtbl**, P1, P1, P1, **P2tog**, P4 (13 sts).

Break off white yarn and continue using black yarn only.

Next row: K1, ssK, K7, K2tog, K1 (11 sts).

Next row: P1, P2tog, purl to last 3 sts, P2togtbl, P1 (9 sts).

Next row: Cast off 2 sts, K4, cast off rem 2 sts.

With RS facing, rejoin black yarn to rem 5 sts.

Starting with a knit row, work 6 rows in SS.

Next row: K1, M1, knit to last st, M1, K1 (7 sts).

Starting with a purl row, work 3 rows in SS.

Next row: K1, K2tog, K1, ssK, K1 (5 sts).

Starting with a purl row, work 7 rows in SS.

Next row: K2tog, K1, ssK (3 sts).

Purl 1 row.

Cast off.

Ears (make two)

Using black yarn and 2.75mm (UK 12, US 2) knitting needles, cast on 5 sts.

Starting with a knit row, work 2 rows in SS.

Next row: ssK, K1, K2tog (3 sts).

Purl 1 row.

Next row: Sl1, K2tog, psso (1 st).

Thread yarn through rem st and fasten off.

Ear linings (make two)

Using pale pink yarn and 2.75mm (UK 12, US 2) knitting needles, cast on 4 sts.

Starting with a knit row, work 2 rows in SS.

Next row: K1, K2tog, K1 (3 sts).

Purl 1 row.

Next row: Sl1, K2tog, psso (1 st).

Thread yarn through rem st and fasten off.

Back leg (left)

Using white yarn and 2.75mm (UK 12, US 2) knitting needles, cast on 8 sts and knit 1 row.

Next row: P5, turn.

Next row: K3, turn.

Next row: P3, turn.

Next row: K3, turn.

Next row: Purl to end (8 sts).

Next row: K3, K3B, K2.

Starting with a purl row, work 5 rows in SS.

Next row: K3, w&t.

Next row: P2, w&t.

Next row: K2, w&t.

Next row: Purl to end (8 sts).

Next row: (K1, M1) twice, K2, M1, K1, M1, K3 (12 sts).

Purl 1 row.

Next row: K2, M1, K1, M1, K4, M1, K1, M1, K4 (16 sts).

Using the Fair Isle technique (see page 14), work as follows:

Work all sts in **bold** using black yarn and all other sts using white yarn.

Next row: P8, **P8**.

Next row: **Cast off 3 sts**, **M1**, **K5**, K6, M1, K1 (15 sts).

Next row: Cast off 5 sts, M1, P1, **P7**, **M1**, **P1** (12 sts).

Break off white yarn and continue using black yarn only.

Starting with a knit row, work 4 rows in SS.

Next row: K1, ssK, knit to last 3 sts, K2tog, K1 (10 sts).

Next row: P1, P2tog, purl to last 3 sts, P2togtbl, P1 (8 sts).

Rep last 2 rows once more (4 sts).

Cast off.

Back leg (right)

Using white yarn and 2.75mm (UK 12, US 2) knitting needles, cast on 8 sts and knit 1 row.

Next row: P6, turn.

Next row: K3, turn.

Next row: P3, turn.

Next row: K3, turn.

Next row: Purl to end (8 sts).

Next row: K2, K3B, K3.

Starting with a purl row, work 5 rows in SS.

Next row: K7, w&t.

Next row: P2, w&t.

Next row: K2, w&t.

Next row: Purl to end (8 sts).

Next row: K3, M1, K1, M1, K2, (M1, K1) twice (12 sts).

Purl 1 row.

Next row: K4, M1, K1, M1, K4, M1, K1, M1, K2 (16 sts).

Using the Fair Isle technique (see page 14), work as follows:

Work all sts in **bold** using black yarn and all other sts using white yarn.

Next row: **P8**, P8.

Next row: Cast off 5 sts, M1, K1, **K8**, **M1**, **K1** (13 sts).

Next row: **Cast off 3 sts**, **M1**, **P8**, M1, P1 (12 sts).

Break off white yarn and continue using black yarn only.

Starting with a knit row, work 4 rows in SS.

Next row: K1, ssK, knit to last 3 sts, K2tog, K1 (10 sts).

Next row: P1, P2tog, purl to last 3 sts, P2togtbl, P1 (8 sts).

Rep last 2 rows once more (4 sts).

Cast off.

Tail

Using black yarn and 2.75mm (UK 12, US 2) knitting needles, cast on 7 sts and work 4.5cm (1¾in) in SS, ending with a knit row.

Change to white yarn.

Starting with a purl row, work 3 rows in SS.

Next row: (K1, K2tog) twice, K1 (5 sts).

Purl 1 row.

Thread yarn through rem sts and fasten off.

Collar

Using red yarn and 2.75mm (UK 12, US 2) knitting needles, cast on 3 sts.

Starting with a knit row, work in SS until collar is long enough to go around the kitten's neck, ending with a purl row.

Cast off.

Making up

Pin the middle of the cast-off end of the kitten's belly to the marker at the tail end of the body and the middle of the cast-on edge to the marker between the front feet. Sew the belly to the sides of the body, being careful not to pucker the front legs when catching the stitches to the belly. Stuff with toy filling as you go. Thread a chenille stick through the front of the body and slide the ends down inside the front legs.

Run a gathering thread through the cast-on stitches of each front leg, pull tightly and secure. Sew the side seam of each front leg, stuffing with toy filling as you go. Sew the cast-off stitches of each front leg to the belly. Sew the foot and leg seams of each back leg, as for the front legs.

Place a length of chenille stick inside each back leg and stuff lightly with toy filling. Using the photograph for guidance, sew each back leg to the body. Sew the cast-off stitches to the belly. Sew the tail seam and slide a length of chenille stick inside. Using the photograph for guidance, sew the tail to the back of the body.

Sew the head seams and stuff the head with toy filling. Using the photograph for guidance, attach the eyes to the head. Fold the head piece in half and sew the back seams, stuffing with toy filling as you go. Using a needle and black yarn, sew from the base of the head to the back of each eye, pull the thread back down to the base and tighten. This gives a realistic shape to the head.

With WS together, sew one ear and one ear lining together to make one ear. Repeat for the second ear. Using the photograph for guidance, sew the ears to the top of the head. Using the photograph for guidance and pale pink yarn, embroider a nose. Using black embroidery thread, embroider a mouth and whiskers. Sew the head to the body. Place the collar around the kitten's neck and sew the cast-on and cast-off edges together. Sew the bell in place.

Mice

A cat's life simply wouldn't be complete without the odd mouse to chase, so here are a few knitted ones that you can make for your little woolly felines. If you prefer, work the tails of the mice as i-cords (see page 14) to avoid having a seam to sew up.

Materials
50g of grey 2-ply (laceweight) yarn (used double throughout)
Small amount of pink 2-ply (laceweight) yarn or embroidery thread
Toy filling
Small black beads

Needles
2.75mm (UK 12, US 2) knitting needles

Tension
Not relevant

Size
Approximately 5cm (2in), 4cm (1½in) and 2.5cm (1in) long, excluding tail

Small mouse

Body
Using a double strand of grey yarn and 2.75mm (UK 12, US 2) knitting needles, cast on 3 sts and knit 1 row.
Next row: K1, M1, knit to last st, M1, K1 (5 sts).
Rep this row six more times (17 sts).
Next row: (K2tog) 4 times, K1, (K2tog) 4 times (9 sts).
Next row: (K2tog) twice, K1, (K2tog) twice (5 sts).
Thread yarn through rem sts and fasten off.

Ears (make two)
Using a double strand of grey yarn and 2.75mm (UK 12, US 2) knitting needles, cast on 4 sts and knit 2 rows.
Next row: ssK, K2tog (2 sts).
Next row: K2tog.
Fasten off rem st.

Tail
Using a double strand of grey yarn and 2.75mm (UK 12, US 2) knitting needles, cast on 3 sts and work in SS until tail measures 2cm (¾in). Thread the yarn through the sts to fasten off. The tail can also be worked using the i-cord technique (see page 14).

Medium mouse

Body

Using a double strand of grey yarn and 2.75mm (UK 12, US 2) knitting needles, cast on 3 sts and knit 1 row.

Next row: K1, M1, knit to last st, M1, K1 (5 sts).

Rep this row 8 more times (21 sts).

Next row: (K2tog) 5 times, K1, (K2tog) five times (11 sts).

Next row: (ssK) twice, sl1, K2tog, psso, (K2tog) twice (5 sts).

Thread yarn through rem sts and fasten off.

Ears (make two)

Using a double strand of grey yarn and 2.75mm (UK 12, US 2) knitting needles, cast on 4 sts and knit 4 rows.

Next row: ssK, K2tog (2 sts).

Next row: K2tog.

Fasten off rem st.

Tail

Using a double strand of grey yarn and 2.75mm (UK 12, US 2) knitting needles, cast on 4 sts and work in SS until tail measures 3cm (1¼in). Thread the yarn through the sts to fasten off. The tail can also be worked using the i-cord technique (see page 14).

Large mouse

Body

Using a double strand of grey yarn and 2.75mm (UK 12, US 2) knitting needles, cast on 3 sts and knit 1 row.

Next row: K1, M1, knit to last st, M1, K1 (5 sts).

Rep this row 11 more times (27 sts).

Next row: (K2tog) 6 times, K1, (K2tog) seven times (14 sts).

Next row: (K2tog) 7 times (7 sts).

Next row: K2tog, K1, (K2tog) twice (4 sts).

Thread yarn through rem sts and fasten off.

Ears (make two)

Using a double strand of grey yarn and 2.75mm (UK 12, US 2) knitting needles, cast on 5 sts and knit 4 rows.

Next row: ssK, K1, K2tog (3 sts).

Next row: sl1, K2tog, psso.

Fasten off rem st.

Tail

Using a double strand of grey yarn and 2.75mm (UK 12, US 2) knitting needles, cast on 4 sts and work in SS until tail measures 4cm (1½in). Thread yarn through rem sts to fasten off. The tail can also be worked using the i-cord technique (see page 14).

Making up

Follow these instructions for each size of mouse. Starting from the base of the mouse, sew the side seam, stuffing with toy filling as you go. Sew the ears to the front of the mouse, using the photographs for guidance.

Using pink yarn (or embroidery thread), oversew a nose on the front of the mouse. Using a single strand of grey yarn and a sewing needle, attach two beads above the nose for eyes. Sew the tail to the base of the mouse.

It's cosy in here! Just right for a cat nap.

Dogs & Puppies

Dress-up Dogs

This cute pair of pups is knitted using a fluffy bouclé yarn to make them very tactile. The pirate dog's jumper is knitted using the Fair Isle technique (see page 14) and his mermaid friend's tail can be taken off.

Materials

60m (66yd) of brown or grey 10-ply (aran) alpaca bouclé yarn
Small amount of black 4-ply (fingering) yarn
Toy filling
Two 6mm (¼in) black beads
Black sewing cotton

Needles

4.5mm (UK 7, US 7) and 2.75mm (UK 12, US 2) knitting needles

Tension

Approximately 18–20 sts measured over 10cm (4in) and worked in SS using 4.5mm knitting needles (UK 7, US 7) and 10-ply (aran) alpaca bouclé yarn

Size

18cm (7in) in length

Note: These dogs are knitted in SS. When you sew each one together, place the WS on the outside as this is the fluffier side.

The materials listed above are sufficient for one of the dogs. The materials for the costumes are listed with the patterns later.

Body

Using brown or grey yarn and 4.5mm (UK 7, US 7) knitting needles cast on 14 sts.

Next row: K3, Kfb, K6, Kfb, K3 (16 sts).
Next row: P4, Pfb, P6, Pfb, P4 (18 sts).
Next row: K4, Kfb, K8, Kfb, K4 (20 sts).
Next row: P5, Pfb, P8, Pfb, P5 (22 sts).
Next row: K5, Kfb, K10, Kfb, K5 (24 sts).
Next row: P6, Pfb, P10, Pfb, P6 (26 sts).
Next row: K6, Kfb, K12, Kfb, K6 (28 sts).
Next row: P7, Pfb, P12, Pfb, P7 (30 sts).
Work 12 rows in SS.
Next row: K6, K2tog, K14, K2tog, K6 (28 sts).
Purl 1 row.
Next row: K6, K2tog, K12, K2tog, K6 (26 sts).
Purl 1 row.
Next row: K4, (K2tog) twice, K10, (K2tog) twice, K4 (22 sts).
Next row: P3, (P2tog) twice, P8, (P2tog) twice, P3 (18 sts).
Next row: K2, (K2tog) twice, K6, (K2tog) twice, K2 (14 sts).
Purl 1 row.
Cast off.

Head

Using brown or grey yarn and 4.5mm (UK 7, US 7) knitting needles, cast on 14 sts and, starting with a knit row, work 6 rows in SS, ending with a purl row.
Next row: K5, (Kfb) four times, K5 (18 sts).
Purl 1 row.
Next row: K5, (Kfb) eight times, K5 (26 sts).
Work 3 rows in SS.
Next row: K5, (K2tog) eight times, K5 (18 sts).
Purl 1 row.
Next row: K5, (K2tog) four times, K5 (14 sts).
Purl 1 row.
Cast off using the three-needle cast-off technique (see page 17).

Legs (make two)

Using brown or grey yarn and 4.5mm (UK 7, US 7) knitting needles, cast on 8 sts.

Starting with a knit row, work 4cm (1½in) in SS, ending with a purl row.

Next row: K3, M1, K2, M1, K3 (10 sts).

Next row: P4, M1, P2, M1, P4 (12 sts).

Next row: K5, M1, K2, M1, K5 (14 sts).

Next row: P6, M1, P2, M1, P6 (16 sts).

Next row: K7, M1, K2, M1, K7 (18 sts).

Work 3 rows in SS.

Cast off using the three-needle cast-off technique (see page 17).

Arms (make two)

Using brown or grey yarn and 4.5mm (UK 7, US 7) knitting needles, cast on 7 sts and, starting with a knit row, work 3cm (1⅛in) in SS, ending with a purl row.

Next row: (K1, M1) six times, K1 (13 sts).

Work 5 rows in SS.

Next row: (K2tog) three times, K1, (K2tog) three times (7 sts).

Purl 1 row.

Leave a length of yarn for sewing up.

Floppy ears (make two)

Worked in GS.

Using brown or grey yarn and 4.5mm (UK 7, US 7) knitting needles, cast on 5 sts and work 3cm (1⅛in) in GS.

Next row: K1, M1, K to last st, M1, K1 (7 sts).

Knit 2 rows.

Next row: K1, K2tog, K1, K2tog, K1 (5 sts).

Knit 1 row.

Cast off.

Nose

Using black yarn and 2.75mm (UK 12, US 2) knitting needles, cast on 3 sts and purl 1 row.

Next row: K1, M1, K1, M1, K1 (5 sts).

Work 2 rows in SS.

Next row: P2tog, P1, P2togtbl (3 sts).

Next row: Sl1, K2tog, psso (1 st).

Cast off, leaving a length of yarn sufficient to embroider the mouth.

Tail

Using brown or grey yarn and 4.5mm (UK 7, US 7) knitting needles, cast on 6 sts and work 3cm (1⅛in) in SS.

Thread yarn through sts and leave a length of yarn for sewing up.

Making up

To make up the body, with the WS on the outside and the cast-off edge at the bottom, sew the back body seam, stuffing with toy filling as you go. This seam will be at the back. Sew the bottom seam closed from side to side.

To make up the head, place the cast-off edge at the back of the head. Sew up the seam (with the WS on the outside) which will go underneath the head, stuffing with toy filling as you go. Sew the cast-on edges together up to the nose. To finish the head, follow the instructions on page 17 to gather the nose.

Pin the 6mm (¼in) black beads in place as eyes, using the photograph for guidance, then sew them in place. Run a thread from the back of the eye down to the base of the head and pull slightly, secure. Repeat for the second eye. This gives the eyes a much more realistic look.

Sew the nose in place and embroider the mouth using the length of yarn left at the end of the nose. Sew the ears in place, using the photographs for guidance. Pin the completed head to the body and sew it in place.

Fold one leg in half with the WS on the outside. Sew the leg seam, stuffing gently with toy filling as you go. The long seam will be at the back of the leg. Sew the seam at the top of the leg together from side to side. Repeat for the second leg.

Using the length of yarn remaining from gathering the cast-off edge, sew along the seam of one arm, stuffing gently with toy filling as you go. Repeat for the second arm. Pin the arms in place on to the side of the body with the seam underneath the arm. Sew in place. Pin the legs in place on to the body, using the photographs for guidance, then sew them in place.

Using the length of yarn remaining from gathering the cast-off edge of the tail, sew along the seam and sew it to the back of the body.

Mermaid costume

Materials

- 110m (120½yd) of green 5-ply (sportweight) yarn
- Small amount of pale pink 5-ply (sportweight) yarn
- Small amount of toy filling
- Four 6mm (¼in) pearl beads
- Cream sewing cotton

Needles

3.25mm (UK 10, US 3) knitting needles

Tension

25 sts measured over 10cm (4in) and worked in SS using 3.25mm (UK 10, US 3) knitting needles and 5-ply (sportweight) yarn

Main tail

Using green yarn and 3.25mm (UK 10, US 3) knitting needles, cast on 36 sts and, starting with a knit row, work 4 rows in SS.

Next row: (K2tog, yo) seventeen times, K2 (36 sts). This row forms picot edge.

Work 21 rows in SS.

Next row: K8, K2tog, K16, K2tog, K8 (34 sts).

Work 3 rows in SS.

Next row: K7, K2tog, K16, K2tog, K7 (32 sts).

Work 3 rows in SS.

Next row: K7, K2tog, K14, K2tog, K7 (30 sts).

Work 3 rows in SS.

Next row: K7, K2tog, K12, K2tog, K7 (28 sts).

Work 3 rows in SS.

Next row: K5, (K2tog) twice, K10, (K2tog) twice, K5 (24 sts).

Work 3 rows in SS.

Next row: K4, (K2tog) twice, K8, (K2tog) twice, K4 (20 sts).

Work 3 rows in SS.

Next row: K3, (K2tog) twice, K6, (K2tog) twice, K3 (16 sts).

Work 3 rows in SS.

Next row: K2, (K2tog) twice, K4, (K2tog) twice, K2 (12 sts).

Purl 1 row.

Next row: K1, (K2tog) twice, K2, (K2tog) twice, K1 (8 sts).

Purl 1 row.

Cast off.

Scales

Using green yarn and 3.25mm (UK 10, US 3) knitting needles, cast on 5 sts and purl 1 row.

*Row 1: K1, M1, K to the end of the row (6 sts).

Row 2: P to last st, M1, P1 (7 sts).

Row 3: K1, M1, K to the end of the row (8 sts).

Row 4: P to last st, M1, P1 (9 sts).

Row 5: K1, M1, K to the end of the row (10 sts).

Row 6: Purl 1 row.

Row 7: K1, ssK, K to end of row (9 sts).

Row 8: P to last 3 sts, ssP, P1 (8 sts).

Row 9: K1, ssK, K to end of row (7 sts).

Row 10: P to last 3 sts, ssP, P1 (6 sts).

Row 11: K1, ssK, K to end of row (5 sts).

Purl 1 row.*

This forms one scale. When you have knitted the right amount of scales cast off. Using the instructions between * and *, make the following rows of scales:

First row (top row): 5 scales.

Second row: 5 scales.

Third row: 5 scales.

Fourth row: 4 scales.

Fifth row: 3 scales.

Sixth row: 2 scales.

Fin (make four)

Using green yarn and 3.25mm (UK 10, US 3) knitting needles, cast on 5 sts.

Row 1: (P1, K1tbl) twice, P1.
Row 2: (K1, P1tbl) twice, K1.
Row 3: P1, M1, K1tbl, P1, K1tbl, M1, P1 (7 sts).
Row 4: K2, P1tbl, K1, P1tbl, K2.
Row 5: P2, M1, K1tbl, P1, K1tbl, M1, P2 (9 sts).
Row 6: (K1, P1tbl) four times, K1.
Row 7: (P1, K1tbl) four times, P1.
Row 8: K1, M1, (P1tbl, K1) three times, P1tbl, M1, K1 (11 sts).
Row 9: P2, (K1tbl, P1) three times, K1tbl, P2.
Row 10: K1, M1, (K1, P1tbl) four times, K1, M1, K1 (13 sts).
Row 11: (P1, K1tbl) six times, P1.
Row 12: (K1tbl, P1) six times, K1tbl.
Rep rows 11 and 12 once more.
Rep row 11 once more.
Row 16: P2tog, (K1tbl, P1) four times, K1tbl, P2tog (11 sts).
Row 17: K3, P1tbl, K3, P1tbl, K3.
Row 18: P1, P2tog, K1tbl, P1, p2tog, K1tbl, P2tog, P1 (8 sts).
Row 19: (K2tog, P1tbl) twice, K2tog (5 sts).
Row 20: (P1, K1tbl) twice, P1.
Cast off.

Making up

Starting with the main part of the tail and with WS on the outside, fold the top four rows over and sew in place, so that the eyelet row forms a picot edging along the top edge of the tail. Sew the back seam of the tail. The seam will be at the back of the tail.

With WS together sew two fin pieces together stuffing gently with toy filling. Repeat for the second fin.

Sew a stuffed fin to each side of the bottom edge of the tail, using the photograph for guidance, and sew the cast-off edge to the tail.

Lightly press the scale rows. Starting with the bottom row, pin in place (see order of scales on opposite page) so that each row overlaps. The top row should rest on the top seam. Sew each row in place, easing to fit. The cast-on and cast-off edges should be at the back.

Bikini shells (make two)

Using pale pink yarn and 3.25mm (UK 10, US 3) knitting needles, cast on 6 sts and knit 2 rows.

Cast off. This forms the bottom of one shell.

With RS facing, pick up and K 3 sts in the middle of the row, leaving a stitch and a half each side.

Next row: P1, M1, P1, M1, P1 (5 sts).

Next row: K1, M1, K3, M1, K1 (7 sts).

Work 3 rows in SS.

Next row: ssK, K3, K2tog (5 sts).

Next row: P2tog, P1, P2togtbl (3 sts).

Cast off.

Halter neck strap

Using green yarn and 3.25mm (UK 10, US 3) knitting needles, cast on 20 sts and work 2 rows in SS.

Cast off.

Lower strap

Using green yarn and 3.25mm (UK 10, US 3) knitting needles, cast on 50 sts and work 2 rows in SS.

Cast off.

Making up

Lightly press the shell pieces and sew three straight stitches along the top of the GS section of each shell, using the photograph as guidance.

Pin each shell in place on the lower strap, with the two ends at the back and the shells evenly spaced at the front. Use the photograph for guidance. Sew the lower edge of the shells to the top edge of the strap.

Sew a small loop on one end of the strap then use cream sewing cotton to sew a pearl bead to the other end. Sew each end of the halter neck strap to the top back edge of each shell. Using cream sewing cotton, sew a group of three pearls to the centre front of the bikini strap as shown in the photograph.

Pirate costume

Materials

45m (49¼yd) of black 4-ply (fingering) yarn
11m (12yd) of red 4-ply (fingering) yarn
Small amount of cream 4-ply (fingering) yarn
Small length of black elastic

Needles

3.25mm (UK 10, US 3) and 2.75mm (UK 12, US 2) knitting needles

Tension

28 sts measured over 10cm (4in) and worked in SS using 3.25mm (UK 10, US 3) knitting needles and black 4-ply (fingering) yarn

Eye patch

Using black yarn and 3.25mm (UK 10, US 3) knitting needles, cast on 3 sts and K 2 rows.

Next row: (K1, M1) twice, K1 (5 sts).

Knit 2 rows.

Cast off.

Measure a piece of elastic to go around the dog's head. Sew each end of the black elastic at the back of the eye patch.

Sweater (front)

Using black yarn and 3.25mm (UK 10, US 3) knitting needles, cast on 28 sts and work four rows in K2, P2 rib.

Following the chart below for the pirate skull and crossbones and using the Fair Isle technique (see page 14), work as follows:

Starting with a knit row, work 14 rows in SS.

Cast off 2 sts at the beginning of the next two rows (24 sts).

Next row: K2, ssK, K to last 4 sts, K2tog, K2 (22 sts).

Next row: P2, P2tog, P to last 4 sts, P2togtbl, P2 (20 sts).

Work 8 rows in SS.*

Next row: K7, turn, leaving rem 13 sts on the needle.

Next row: P1, P2tog, P4 (6 sts).

Next row: K3, K2tog, K1 (5 sts).

Cast off.

With RS facing, rejoin yarn to rem 13 sts and cast off 6 sts, K to end of row (7 sts).

Next row: P4, P2togtbl, P1 (6 sts).

Next row: K1, ssK, K3 (5 sts).

Cast off.

Chart for the pirate sweater

Sweater (back)

Work as for front to * and continue as follows.

Next row: K8, turn, leaving rem 12 sts on the needle.

Next row: P1, P2tog, P5 (7 sts).

Next row: K4, K2tog, K1 (6 sts).

Next row: P1, P2tog, P3 (5 sts).

Cast off.

With RS facing rejoin yarn to rem 12 sts and cast off 4 sts, K to end of row (8 sts).

Next row: P5, P2togtbl, P1 (7 sts).

Next row: K1, ssK, K4 (6 sts).

Next row: P3, P2tog, P1 (5 sts).

Cast off.

Join the right shoulder seam and pick up and K 12 sts around the front neck shaping. Pick up and K 12 sts around the back of the neck shaping (24 sts).

Work four rows in K2, P2 rib.

Cast off loosely and evenly.

Sew left shoulder and neckband seam.

Sleeves

Taking the joined front and back of the jumper, pick up and K 24 sts along the edge of one armhole.

Starting with a purl row, work 3 rows in SS.

Next row: K1, ssK, K to last 3 sts, K2tog, K1 (22 sts).

Work 3 rows in SS.

Rep the last four rows once more (20 sts).

Work 4 rows in K2, P2 rib.

Cast off.

Repeat for the second sleeve.

Sew each underarm and side seam.

Bandana

Using red yarn and 3.25mm (UK 10, US 3) knitting needles, cast on 3 sts.

Next row: (K1, M1) twice, K1 (5 sts).

Next row: K2, P1, K2.

Next row: K1, M1, K to last st, M1, K1 (7 sts).

Next row: K2, P3, K2.

Next row: K2, M1, K to last 2 sts, M1, K2 (9 sts).

Next row: K2, P5, K2.

Next row: K2, M1, K to last 2 sts, M1, K2 (11 sts).

Next row: K2, P7, K2.

Next row: K2, M1, K to last 2 sts, M1, K2 (13 sts).

Next row: K2, P9, K2.

Next row: K2, M1, K to last 2 sts, M1, K2 (15 sts).

Next row: K2, P11, K2.

Working in GS from now on, cast on 12 sts at the beginning of the next two rows (39 sts).

Knit 2 rows. Cast off.

Using cream yarn, embroider spots on to the bandana using French knots (see page 16).

Flag

Using red yarn and 2.75mm (UK 12, US 2) knitting needles, cast on 14 sts and work 4 rows in GS.

Next row: Knit all sts.

Next row: K3, P to last 3 sts, K3.

Rep last two rows once more.

Next row: K2, ssK, K to last 4 sts, K2tog, K2 (12 sts).

Next row: K3, P to last 3 sts, K3.

Rep last two rows three more times (6 sts).

Next row: K1, (K2tog) twice, K1 (4 sts).

Next row: K2tog twice (2 sts).

Thread yarn through rem 2 sts and fasten.

Using cream yarn, embroider spots on to the flag using French knots (see page 16j).

If you want to attach your flag to a stick as on page 107 (I used a dog treat), then use loops of red yarn to secure it.

Stripy Sausage

Stripy Sausage is a useful little chap: lay him in front of a door to keep your draughts out! He is a fat little sausage dog whose legs are sticking out in front and behind him, just like my dog when he is fast asleep. You can vary the colours used to fit in with your own colour scheme.

Materials
375m (410yd) of brown 5-ply (sportweight) yarn (used double throughout)
The following amounts of 5-ply (sportweight) yarn (used double throughout): 50m (55yd) purple, 34m (37¼yd) turquoise, 39m (43yd) teal, 24m (26¼yd) light brown, 44m (48¼yd) bright green and 60m (66yd) red
Small amount of black 4-ply (fingering) yarn
Toy filling
Two 10mm (⅜in) black shanked buttons

Tools
4.5mm (UK 7, US 7) 2.75mm (UK 12, US 2) knitting needles
Stitch holders

Tension
18 sts measured over 10cm (4in) and worked in SS using 4.5mm (UK 7, US 7) knitting needles and 5-ply (sportweight) yarn.

Size
64cm (25¼in) from the tip of the nose to the end of the back leg

Note: This dog is knitted using a double strand of yarn throughout, except for the nose.

Head
Cast on 14 sts using a double strand of brown yarn and 4.5mm (UK 7, US 7) knitting needles and purl 1 row.
Next row: K1, M1, K to last st, M1, K1 (16 sts).
Next row: P1, M1, P to last st, M1, P1 (18 sts).
Rep last 2 rows twice more (26 sts).
Next row: K1, M1, K to last st, M1, K1 (28 sts).
Purl 1 row.
Rep last 2 rows twice more (32 sts).
Next row: K15, M1, K2, M1, K15 (34 sts).
Next row: P16, M1, P2, M1, P16 (36 sts).
Next row: K17, M1, K2, M1, K17 (38 sts).
Next row: P18, M1, P2, M1, P18 (40 sts).
Next row: K19, M1, K2, M1, K19 (42 sts).
Next row: P20, M1, P2, M1, P20 (44 sts).
Next row: K21, M1, K2, M1, K21 (46 sts).
Purl 1 row.
Next row: K22, M1, K2, M1, K22 (48 sts).
Work 9 rows in SS.
Next row: K1, ssK, K18, ssK, K2, K2tog, K18, K2tog, K1 (44 sts).
Purl 1 row.
Next row: K1, ssK, K16, ssK, K2, K2tog, K16, K2tog, K1 (40 sts).
Purl 1 row.
Next row: K1, ssK, K14, ssK, K2, K2tog, K14, K2tog, K1 (36 sts).
Next row: P1, P2tog, P12, P2tog, P2, P2togtbl, P12, P2togtbl, P1 (32 sts).
Next row: K1, ssK, K10, ssK, K2, K2tog, K10, K2tog, K1 (28 sts).
Next row: P1, P2tog, P8, P2tog, P2, P2togtbl, P8, P2togtbl, P1 (24 sts).
Next row: K1, ssK, K6, ssK, K2, K2tog, K6, K2tog, K1 (20 sts).
Next row: P1, P2tog, P4, P2tog, P2, P2togtbl, P4, P2togtbl, P1 (16 sts).
Cast off using the three-needle cast-off technique (see page 17).

Body, front legs and tail

Start at the front legs as follows:

Left front leg

Cast on 11 sts using a double strand of brown yarn and 4.5mm (UK 7, US 7) knitting needles, and purl 1 row.

Next row: K9, w&t.

Next row: P6, w&t.

Next row: K5, w&t.

P to end of row.*

Next row: Cast on 5 sts, K to end of row (16 sts).

Work 13 rows in SS.

Next row: Cast off 6 sts, K3, cast off 6 sts (4 sts).

Place rem 4 sts on a stitch holder.

Right front leg

Work as for left front leg to *.

Knit 1 row.

Next row: Cast on 5 sts, P to end of row (16 sts).

Work 12 rows in SS.

Next row: Cast off 6 sts, K3, cast off 6 sts (4 sts).

Place rem 4 sts on a stitch holder.

With RS facing knit across 4 sts of left front leg, turn work and cast on 32 sts, turn work and knit across 4 sts of right leg (40 sts).

Work 17 rows in SS.

Next row: K1, M1, K to last st, M1, K1 (42 sts).

Work 3 rows in SS.

Continue in SS, changing colour and working in stripe pattern as follows, using a double strand of each colour yarn:

Purple – Work 18 rows.

Turquoise – Work 16 rows.

Teal – Work 8 rows.

Light brown – Work 12 rows.

Bright green – Work 14 rows.

Red – Work 18 rows.

Finally, change back to brown yarn and work a further 8 rows.

Next row: K1, ssK, K to last 3 sts, K2tog, K1 (40 sts).

Work 3 rows in SS.

Next row: K1, ssK, K to last 3 sts, K2tog, K1 (38 sts).

Purl 1 row.

Rep last two rows once more (36 sts).

Next row: K1, ssK, K14, M1, K2, M1, K14, K2tog, K1 (36 sts).

Next row: P17, M1, P2, M1, P17 (38 sts).

Next row: K1, ssK, K15, M1, K2, M1, K15, K2tog, K1 (38 sts).

Next row: P1, P2tog, P15, M1, P2, M1, P15, P2togtbl, P1 (38 sts).

Next row: Cast off 13 sts, K4, M1, K2, M1, K to last 3 sts, K2tog, K1 (26 sts).

Next row: Cast off 13 sts, P to last 3 sts, P2togtbl, P1 (12 sts).

Next row: K1, ssK, K2, M1, K2, M1, K2, K2tog, K1 (12 sts).

Next row: P1, P2tog, P2, M1, P2, M1, P2, P2togtbl, P1 (12 sts).

Next row: K1, ssK, K to last 3 sts, K2tog, K1 (10 sts).

Next row: P1, P2tog, P4, P2togtbl, P1 (8 sts).

Next row: (K2tog) four times (4 sts).

Thread yarn through rem sts and fasten.

117

Bottom gusset

Cast on 8 sts using a double strand of brown yarn and 4.5mm (UK 7, US 7) knitting needles. Starting with a knit row, work 2 rows in SS.

Next row: K1, M1, K to last st, M1, K1 (10 sts).

Next row: P1, M1, P to last st, M1, P1 (12 sts).

Rep last 2 rows once more (16 sts).

Work 2 rows in SS.

Next row: K1, M1, K to last st, M1, K1 (18 sts).

Work 25 rows in SS.

Next row: K1, M1, K to last st, M1, K1 (20 sts).

Work 95 rows in SS.

Next row: K1, ssK, K to last 3 sts, K2tog, K1 (18 sts).

Work 11 rows in SS.

Next row: K1, ssK, K to last 3 sts, K2tog, K1 (16 sts).

Purl 1 row.

Rep the last two rows four more times (8 sts).

Work 4 rows in SS.

Next row: K1, ssK, K to last 3 sts, K2tog, K1 (6 sts).

Work 3 rows in SS.

Rep last 4 rows once more (4 sts).

Next row: (K2tog) twice (2 sts).

Next row: P2tog.

Fasten off rem st.

Nose

Cast on 10 sts using black yarn and 2.75mm (UK 12, US 2) knitting needles and, starting with a knit row, work 2 rows in SS.

Next row: K7, w&t.

Next row: P4, w&t.

Nothing beats a good sleep.

Next row: K to end of row.

Purl 1 row.

Next row: K3, ssK, K2tog, K3 (8 sts).

Purl 1 row.

Next row: K2, ssK, K2tog, K2 (6 sts).

Purl 1 row.

Next row: K1, ssK, K2tog, K1 (4 sts).

Purl 1 row.

Thread yarn through rem sts and fasten, leaving a length of yarn to use to embroider the mouth.

Ears (make two)

Cast on 11 sts using a double strand of brown yarn and 4.5mm (UK 7, US 7) knitting needles. Starting with a knit row, work 6 rows in SS.

Next row: K1, M1, K to last st, M1, K1 (13 sts).

Work 3 rows in SS.

Next row: K1, M1, K to last st, M1, K1 (15 sts).

Work 9 rows in SS.

Next row: K1, ssK, K to last 3 sts, K2tog, K1 (13 sts).

Purl 1 row.

Rep last 2 rows twice more (9 sts).

Cast off.

Ear linings (make two)

Each ear lining is knitted using a different shade. I chose teal and purple.

Cast on 9 sts using a double strand of yarn in the colour of your choice and 4.5mm (UK 7, US 7) knitting needles. Starting with a knit row, work 4 rows in SS.

Next row: K1, M1, K to last st, M1, K1 (11 sts).

Work 3 rows in SS.

Next row: K1, M1, K to last st, M1, K1 (13 sts).

Work 7 rows in SS.

Next row: K1, ssK, K to last 3 sts, K2tog, K1 (11 sts).

Next row: P1, P2tog, P to last 3 sts, P2togtbl, P1 (9 sts).

Next row: K1, ssK, K to last 3 sts, K2tog, K1 (7 sts).

Cast off.

Back legs (make two)

Cast on 11 sts using a double strand of brown yarn and 4.5mm (UK 7, US 7) knitting needles and purl 1 row.

Next row: K9, w&t.

Next row: P6, w&t.

Next row: K5, w&t.

P to end of row.

Next row: Cast on 5 sts, K to end of row (16 sts).

Work 12 rows in SS.

Cast off.

Collar

Cast on 7 sts using a double strand of red yarn and 4.5mm (UK 7, US 7) knitting needles and work in SS until collar is long enough to go around the dog's neck.

Cast off.

Making up

Pin and sew one front leg seam, folding the shapings to make the foot and stuff with toy filling. Repeat for second front leg.

Pin the bottom gusset on to the body, matching the cast-off end of the gusset (thinner end) to the tail of the dog. Sew the gusset in place, stuffing firmly with toy filling as you go. Fold the front legs over on to the gusset, making sure they will lie flat and sew in place using the photograph as guidance.

Pin and sew the back leg seam, folding the shapings to make the foot and stuff with toy filling. Repeat for second back leg.

Sew the two legs to the back of the dog, using the photograph for guidance and placing at the same level as the front legs.

Placing the cast-off edge at the back of the head, sew the seam that will go underneath the head, stuffing with toy filling as you go. Sew the cast-on edges together up to the nose. To finish the head, see page 17 for instructions on how to gather the nose.

Pin the black shanked buttons in place as eyes, using the photographs for guidance. Sew in place. Run the yarn from the back of the eye down to the base of the head and pull slightly, secure. Repeat for the second eye. This gives the eyes a much more realistic look.

With WS together, pin one ear to one ear lining and carefully sew the seam around the ear. Repeat for second ear. Pin the ears in place on the top of the head, using the photograph for guidance. Sew in place.

Sew the nose to the front of the face and embroider on the mouth, using the length of yarn left at the end of the nose and straight stitches.

Firmly sew the head to the body. Sew the cast-on and cast-off edges of the collar together and place around the dog's neck.

Fluffy Floppy Dog

Everyone loves Fluffy, because his silky fur is super soft and cuddly. His body and legs are knitted in one piece, making him an easy project to sew together.

Materials
- 75m (82yd) of faux fur yarn
- 20m (22yd) of grey 5-ply (sportweight) yarn
- Small amount of black 4-ply (fingering) yarn
- Small amount of blue 5-ply (sportweight) yarn
- Two 16mm (⅝in) black buttons for eyes
- Toy filling

Needles
4.5mm (UK 7, US 7), 2.75mm (UK 12, US 2) and 3.25mm (UK 10, US 3) knitting needles

Tension
15–16 sts worked in SS using 4.5mm (UK 7, US 7) knitting needles and faux fur yarn; measured over 10cm (4in)

Size
25cm (10in) from nose to tail

Note: This dog is knitted in SS. When you sew him together, place the WS on the outside as this is the fluffier side.

Body and legs (made in one piece)
Cast on 42 sts using faux fur yarn and 4.5mm (UK 7, US 7) knitting needles.
Starting with a purl row, work 3 rows in SS.
Next row: K1, M1, K to last st, M1, K1 (44 sts).
Work 3 rows in SS.
Next row: K1, K2tog, K to last 3 sts, K2tog, K1 (42 sts).
Work 3 rows in SS.
Cast off 12 sts at the beg of the next 2 rows (18 sts).
Starting with a knit row, work 16 rows in SS.
Cast on 12 sts at the beg of the next 2 rows (42 sts).

Starting with a knit row, work 3 rows in SS.
Next row: P1, M1, P to last st, M1, P1 (44 sts).
Work 3 rows in SS.
Next row: P1, P2tog, P to last 3 sts, P2tog, P1 (42 sts).
Work 6 rows in SS.
Next row: K1, M1, K to last st, M1, K1 (44 sts).
Work 3 rows in SS.
Next row: K1, K2tog, K to last 3 sts, K2tog, K1 (42 sts).
Work 3 rows in SS.
Cast off 12 sts at the beg of the next two rows (18 sts).
Next row: K1, M1, K to last st, M1, K1 (20 sts).
Work 14 rows in SS.
Next row: P1, P2tog, P to last 3 sts, P2tog, P1 (18 sts).
Cast on 12 sts at the beg of the next two rows (42 sts).
Starting with a knit row, work 3 rows in SS.
Next row: P1, M1, P to last st, M1, P1 (44 sts).
Work 3 rows in SS.
Next row: P1, P2tog, P to last 3 sts, P2tog, P1 (42 sts).
Work 3 rows in SS.
Cast off.

Head
Cast on 12 sts using faux fur yarn and 4.5mm (UK 7, US 7) knitting needles.
Next row: (Kfb) twelve times (24 sts).
Starting with a purl row, work 13 rows in SS.
Next row: K8, (Kfb) eight times, K8 (32 sts).
Purl 1 row.
Next row: K8, (Kfb) sixteen times, K8 (48 sts).
Work 5 rows in SS.
Next row: K8, (K2tog) sixteen times, K8 (32 sts).
Purl 1 row.
Cast off using the three-needle cast-off technique (see page 17).

Nose

Cast on 5 sts using black yarn and 2.75mm (UK 12, US 2) knitting needles.

Purl 1 row.

Next row: K1, M1, K to last st, M1, K1 (7 sts).

Purl 1 row.

Rep last 2 rows once more (9 sts).

Work 4 rows in SS.

Next row: K1, ssK, K to last 3 sts, K2tog, K1 (7 sts).

Purl 1 row.

Rep last 2 rows once more (5 sts).

Cast off.

Outer ears (make two)

Using faux fur yarn and 4.5mm (UK 7, US 7) knitting needles, cast on 8 sts and, starting with a knit row, work 4 rows in SS.

Next row: K1, M1, K to last st, M1, K1 (10 sts).

Work 5 rows in SS.

Rep last 6 rows once more (12 sts).

Next row: K1, K2tog, K to last 3 sts, K2tog, K1 (10 sts).

Purl 1 row.

Work last 2 rows once more (8 sts).

Cast off.

Ear linings (make two)

Using grey yarn and 3.25mm (UK 10, US 3) knitting needles, cast on 8 sts and, starting with a knit row, work 6 rows in SS.

Next row: K1, M1, K to last st, M1, K1 (10 sts).

Work 7 rows in SS.

Rep last 8 rows once more (12 sts).

Next row: K1, ssK, K to last 3 sts, K2tog, K1 (10 sts).

Purl 1 row.

Next row: K1, ssK, K to last 3 sts, K2tog, K1 (8 sts).

Next row: P1, P2tog, P to last 3 sts, P2togtbl, P1 (6 sts).

Cast off.

Tail

Using faux fur yarn and 4.5mm (UK 7, US 7) knitting needles, cast on 10 sts and, starting with a knit row, work 6 rows in SS.

Next row: K1, M1, K3, M1, K2, M1, K3, M1, K1 (14 sts).

Work 5 rows in SS.

Next row: (K2tog) seven times (7 sts).

Thread yarn through rem sts and sew closed, sew side seam of tail.

Collar

Using blue yarn and 3.25mm (UK 10, US 3) knitting needles, cast on 6 sts and work in SS until the collar fits around the neck. Cast off.

Making up

With the WS on the outside, slightly gather the cast-on end of the head and sew together: this forms the front of the face. Sew the seam that forms the bottom of the head, stuffing with toy filling as you go. The cast-off edge forms the back of the head.

Slightly gather the nose and sew to the front top edge of the face, placing a small amount of toy filling inside. Sew the black buttons in place as eyes using the photographs as guidance.

Pin one ear lining piece to one outer ear piece making sure that the RS of the ear lining piece and the WS (fluffier side) of the ear piece face outwards. Carefully sew the lining to the outer ear. Repeat for the second ear. Pin both completed ears in place on the head and sew on firmly.

To put the body together, fold it in half so that the cast-on and cast-off edges are together (use the diagram on the right for guidance). You can then see the finished shape of the dog's legs and body.

Sew up the side and leg seams of the body, stuffing lightly with toy filling as you go. When you stroke the body of the dog the 'pile' of the fur will go one way; the pile should go towards the back of the dog.

Sew the head firmly to the front of the body.

Place a small amount of toy filling in the end of the tail and sew it in place on the back of the dog using the photograph for guidance.

Place the collar around the dog's neck and sew the cast-on and cast-off edges together.

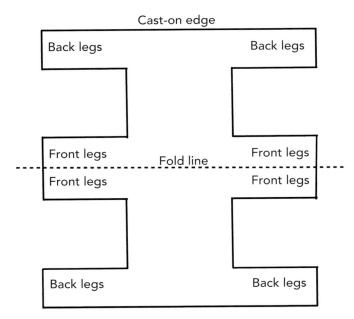

Cast-on edge

Back legs		Back legs
Front legs	Fold line	Front legs
Front legs		Front legs
Back legs		Back legs

Circus Dogs

These playful characters fit into your hand perfectly and their cheerful expressions are enough to make anyone smile. With a small bag of weighting beads inside them, you can use them as little juggling dogs.

Materials

40m (43¾yd) of 5-ply (sportweight) yarn in orange, turquoise, citron and brown (this is enough to make all three dogs)
Toy filling
Small fabric bag filled with weighting beads
Two 6mm (¼in) black beads
Black sewing cotton

Tools

3.25mm (UK 10, US 3) knitting needles
Stitch holders or spare needle

Tension

5 sts measured over 2cm (¾in) and worked in SS using 3.25mm (UK 10, US 3) knitting needles and 5-ply (sportweight) yarn

Size

Approximately 8cm (3⅛in) tall

Note: You will need to choose one shade to use as the main colour (MC). The other two will be contrast colour 1 (CC1) and contrast colour 2 (CC2). The brown is used for the nose and ears.

Body, head and tail

Starting at the tail, cast on 4 sts using MC. Work 4 rows in SS, starting with a knit row.
Next row: K1, M1, K2, M1, K1 (6 sts).
Work 3 rows in SS.
Cast on 9 sts at the beginning of the next 2 rows (24 sts).
Next row: K1, M1, K to last st, M1, K1 (26 sts).
Purl 1 row.
Next row: K1, ssK, K7, K2tog, K2, ssK, K7, K2tog, K1 (22 sts).

Work 3 rows in SS.
Next row: K1, ssK, K5, K2tog, K2, ssK, K5, K2tog, K1 (18 sts).
Work 3 rows in SS.
Next row: K1, ssK, K3, K2tog, K2, ssK, K3, K2tog, K1 (14 sts).
Purl 1 row.
Next row: Cast off 4 sts, K5, cast off rem 4 sts (6 sts).
Place rem 6 sts on a stitch holder or spare needle.
Now work the two sides that form the bottom part of the head when sewn together, using MC.
Cast on 8 sts and, starting with a P row, work 3 rows in SS.
Place sts on a holder.
Rep from * to * in order to make the second section.
With RS facing, K1, M1, K across rem 7 sts, K across 6 sts from body and then K across first 7 sts of second head section on the holder, M1, K1 (24 sts).
Next row: P11, M1, P2, M1, P11 (26 sts).
Work 4 rows in SS.
Next row: K1, ssK, K6, K2tog, K4, ssK, K6, K2tog, K1 (22 sts).
Next row: P8, P2tog, P2, P2togtbl, P8 (20 sts).
Next row: Cast off 8 sts, K3, cast off rem 8 sts (4 sts).
With WS facing rejoin yarn to rem 4 sts and work 3 rows in SS.
Next row: K1, M1, K2, M1, K1 (6 sts).
Work 13 rows in SS.
Next row: K1, ssK, K2tog, K1 (4 sts).
Purl 1 row.
Cast off.

Drum roll, please!

Arms and legs (make four)

Using CC1 yarn, cast on 4 sts and, starting with a knit row, work 4 rows in SS.
Next row: K1, K2tog, K1 (3 sts).
Next row: P1, M1, P2 (4 sts).
Work 4 rows in SS.
Cast off.

Nose

Using brown yarn, cast on 3 sts and purl 1 row.
Next row: K1, M1, K to last st, M1, K1 (5 sts).
Purl 1 row.
Rep last 2 rows once more (7 sts).
Next row: K1, ssK, K1, K2tog, K1 (5 sts).
Purl 1 row.
Cast off.

Ears (make two)

Using brown yarn, cast on 4 sts and, starting with a knit row, work 4 rows in SS.
Next row: K1, M1, K2, M1, K1 (6 sts).
Work 3 rows in SS.
Next row: K1, ssK, K2tog, K1 (4 sts).
Purl 1 row.
Cast off.

Ear linings (make two)

Using CC2 yarn, cast on 3 sts and, starting with a knit row, work 4 rows in SS.
Next row: K1, M1, K1, M1, K1 (5 sts).
Work 3 rows in SS.
Next row: ssK, K1, K2tog (3 sts).
Purl 1 row.
Cast off.

Front

Using CC1 yarn, cast on 12 sts and work as follows:
Next row: K1, M1, K to last st, M1, K1 (14 sts).
Purl 1 row.
Next row: K1, ssK, K to last 3 sts, K2tog, K1 (12 sts).
Work 3 rows in SS.
Rep last 4 rows twice more (8 sts).
Next row: K1, ssK, K to last 3 sts, K2tog, K1 (6 sts).
Purl 1 row.
Cast off.

Base and tummy

Starting at the tail end, cast on 3 sts using CC2 yarn and purl 1 row.
Next row: K1, M1, K to last st, M1, K1 (5 sts).
Work 3 rows in SS.
Rep last 4 rows three more times (11 sts).
Next row: Cast off 3 sts, K4, cast off rem 3 sts (5 sts).
With WS facing rejoin yarn to rem 5 sts and P 1 row.
Next row: K1, M1, K to last st, M1, K1 (7 sts).
Work 5 rows in SS.
Next row: K1, ssK, K1, K2tog, K1 (5 sts).
Purl 1 row.
Next row: ssK, K1, K2tog (3 sts).
Cast off.

Making up

Starting with the head, sew the bottom edge of each of the head sections together as shown. Sew the top gusset along the top edges of the head sections to form the top of the head. Sew the cast-off edge in place along the side flaps (see right). Stuff with toy filling.

Sew the tail seam, then sew the front of the body in place along the side edges of the body, placing the cast-on edge at the bottom. Stuff gently, placing the small fabric bag inside the stuffing. Starting at the tail end, sew the base in place, folding the tummy up over the front of the dog and sewing it in place.

Sew each arm and leg in the same way: fold in half and sew up the seams. Sew each arm and leg in place, using the photographs for guidance. The legs are sewn either side of the tummy along the bottom seam and the arms a short way down the side seams.

Sew the ears and ear linings together, then sew the ears to the back of the seam created at the top of the head, using the photograph for guidance.

Sew the nose in place as shown, placing the cast-off edge at the top, then sew the mouth using straight stitches.

Using black sewing cotton and a sewing needle, sew the black beads in place for eyes using the photograph for guidance.

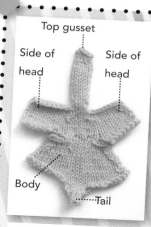

Top gusset

Side of head

Side of head

Bottom seam of head

Body

Tail

Sewing up the head

Upper left: The body and head, ready to be sewn up.
Upper right: Stuff the piece after you sew the narrow central flap to the side flaps.
Lower left: The body pieces folded in, ready for the front to be sewn on.

That didn't happen in rehearsal...

127

Black and White Terriers

If you are relatively new to knitting then have a go at these cute chaps. They are knitted in garter stitch (just knit) and every part of the dog is just a knitted rectangle. The only bit of shaping is on the ears to make them triangular. A super-easy, super-cute project!

Materials
36m (39⅜yd) of DK (8-ply) eyelash yarn
Small amount of black 4-ply (fingering) yarn
Two 6mm (¼in) black beads
Toy filling
Chenille sticks
Small amount of tartan ribbon
Black sewing cotton

Needles
3.5mm (UK 9/10, US 4) and 2.75mm (UK 12, US 2) knitting needles

Tension
18 sts worked in GS using 3.5mm (UK 9/10, US 4) knitting needles and DK (8-ply) eyelash yarn measured over 10cm (4in)

Size
14cm (5½in) from nose to tail, and 12cm (4¾in) from tip of ear to toe

Body
Using eyelash yarn and 3.5mm (UK 9/10, US 4) knitting needles, cast on 26 sts.
Work 8cm (3⅛in) in GS.
Cast off.

Legs (make four)
Using eyelash yarn and 3.5mm (UK 9/10, US 4) knitting needles, cast on 8 sts.
Work 4cm (1½in) in GS.
Thread yarn through sts and fasten.

Head
Using eyelash yarn and 3.5mm (UK 9/10, US 4) knitting needles, cast on 10 sts.
Work 15cm (6in) in GS.
Cast off.

Nose
Using black yarn and 2.75mm (UK 12, US 2) knitting needles, cast on 5 sts.
Work 5 rows in GS.
Cast off, leaving a length of yarn long enough to embroider the mouth.

Ears (make two)
Using white eyelash yarn and 3.5mm (UK 9/10, US 4) knitting needles, cast on 6 sts.
Work 6 rows in GS.
Next row: K2tog, K2, K2tog (4 sts).
Work 2 rows in GS.
Next row: K2tog, K2tog (2 sts).
Next row: K2tog and fasten off rem st.

Tail
Using eyelash yarn and 3.5mm (UK 9/10, US 4) knitting needles, cast on 6 sts.
Work 3cm (1⅛in) in GS.
Thread yarn through sts and gather. Fasten off yarn and sew side seam of tail.

Making up

The head is made from one long knitted rectangle, which is folded to form the head shape. Start by folding the cast-on or cast-off edge as shown by fold line 1 on the diagram opposite. Sew the side seams this creates and stuff this section with toy filling. Fold the rest of the head over (fold line 2) and sew the other cast-on/off end to the stuffed head section you have made. You will now have a seam to sew for the back of the head, on either side, which runs from the top of the bottom of the head. Sew one side seam, stuff with toy filling and sew the second seam closed.

Using black sewing cotton, sew the black beads in place as eyes, using the photographs for guidance, then sew the nose to the front of the face, folding the corners under to give a rounded look. Embroider the mouth using the black yarn. Sew the ends of yarn in on the ears and sew both ears on to the top of the head.

Fold the body in half and sew the cast on-edge together, then sew up the side seam, stuffing with toy filling as you go. Sew the cast-off edge together to form the back of the dog. Placing the seam underneath, sew the head to the body.

Sew the side seam of one leg and place a small amount of toy filling inside. Slide a chenille stick inside the leg and slide the chenille stick up inside the body of the dog, using the photograph to guide you where to place the leg. Sew the leg to the body, then repeat for the other three legs. Sew the tail to the back of the body. You do not need to stuff the tail, but if you wish you can place a small length of chenille stick inside it.

Finally, sew a length of tartan ribbon around the dog's neck as a collar. If necessary, use some sharp scissors to trim some of the longer hairs around the eyes to help them show more.

Diagrams for making up the Terrier's head

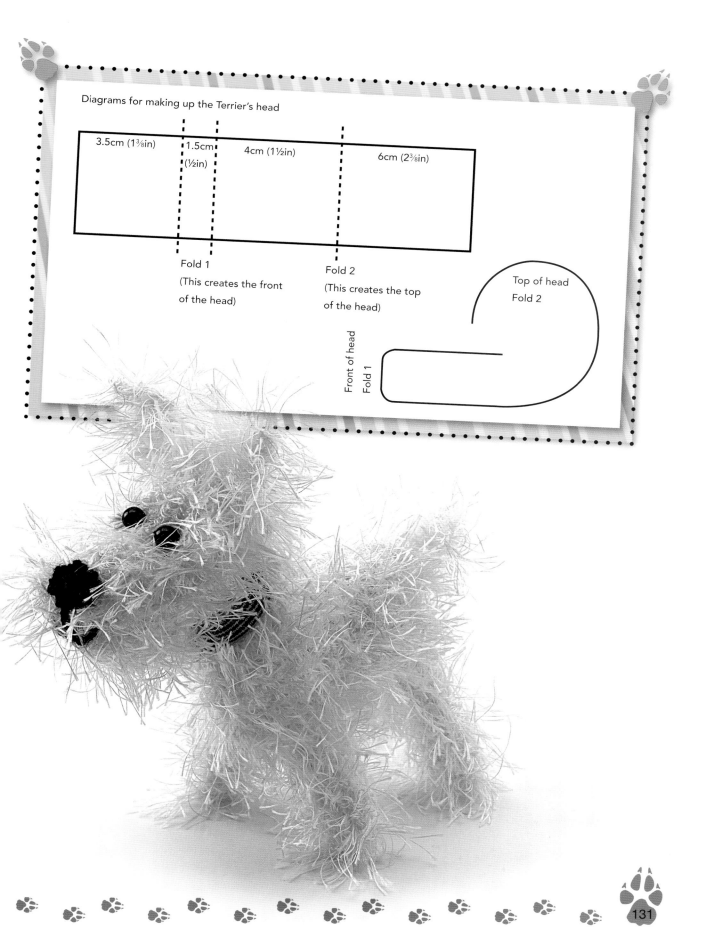

3.5cm (1⅜in) 1.5cm (½in) 4cm (1½in) 6cm (2⅜in)

Fold 1
(This creates the front of the head)

Fold 2
(This creates the top of the head)

Top of head
Fold 2

Front of head
Fold 1

Chic Chihuahua

This young lady has such an appealing expression that you will just want to make her. She is knitted using DK (8-ply) yarn and even has a smart diamanté collar and a bag to be carried around in so she does not get her delicate feet dirty.

Materials
- 45m (49¼yd) of cream DK (8-ply) yarn
- 60m (66yd) of beige DK (8-ply) yarn
- Small amounts of 4-ply (fingering) yarn in cream, black and fuchsia pink
- Toy filling
- Two 12mm (½in) black shanked buttons
- 10cm (4in) of rhinestone trim
- Black sewing cotton
- Safety pin
- Chenille sticks

Tools
- 2.75mm (UK 12, US 2) and 3.75mm (UK 9, US 5) knitting needles
- Two stitch markers

Tension
20–22 sts measured over 10cm (4in) and worked in SS using 3.75mm (UK 9, US 5) knitting needles and DK (8-ply) yarn

Size
16cm (6¼in) from nose to tail, and 16cm (6¼in) from top of the head to bottom of feet

Body and front legs
Start at bottom edge of right foot.
Using cream DK (8-ply) yarn and 3.75mm (UK 9, US 5) knitting needles, cast on 10 sts.
*Next row: K5, turn.
Next row: P3, turn.
Next row: K3, turn.
Next row: P3, turn.
Next row: Knit to end of row.
Next row: P5, P3B, P2.*
Work 12 rows in SS.

Next row: Cast off 5 sts, K to end of row (5 sts).
Next row: Cast off 2 sts, P to end of row (3 sts).
Change to beige yarn.
Next row: K1, M1, K to end of row (4 sts).
Next row: Cast on 12 sts, P to last st, M1, P1 (17 sts).
Knit 1 row.
Next row: Cast on 4 sts and P to end of row (21 sts).
Next row: K1, M1, K to last st, M1, K1 (23 sts).
Work 25 rows in SS, placing a stitch marker at either end of row 13.
Next row: K1, ssK, K to last 3 sts, K2tog, K1 (21 sts).
Next row: Cast off 4 sts, P to end of row (17 sts).
Knit 1 row.
Next row: Cast off 12 sts, P to last 3 sts, P2togtbl, P1 (4 sts).
Next row: K1, K2tog, K1 (3 sts).
Change to cream DK (8-ply) yarn.
Next row: Cast on 2 sts, P to end of row (5 sts).
Next row: Cast on 5 sts, K to end of row (10 sts).
Work 13 rows in SS.
Work from * to * as for right foot.
Cast off.

Belly
Using cream DK (8-ply) yarn and 3.75mm (UK 9, US 5) knitting needles, cast on 5 sts and, starting with a knit row, work 6 rows in SS.
Next row: K1, M1, K3, M1, K1 (7 sts).
Work 5 rows in SS.
Next row: K1, M1, K5, M1, K1 (9 sts).
Work 11 rows in SS.
Next row: K1, ssK, K3, K2tog, K1 (7 sts).
Work 15 rows in SS.
Next row: K1, ssK, K1, K2tog, K1 (5 sts).
Work 5 rows in SS.
Cast off.

Head

Using beige yarn and 3.75mm (UK 9, US 5) knitting needles, cast on 14 sts and purl 1 row.

Next row: K1, M1, K to last st, M1, K1 (16 sts).

Next row: P1, M1, P to last st, M1, P1 (18 sts).

Rep last 2 rows once more (22 sts).

Next row: K6, M1, (K2, M1) twice, (K1, M1) twice, (K2, M1) twice, K6 (29 sts).

Work 3 rows in SS.

Next row: K8, M1, (K2, M1) three times, K1, (M1, K2) three times, M1, K8 (37 sts).

Work 3 rows in SS.

Next row: K10, (M1, K2) four times, M1, K1, (M1, K2) four times, M1, K10 (47 sts).

Work 3 rows in SS.

Next row: K1, ssK, K17, ssK, K3, K2tog, K17, K2tog, K1 (43 sts).

Purl 1 row.

Next row: K1, ssK, K15, ssK, K3, K2tog, K15, K2tog, K1 (39 sts).

Purl 1 row.

Next row: K1, ssK, K13, ssK, K3, K2tog, K13, K2tog, K1 (35 sts).

Next row: P1, P2tog, P to last 3 sts, P2togtbl, P1 (33 sts).

Cast off 13 sts at the beginning of the next 2 rows (7 sts).

Work 12 rows in SS.

Next row: K1, ssK, K1, K2tog, K1 (5 sts).

Purl 1 row.

Cast off.

Snout

Using cream DK (8-ply) yarn and 3.75mm (UK 9, US 5) needles, cast on 14 sts and purl 1 row.

Next row: K1, M1, K to last st, M1, K1 (16 sts).

Next row: P1, M1, P to last st, M1, P1 (18 sts).

Rep last two rows once more (22 sts).

Work 2 rows in SS.

Cast off 9 sts at the beginning of the next 2 rows (4 sts).

Next row: (K2tog) twice (2 sts).

Purl 1 row.

Next row: K1, M1, K1 (3 sts).

Work 5 rows in SS.

Next row: Sl1, K2tog, psso (1 st).

Fasten off rem st.

Back leg (right)

Using cream DK (8-ply) yarn and 3.75mm (UK 9, US 5) knitting needles, cast on 10 sts.

Next row: K5, turn.

Next row: P3, turn.

Next row: K3, turn.

Next row: P3, turn.

Next row: K to end of row.

Next row: P5, P3B, P2.

Work 12 rows in SS.

Next row: Cast off 5 sts, K to end of row (5 sts).

Next row: Cast off 1 st, P to end of row (4 sts).

Change to beige yarn.

**Next row: K1, M1, K to last st, M1, K1 (6 sts).

Next row: P1, M1, P to last st, M1, P1 (8 sts).

Rep last 2 rows once more (12 sts).

Work 6 rows in SS.

Next row: K1, ssK, K to last 3 sts, K2tog, K1 (10 sts).

Next row: P1, P2tog, P to last 3 sts, P2togtbl, P1 (8 sts).

Next row: K1, ssK, K to last 3 sts, K2tog, K1 (6 sts).

Cast off.

Back leg (left)

Using cream DK (8-ply) yarn and 3.75mm (UK 9, US 5) knitting needles, cast on 10 sts.

Next row: K8, turn.

Next row: P3, turn.

Next row: K3, turn.

Next row: P3, turn.

Next row: K to end of row.

Next row: P2, P3B, P5.

Work 12 rows in SS.

Next row: Cast off 1 st, K to end of row (9 sts).

Next row: Cast off 5 sts, P to end of row (4 sts).

Change to beige yarn.

Work as for back leg (right) from ** to end.

Ears (make two)

Using beige yarn and 3.75mm (UK 9, US 5) knitting needles, cast on 14 sts and, starting with a knit row, work 6 rows in SS.

Next row: K1, ssK, K to last 3 sts, K2tog, K1 (12 sts).

Work 3 rows in SS.

Next row: K1, ssK, K to last 3 sts, K2tog, K1 (10 sts).

Purl 1 row.

Rep last two 2 once more (8 sts).

Next row: K1, ssK, K2, K2tog, K1 (6 sts).

Next row: P1, P2tog, P2togtbl, P1 (4 sts).

Next row: (K2tog) twice (2 sts).

Next row: P2tog (1 st). Fasten off rem st.

Ear linings (make two)

Using cream 4-ply (fingering) yarn and 2.75mm (UK 12, US 2) knitting needles, cast on 14 sts and, starting with a knit row, work 6 rows in SS.

Next row: K1, ssK, K to last 3 sts, K2tog, K1 (12 sts).

Work 3 rows in SS.

Rep last 4 rows once more (10 sts).

Next row: K1, ssK, K to last 3 sts, K2tog, K1 (8 sts).

Purl 1 row.

Rep last 2 rows twice more (4 sts).

Next row: ssK, K2tog (2 sts).

Next row: P2tog (1 st). Fasten off rem st.

Tail

Using beige yarn and 3.75mm (UK 9, US 5) knitting needles, cast on 8 sts and, starting with a knit row, work 4 rows in SS.

Next row: K6, w&t.

Next row: P4, w&t.

Next row: K3, w&t.

Next row: P to end of row.

Work 4 rows in SS.

Next row: K1, ssK, K2, K2tog, K1 (6 sts).

Work 3 rows in SS.

Next row: K1, ssK, K2tog, K1 (4 sts).

Purl 1 row.

Thread yarn through rem sts and fasten.

Nose

Using black yarn and 2.75mm (UK 12, US 2) knitting needles, cast on 5 sts. Starting with a knit row, work 4 rows in SS.

Next row: ssK, K1, K2tog (3 sts).

Next row: Sl1, P2tog, psso (1 st).

Thread yarn through rem st to fasten.

Making up

Starting with one of the front legs, thread a length of yarn through the bottom edge of the foot and gather to form the bottom of the foot. Sew the side seam and stuff with toy filling, placing a chenille stick inside the toy filling. Repeat for the second front leg.

Matching the middle of the cast-off edge of the belly to the stitch marker at the back of the body, and the middle of the cast-on edge of the belly to the stitch marker at the front of the body, pin the belly in place. Stuff the body firmly with toy filling, sewing the seams of the belly in place. Sew the cast-off edge of the top of each front leg to the belly.

Sew each back leg in the same way as the front legs. Pin the top of each back leg to the body as shown in the photographs, stuff gently with toy filling and sew in place, sewing the cast-off edge of the top of the leg to the belly. Push one end of the chenille stick from the leg into the body.

Sew the gusset at the back of the head (using the photograph on page 136 as guidance), stuffing the head with toy filling as you work. Starting at the cast-on edge, sew the seam on the snout and pin to the front of the face, stuffing with toy filling as you go. The seam goes underneath the head. Sew in place and sew the cream stripe up the centre of the head as shown.

With WS together, sew one ear lining to one ear. Repeat for the second ear. Pin the ears in place using the photograph as guidance and then sew in place. Using black sewing cotton, sew the two black shanked buttons in place for eyes. Sew the black nose to the front of the head using black yarn. Sew the head firmly to the front of the body. The head will be a bit wobbly but the collar will stabilise it once it is sewn on.

Fold the tail in half and sew the side seam, stuffing the cast-on end with toy filling. Sew in place, using the photographs for guidance.

Collar

Using fuchsia pink yarn and 2.75mm (UK 12, US 2) knitting needles, cast on 5 sts and work in SS until the collar fits snugly around dog's neck. Cast off.

Place the collar around the dog's neck and sew the cast-on and cast-off edges together. Sew the rhinestone trim in place.

Chihuahua's doggy bag

Materials

75m (82yd) of sparkly pink DK (8-ply) cotton yarn
Small amount of fuchsia pink 4-ply (fingering) yarn

Needles

3.5mm (UK 9/10, US 4) and 2.75mm (UK 12, US 2) knitting needles

Tension

24 sts measured over 10cm (4in) using 3.5mm (UK 9/10, US 4) knitting needles and DK (8-ply) yarn

Bag

Starting with the base and using sparkly pink yarn, cast on 24 sts using 3.5mm (UK 9/10, US 4) knitting needles.
Work 7cm (2¾in) in GS.
Next row: Cast on 52 sts, K to end of row (76 sts).
Starting with a WS row, work 6cm (2⅜in) in SS ending with a WS row.
Next row: Cast off 17 sts, K to the end of the row (59 sts).
Next row: Cast off 3 sts, P to the end of the row (56 sts).
Cast off 2 sts at the beg of the next 2 rows (52 sts).
Rep last 2 rows once more (48 sts).
Work 2 rows in SS.
Cast off.

Top of bag

Using sparkly pink yarn and 3.5mm (UK 9/10, US 4) knitting needles, cast on 5 sts and work in SS until the strip is long enough to go all around the top edge of the bag when slightly stretched. Cast off.
Note: Alternatively, this can be knitted as an i-cord (see page 14).

Handles (make two)

Using sparkly pink yarn and 3.5mm (UK 9/10, US 4) knitting needles, cast on 5 sts and work in SS until handle measures 11cm (4⅜in). Cast off.
Note: Alternatively, these be knitted as an i-cord (see page 14).

Paw prints (make two)

Using fuchsia pink yarn and 2.75mm (UK 12, US 2) knitting needles, cast on 5 sts and purl 1 row.

Next row: K1, M1, K to last st, M1, K1 (7 sts).

Purl 1 row.

Cast off 2 sts at beg of the next 2 rows (3 sts).

Work 2 rows in SS.

Next row: Sl1, K2tog, psso (1 st).

Fasten off rem st.

Making up

Lay your knitted bag out and sew the two edges marked 1 to each other. Repeat for 2, 3 and 4 to make the bag shape. Pin the bag edging in place along the top shaped edge of the bag, covering the cast-off edge. Sew in place.

Pin the handles in place (see photograph for guidance) and sew securely to the inside edge of the bag. Using fuchsia pink yarn, sew one paw print to one side of the bag and embroider four French knots (see page 16) as pads, using the photograph for guidance on placement. Repeat with the second paw on the other side of the bag.

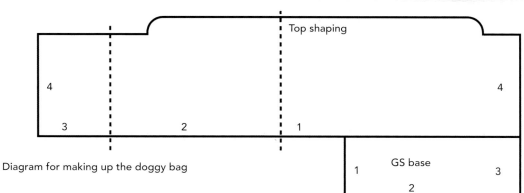

Diagram for making up the doggy bag

Mischief-makers

These cute little pups are irresistible. Made using a fluffy yarn, they are easy to knit and quick to make, so why not have a whole litter?

Materials
- 60m (66yd) of fluffy grey 10-ply (aran) yarn
- Small amount of black 4-ply (fingering) yarn
- Two 8mm (⅜in) black shanked buttons
- Toy filling

Needles
5mm (UK 6, US 8) and 2.75mm (UK 12, US 2) knitting needles

Tension
8–9 sts measured over 5cm (2in) and worked in SS using 5mm (UK 12, US 2) knitting needles and 10-ply (aran) yarn

Size
26cm (10¼in) from top of head to bottom of feet

Notes: Each pup is knitted in SS but sewn together with the WS on the outside to give a fluffier appearance.

The yarn listed above is sufficient to make one of the dogs – simply double the amount to make sure you have enough for his playmate.

Head
Using fluffy grey yarn and 5mm (UK 6, US 8) knitting needles, cast on 10 sts.
Next row: K2, M1, K1, M1, K4, M1, K1, M1, K2 (14 sts).
Next row: P3, M1, P1, M1, P6, M1, P1, M1, P3 (18 sts).
Next row: K4, M1, K1, M1, K8, M1, K1, M1, K4 (22 sts).
Purl 1 row.
Next row: K5, M1, K1, M1, K10, M1, K1, M1, K5 (26 sts).
Purl 1 row.
Next row: K6, M1, K1, M1, K12, M1, K1, M1, K6 (30 sts).
Work 3 rows in SS.
Next row: K5, ssK, K1, K2tog, K10, ssK, K1, K2tog, K5 (26 sts).
Purl 1 row.

Next row: K4, ssK, K1, K2tog, K8, ssK, K1, K2tog, K4 (22 sts).
Purl 1 row.
Next row: K3, ssK, K1, K2tog, K6, ssK, K1, K2tog, K3 (18 sts).
Work 3 rows in SS.
Cast off rem sts.

Legs (make two)
Using fluffy grey yarn and 5mm (UK 6, US 8) knitting needles, cast on 18 sts.
Next row: K8, M1, K2, M1, K8 (20 sts).
Work 3 rows in SS.
Next row: K7, K2tog, K2, ssK, K7 (18 sts).
Next row: P6, P2tog, P2, P2togtbl, P6 (16 sts).
Next row: K5, K2tog, K2, ssK, K5 (14 sts).
Next row: P4, P2tog, P2, P2togtbl, P4 (12 sts).
Work 12 rows in SS.
Cast off.

Arms (make two)
Using fluffy grey yarn and 5mm (UK 6, US 8) knitting needles, cast on 8 sts.
Next row: K1, M1, (K2, M1) three times, K1 (12 sts).
Work 5 rows in SS.
Next row: K2, K2tog, K4, K2tog, K2 (10 sts).
Work 11 rows in SS.
Cast off.

Ears (make four)
Using fluffy grey yarn and 5mm (UK 6, US 8) knitting needles, cast on 4 sts and purl 1 row.
Next row: K1, M1, K2, M1, K1 (6 sts).
Next row: P1, M1, P4, M1, P1 (8 sts).
Work 2 rows in SS.
Next row: K1, K2tog, K2, K2tog, K1 (6 sts).
Work 3 rows in SS.
Next row: K1, (K2tog) twice, K1 (4 sts).
Purl 1 row.
Cast off rem sts.

Nose

Using black yarn and 2.75mm (UK 12, US 2) knitting needles, cast on 3 sts and purl 1 row.

Next row: (K1, M1) twice, K1 (5 sts).

Work 2 rows in SS.

Next row: P2tog, P1, P2togtbl (3 sts).

Knit 1 row.

Cast off, leaving a length of yarn long enough to embroider the mouth.

Body

Using fluffy grey yarn and 5mm (UK 6, US 8) knitting needles, cast on 12 sts.

Next row: K3, Kfb, K4, Kfb, K3 (14 sts).

Next row: P3, Kfb, P6, Kfb, P3 (16 sts).

Next row: K4, Kfb, K6, Kfb, K4 (18 sts).

Next row: P4, Kfb, P8, Kfb, P4 (20 sts).

Next row: K5, Kfb, K8, Kfb, K5 (22 sts).

Next row: P5, Kfb, P10, Kfb, P5 (24 sts).

Next row: K6, Kfb, K10, Kfb, K6 (26 sts).

Next row: P6, Kfb, P12, Kfb, P6 (28 sts).

Next row: K7, Kfb, K12, Kfb, K7 (30 sts).

Next row: P7, Kfb, P14, Kfb, P7 (32 sts).

Knit 1 row.

Next row: P8, Kfb, P14, Kfb, P8 (34 sts).

Knit 1 row.

Next row: P8, Kfb, P16, Kfb, P8 (36 sts).

Work 4 rows in SS.

Next row: K8, ssK, K16, K2tog, K8 (34 sts).

Purl 1 row.

Next row: K8, ssK, K14, K2tog, K8 (32 sts).

Purl 1 row.

Next row: K7, ssK, K14, K2tog, K7 (30 sts).

Purl 1 row.

Next row: K7, ssK, K12, K2tog, K7 (28 sts).

Purl 1 row.

Next row: K6, ssK, K12, K2tog, K6 (26 sts).

Purl 1 row.

Next row: K6, ssK, K10, K2tog, K6 (24 sts).

Purl 1 row.

Next row: K5, ssK, K10, K2tog, K5 (22 sts).
Purl 1 row.
Next row: K5, ssK, K8, K2tog, K5 (20 sts).
Purl 1 row.
Next row: K4, ssK, K8, K2tog, K4 (18 sts).
Purl 1 row.
Next row: K4, ssK, K6, K2tog, K4 (16 sts).
Purl 1 row.
Next row: K3, ssK, K6, K2tog, K3 (14 sts).
Purl 1 row.
Cast off.

Tail
Using fluffy grey yarn and 5mm (UK 6, US 8) knitting needles, cast on 8 sts. Starting with a knit row, work 8 rows in SS.
Next row: K1, M1, (K2, M1) three times, K1 (12 sts).
Purl 1 row.
Next row: K1, K2tog, K1, (K2tog) twice, K1, K2tog, K1 (8 sts).
Cast off.

Making up
With the WS facing outwards and starting at the cast-on end of the body (bottom), sew up the back seam. Stuff with toy filling as you sew. Sew the cast-on edge together to form the bottom seam, ensuring the back seam is in the centre of the back. Sew the cast-off edge together to form the top seam.

With the WS facing outwards, sew up the back seam of the head. This seam will be underneath the head. Stuff with toy filling and sew the top and bottom seams as for the body.

Using black yarn, sew the nose in place, embroider the mouth, and then sew on the black shanked buttons as eyes. Use the photographs for guidance on where to place them.

Attach fluffy grey yarn to the centre back of the head, then sew the head to the top edge of the body using the photographs for guidance.

With the WS facing outwards sew two ear pieces together. Repeat for the second ear. Sew the ears to the top of the head using the photographs for guidance and leaving approximately 1cm (⅜in) in between the ears.

With WS facing outwards, sew up the side seam of the arm. Stuff with toy filling and sew up the top and bottom seams. The cast-off end forms the top of the arm. Repeat for the second arm.

With the seam facing towards the back of the pup, sew the cast-off edge of the arm to the side of the body just under the head, using the photographs for guidance. Repeat for the second arm.

Sew up the back seam of the leg, stuff it with toy filling, then sew the foot closed. Sew up the top seam of the leg horizontally, so that the back seam is in the centre. Repeat for the second leg and sew the legs to the bottom of the body, towards the front of the pup. Sew up the side and bottom seams of the tail, but do not stuff it. Sew the top of the tail (cast-on end) to the back of the body. See photographs for guidance.

Bullseye

Bullseye has real character in his gleaming black eyes and just wants a hug. His black patches are knitted separately and sewn on after making him up; if you want to give him a few more patches you can easily make two or three more to sew on.

Materials
62m (68yd) of cream 10-ply (aran) yarn
25m (27½yd) of black 10-ply (aran) yarn
Toy filling
Two 10mm (⅜in) black shanked buttons
Black sewing cotton

Needles
4mm (UK 8, US 6) knitting needles

Tension
9–10 sts measured over 5cm (2in) and worked in SS using 4mm (UK 8, US 6) knitting needles and 10-ply (aran) yarn

Size
Approximately 20cm (8in) tall when sitting down as shown opposite

Body front
Using cream yarn, cast on 20 sts and work 4 rows in SS, starting with a knit row.
Next row: K1, M1, K8, M1, K2, M1, K8, M1, K1 (24 sts).
Purl 1 row.
Next row: K1, M1, K10, M1, K2, M1, K10, M1, K1 (28 sts).
Purl 1 row.
Next row: K1, M1, K12, M1, K2, M1, K12, M1, K1 (32 sts).
Purl 1 row.
Next row: K1, M1, K14, M1, K2, M1, K14, M1, K1 (36 sts).
Work 15 rows in SS.
Next row: K1, ssK, K12, K2tog, K2, ssK, K12, K2tog, K1 (32 sts).
Work 3 rows in SS.
Next row: K1, ssK, K10, K2tog, K2, ssK, K10, K2tog, K1 (28 sts).
Purl 1 row.
Next row: K1, ssK, K8, K2tog, K2, ssK, K8, K2tog, K1 (24 sts).
Purl 1 row.
Next row: K1, ssK, K to last 3 sts, K2tog, K1 (22 sts).
Purl 1 row.
Rep last 2 rows three more times (16 sts).
Next row: K1, ssK, K2, K2tog, K2, ssK, K2, K2tog, K1 (12 sts).
Cast off (WS).

Body back

Using cream yarn, cast on 20 sts and work 2 rows in SS, starting with a knit row.

Next row: K1, M1, K8, M1, K2, M1, K8, M1, K1 (24 sts).
Purl 1 row.

Next row: K1, M1, K10, M1, K2, M1, K10, M1, K1 (28 sts).
Purl 1 row.

Next row: K1, M1, K12, M1, K2, M1, K12, M1, K1 (32 sts).
Work 15 rows in SS.

Next row: K1, ssK, K to last 3 sts, K2tog, K1 (30 sts).
Purl 1 row.
Rep last 2 rows eleven more times (8 sts).
Cast off.

Base

Using cream yarn, cast on 16 sts and, starting with a knit row, work 2 rows in SS.

Next row: K1, M1, K to last st, M1, K1 (18 sts).
Work 9 rows in SS.

Next row: K1, ssK, K to last 3 sts, K2tog, K1 (16 sts).
Purl 1 row.

Next row: K1, ssK, K to last 3 sts, K2tog, K1 (14 sts).

Next row: P1, P2tog, P to last 3 sts, P2togtbl, P1 (12 sts).
Cast off.

Legs (make two)

Using cream yarn, cast on 18 sts.

Next row: K8, M1, K2, M1, K8 (20 sts).
Work 3 rows in SS.

Next row: K9, M1, K2, M1, K9 (22 sts).
Work 3 rows in SS.

Next row: K10, M1, K2, M1, K10 (24 sts).
Purl 1 row.

Next row: K11, M1, K2, M1, K11 (26 sts).
Purl 1 row.

Next row: K12, M1, K2, M1, K12 (28 sts).
Purl 1 row.

Next row: K13, M1, K2, M1, K13 (30 sts).

Next row: P14, M1, P2, M1, P14 (32 sts).

Next row: K15, M1, K2, M1, K15 (34 sts).

Next row: P16, M1, P2, M1, P16 (36 sts).
Work 2 rows in SS.

Next row: K1, ssK, K12, K2tog, K2, K2tog, K12, ssK, K1 (32 sts).

Next row: P1, P2tog, P10, P2togtbl, P2, P2tog, P10, P2togtbl, P1 (28 sts).

Cast off 11 sts at the beginning of the next two rows (6 sts).

Work 2 rows in SS.

Next row: K1, M1, K to last st, M1, K1 (8 sts).
Purl 1 row.
Rep last 2 rows once more (10 sts).
Work 2 rows in SS.

Next row: K1, ssK, K to last 3 sts, K2tog, K1 (8 sts).
Purl 1 row.
Rep last 2 rows once more (6 sts).
Cast off.

Arms (make two)

Using cream yarn and 4mm (UK 8, US 6) needles, cast on 16 sts and, starting with a knit row, work 12 rows in SS.

Next row: K1, M1, K6, M1, K2, M1, K6, M1, K1 (20 sts).
Purl 1 row.

Next row: K1, M1, K8, M1, K2, M1, K8, M1, K1 (24 sts).
Work 3 rows in SS.

Next row: K1, ssK, K6, K2tog, K2, ssK, K6, K2tog, K1 (20 sts).
Next row: P1, P2tog, P4, P2togtbl, P2, P2tog, P4, P2togtbl, P1 (16 sts).
Cast off using the three-needle cast-off technique (see page 17).

Head

Using cream yarn, cast on 14 sts and purl 1 row.
Next row: K1, M1, K to last st, M1, K1 (16 sts).
Next row: P1, M1, P to last st, M1, P1 (18 sts).
Rep last 2 rows twice more (26 sts).
Next row: K1, M1, K to last st, M1, K1 (28 sts).
Purl 1 row.
Rep last 2 rows once more (30 sts).
Next row: K14, M1, K2, M1, K14 (32 sts).
Next row: P15, M1, P2, M1, P15 (34 sts).
Next row: K16, M1, K2, M1, K16 (36 sts).

Next row: P17, M1, P2, M1, P17 (38 sts).
Next row: K18, M1, K2, M1, K18 (40 sts).
Next row: P19, M1, P2, M1, P19 (42 sts).
Next row: K20, M1, K2, M1, K20 (44 sts).
Work 9 rows in SS.
Next row: K1, ssK, K16, K2tog, K2, ssK, K16, K2tog, K1 (40 sts).
Purl 1 row.
Next row: K1, ssK, K14, K2tog, K2, ssK, K14, K2tog, K1 (36 sts).
Purl 1 row.
Next row: K1, ssK, K12, K2tog, K2, ssK, K12, K2tog, K1 (32 sts).
Next row: P1, P2tog, P10, P2togtbl, P2, P2tog, P10, P2togtbl, P1 (28 sts).
Next row: K1, ssK, K8, K2tog, K2, ssK, K8, K2tog, K1 (24 sts).
Next row: P1, P2tog, P6, P2togtbl, P2, P2tog, P6, P2togtbl, P1 (20 sts).
Next row: K1, ssK, K4, K2tog, K2, ssK, K4, K2tog, K1 (16 sts).
Cast off using the three-needle cast-off technique (see page 17).

Ears (make two in cream and two in black)

Cast on 8 sts and, starting with a knit row, work 6 rows in SS.
Next row: K1, M1, K to last st, M1, K1 (10 sts).
Work 7 rows in SS.
Next row: K1, M1, K to last st, M1, K1 (12 sts).
Work 3 rows in SS.
Next row: K1, ssK, K to last 3 sts, K2tog, K1 (10 sts).
Next row: P1, P2tog, P to last 3 sts, P2togtbl, P1 (8 sts).
Cast off.

I've got a bone to pick with you...

Nose

Using black yarn, cast on 5 sts and, starting with a knit row, work 4 rows in SS.

Next row: SsK, K1, K2tog (3 sts).

Purl 1 row.

Next row: Sl1, K2tog, psso (1 st).

Fasten off rem st, leaving a length of yarn long enough to embroider the mouth.

Patch on face

Using black yarn, cast on 4 sts and purl 1 row.

Next row: K1, M1, K2, M1, K1 (6 sts).

Next row: P1, M1, K4, M1, P1 (8 sts).

Work 2 rows in SS.

Next row: K1, ssK, K2, K2tog, K1 (6 sts).

Next row: P1, P2tog, P2togtbl, P1 (4 sts).

Cast off (RS).

Tail

Using black yarn, cast on 10 sts and, starting with a knit row, work 4 rows in SS.

*__Next row:__ K8, w&t.

Next row: P6, w&t.

Next row: K to end of row.

Purl 1 row.*

Rep from * to * once more.

Next row: K1, ssK, K to last 3 sts, K2tog, K1 (8 sts).

Purl 1 row.

Rep last 2 rows once more (6 sts).

Next row: (K2tog) three times (3 sts).

Thread yarn through rem sts and fasten, leaving enough yarn to sew the side seam of the tail.

Patch on body

Using black yarn, cast on 7 sts and knit 1 row.

Next row: P1, M1, P to last st, M1, P1 (9 sts).

Work 2 rows in SS.

Next row: K1, M1, K to last st, M1, K1 (11 sts).

Work 3 rows in SS.

Next row: K1, ssK, K to last 3 sts, K2tog, K1 (9 sts).

Purl 1 row.

Rep last 2 rows once more (7 sts).

Cast off.

... I think you're trying to stitch me up!

Making up

Pin and sew the side seams of the body pieces together, placing the cast-on edges at the bottom. Stuff the body with toy filling, pin the base in place then sew the base to the body, placing the cast-on edge at the front.

With the head shaping forming the top of the head and the cast-off edge forming the back of the head, sew up the seam along the bottom of the head and up the front. When you get to the cast-on edges, run a length of cream yarn through a row of stitches a couple of stitches in from the cast-off edge and gather. This gives a rounder finish to the nose (see page 17).

Sew the black patch on to the face using the photograph for guidance. Sew the black shanked buttons in place as eyes using black sewing cotton. Run the thread from the back of each eye down to the base of the head and pull slightly to secure. This gives the eyes a much more realistic look.

With the WS together, sew the two black ear pieces together. Repeat for the cream ear. Pin the ears in place on the top of the head, making sure that the black ear is on the opposite side of the head to the black eye patch. Sew in place.

Sew the nose to the front of the face, placing the cast-on edge at the top, and embroider the mouth using straight stitches and the length of black yarn left from the nose.

Sew up the side seam of the first arm and fold so that this seam is beneath the arm. Sew the cast-off stitches of the arm together, then stuff with toy filling and embroider the spaces between the fingers on the paw using black yarn and straight stitches. Repeat for the second arm, then pin the arms on the body and sew in place.

Sew up the back seam of the leg, stuff with toy filling and sew the base of the foot in place. Repeat for the second leg, then pin both in place so that the back of the leg is just above the base/body seam and the seam is underneath the leg. Use the photograph for guidance when placing the legs.

Sew the black body patch in place. Sew up the seam of the tail (this will be at the top when it is sewn on to the body) and place a small amount of toy filling inside. Sew it in place at the bottom of the body using the photographs for guidance.

Stripes

Daredevil Stripes has a look of fun on his stripy face. Follow the colour sequence and you will end up with your very own colourful dog. Why not knit him in shades of blue for a baby boy? Just remember to use safety eyes in place of buttons.

Materials
70m (76½yd) of pink 10-ply (aran) cotton yarn (MC)
62m (68yd) of purple 10-ply (aran) cotton yarn (CC)
Small amount of black 4-ply (fingering) cotton yarn
Toy filling
Chenille sticks

Needles
3.75mm (UK 9, US 5) and 2.75mm (UK 12, US 2) knitting needles

Tension
20 sts measured over 10cm (4in) and worked in SS using 3.75mm (UK 9, US 5) knitting needles and 10-ply (aran) cotton yarn

Size
18cm (7in) tall when sitting down as shown on page 150

Note: The six-row stripe pattern is worked as follows:
Starting with a knit row and working in SS:
Work 2 rows in CC.
Work 4 rows in MC.
Four-row stripe pattern:
Starting with a knit row and working in SS:
Work 2 rows in CC.
Work 2 rows in MC.

Head
Cast on 10 sts using MC and 3.75mm (UK 9, US 5) knitting needles and purl 1 row.
Next row: K1, M1, K to last st, M1, K1 (12 sts).
Next row: P1, M1, P to last st, M1, P1 (14 sts).
Next row: K1, M1, K4, M1, K4, M1, K4, M1, K1 (18 sts).
Purl 1 row.

Next row: K1, M1, K5, M1, K6, M1, K5, M1, K1 (22 sts).
Purl 1 row.
Next row: K1, M1, K6, M1, K8, M1, K6, M1, K1 (26 sts).
Purl 1 row.
Next row: K1, M1, K7, M1, K10, M1, K7, M1, K1 (30 sts).
Purl 1 row.
Join in CC and work next 14 rows in the six-row stripe pattern (see notes).
Next row: K12, M1, K6, M1, K12 (32 sts).
Next row: P13, M1, P6, M1, P13 (34 sts).
Next row: K14, M1, K6, M1, K14 (36 sts).
Purl 1 row.
Next row: K15, M1, K6, M1, K15 (38 sts).
Purl 1 row.
Next row: K16, M1, K6, M1, K16 (40 sts).
Work 7 rows in SS.
Continue in MC.
Work 2 rows in SS.
Next row: K1, ssK, K14, K2tog, K2, ssK, K14, K2tog, K1 (36 sts).
Purl 1 row.
Next row: K1, ssK, K12, K2tog, K2, ssK, K12, K2tog, K1 (32 sts).
Purl 1 row.
Next row: K1, ssK, K10, K2tog, K2, ssK, K10, K2tog, K1 (28 sts).
Next row: P1, P2tog, P8, P2togtbl, P2, P2tog, P8, P2togtbl, P1 (24 sts).
Next row: K1, ssK, K6, K2tog, K2, ssK, K6, K2tog, K1 (20 sts).
Next row: P1, P2tog, P4, P2togtbl, P2, P2tog, P4, P2togtbl, P1 (16 sts).
Cast off using the three-needle cast-off technique (see page 17).

Body (make two)

Cast on 10 sts using MC and 3.75mm (UK 9, US 5) knitting needles and, starting with a knit row, work 2 rows in SS.

The body is worked in the six-row stripe pattern from now on.

Next row: K1, M1, K to last st, M1, K1 (12 sts).
Purl 1 row.
Rep last 2 rows four more times (20 sts).
Next row: K1, M1, K to last st, M1, K1 (22 sts).
Work 3 rows in SS.
Rep last 4 rows four more times (30 sts).
Work 6 rows in SS.
Next row: K1, ssK, K9, K2tog, K2, ssK, K9, K2tog, K1 (26 sts).
Purl 1 row.
Next row: K1, ssK, K7, K2tog, K2, ssK, K7, K2tog, K1 (22 sts).
Purl 1 row.
Next row: K1, ssK, K5, K2tog, K2, ssK, K5, K2tog, K1 (18 sts).
Next row: P1, P2tog, P3, P2togtbl, P2, P2tog, P3, P2togtbl, P1 (14 sts).
From now on, work only in MC.

Next row: K1, ssK, K1, K2tog, K2, ssK, K1, K2tog, K1 (10 sts).
Cast off.

Nose

Using black yarn and 2.75mm (UK 12, US 2) knitting needles, cast on 5 sts and purl 1 row.
Next row: K1, M1, K to last st, M1, K1 (7 sts).
Work 3 rows in SS.
Next row: K1, ssK, K1, K2tog, K1 (5 sts).
Purl 1 row.
Cast off, leaving a long enough length of yarn to embroider the mouth.

Ears (make two)

Using CC and 3.75mm (UK 9, US 5) knitting needles, cast on 6 sts starting with a knit row, and work 18 rows in SS.
Next row: K1, ssK, K2tog, K1 (4 sts).
Purl 1 row.
Next row: K1, M1, K2, M1, K1 (6 sts).
Work 18 rows in SS.
Cast off.

Arms (make two)

Using MC and 3.75mm (UK 9, US 5) knitting needle, cast on 12 sts starting with a knit row, and work 2 rows in SS.

From now on work in the four-row stripe pattern.

Work 12 rows in SS.

Continue in CC only.

Next row: K1, M1, K4, M1, K2, M1, K4, M1, K1 (16 sts).

Purl 1 row.

Next row: K1, M1, K6, M1, K2, M1, K6, M1, K1 (20 sts).

Work 5 rows in SS.

Next row: K1, ssK, K4, K2tog, K2, ssK, K4, K2tog, K1 (16 sts).

Next row: P1, P2tog, P2, P2togtbl, P2, P2tog, P2, P2togtbl, P1 (12 sts).

Cast off, using the three-needle cast-off technique (see page 17).

Tail

Using CC and 3.75mm (UK 9, US 5) knitting needles, cast on 10 sts starting with a knit row, and work 10 rows in SS.

Next row: (K2tog) five times (5 sts).

Thread yarn through rem sts, gather and sew the side seam of the tail. Fasten off yarn.

Legs (make two)

Using CC and 3.75mm (UK 9, US 5) knitting needles, cast on 14 sts starting with a knit row, and work 16 rows in the four-row stripe pattern.

Cast off.

Feet (make two)

Using CC and 3.75mm (UK 9, US 5) knitting needles, cast on 8 sts and purl 1 row.

Next row: K1, M1, K to last st, M1, K1 (10 sts).

Next row: P1, M1, P to last st, M1, P1 (12 sts).

Work 6 rows in SS.

Next row: K1, ssK, K to last 3 sts, K2tog, K1 (10 sts).

Work 2 rows in SS.

Next row: P1, M1, P to last st, M1, P1 (12 sts).

Work 6 rows in SS.

Next row: K1, ssK, K to last 3 sts, K2tog, K1 (10 sts).

Next row: P1, P2tog, P to last 3 sts, P2togtbl, P1 (8 sts).

Knit 1 row.

Cast off.

Making up

Sew the side seams of the body with the cast-off end forming the base. Stuff with toy filling. Sew the head seam that forms the bottom and front of the head. Stuff the head with toy filling as you sew.

Slightly gather the nose and sew to the front top edge of the face, placing a small amount of toy filling inside. Using the length of yarn left from the nose, embroider the mouth using straight stitches. Using black cotton yarn, embroider two French knots (see page 16) for eyes just behind the first purple stripe.

Fold one ear in half lengthways and sew the seams. Fold a chenille stick in half and place it inside the ear around the outside edge so you can bend it into position. Repeat for the second ear. Pin the ears in place using the photograph as guidance, then sew them in place, pushing the two ends of the chenille stick inside the head to avoid any sharp ends protruding. Sew the head to the body.

Sew the side seam of the arm stuffing with toy filling as you go. Using MC, work three stitches over the paw to give the appearance of separate fingers. Repeat for the second arm. Sew it to the side seam of the dog, using the photograph for guidance and placing the seam underneath the arm.

Sew the foot seam, stuffing with toy filling as you go. Sew the side seam of the leg and stuff with toy filling. Sew the stuffed foot to the end of the leg with the leg seam at the back. The cast-off end of the foot should be at the back. Sew the seam at the top of the leg together from side to side. Using MC work three stitches over the paw to give the appearance of separate toes. Repeat for the second foot and leg. Using the photograph for guidance, sew the legs to the body, making sure you sew them to a MC stripe. Sew the tail to the lowest CC stripe on the back of the body. The tail is not stuffed.

Pink Poodle

Glamorous Pink Poodle is a rosy delight! She is easy to make, as her fluffy wristlets and anklets are knitted separately and sewn on after making up. Don't forget to give her some long eyelashes.

Materials

- 80m (87½yd) of pale pink 5-ply (sportweight) yarn
- 45m (49¼yd) of pale pink fluffy 10-ply (aran) yarn
- Small amount of black 4-ply (fingering) yarn
- Two 6mm (¼in) black beads
- Toy filling
- Black and pink sewing cotton
- Small amount of narrow pink ribbon

Needles

3.25mm (UK 10, US 3), 4.5mm (UK 7, US 7) and 2.75mm (UK 12, US 2) knitting needles

Tension

25 sts measured over 10cm (4in) and worked in SS using 3.25mm (UK 10, US 3) knitting needles and 5-ply (sportweight) yarn

Size

21cm (8¼in) from the bottom of the feet to top of the head

Body

Using pale pink fluffy 10-ply (aran) yarn and 4.5mm (UK 7, US 7) knitting needles, cast on 12 sts and, starting with a knit row, work 4 rows in SS.

Next row: K2, (Kfb) twice, K4, (Kfb) twice, K2 (16 sts).
Work 3 rows in SS.
Next row: K3, (Kfb) twice, K6, (Kfb) twice, K3 (20 sts).
Work 3 rows in SS.
Next row: K4, (Kfb) twice, K8, (Kfb) twice, K4 (24 sts).
Purl 1 row.
Next row: K5, (Kfb) twice, K10, (Kfb) twice, K5. (28 sts).
Purl 1 row.
Next row: K6, (Kfb) twice, K12, (Kfb) twice, K6 (32 sts).
Work 7 rows in SS.
Next row: K6, (K2tog) twice, K12, (K2tog) twice, K6 (28 sts).
Purl 1 row.
Next row: K5, (K2tog) twice, K10, (K2tog) twice, K5 (24 sts).
Purl 1 row.
Next row: K4, (K2tog) twice, K8, (K2tog) twice, K4 (20 sts).
Next row: P3, (P2tog) twice, P6, (P2tog) twice, P3 (16 sts).
Cast off.

Legs (make two)

Using pale pink 5-ply (sportweight) yarn and 3.25mm (UK 10, US 3) knitting needles, cast on 14 sts. Starting with a knit row, work 14 rows in SS.
Cast off.

I'm feeling in the pink!

Feet (make two)

Using pale pink 5-ply (sportweight) yarn and 3.25mm (UK 10, US 3) knitting needles, cast on 7 sts and purl 1 row.

Next row: K1, M1, K to last st, M1, K1 (9 sts).

Next row: P1, M1, P to last st, M1, P1 (11 sts).

Work 6 rows in SS.

Next row: K1, ssK, K to last 3 sts, K2tog, K1 (9 sts).

Work 2 rows in SS.

Next row: P1, M1, P to last st, M1, P1 (11 sts).

Work 6 rows in SS.

Next row: K1, ssK, K to last 3 sts, K2tog, K1 (9 sts).

Next row: P1, P2tog, P to last 3 sts, P2togtbl, P1 (7 sts).

Knit 1 row.

Cast off.

Arms (make two)

Using pale pink 5-ply (sportweight) yarn and 3.25mm (UK 10, US 3) knitting needles, cast on 12 sts and, starting with a knit row, work 12 rows in SS.

Next row: K1, M1, K4, M1, K2, M1, K4, M1, K1 (16 sts).

Purl 1 row.

Next row: K1, M1, K6, M1, K2, M1, K6, M1, K1 (20 sts).

Work 3 rows in SS.

Next row: K1, ssK, K4, K2tog, K2, ssK, K4, K2tog, K1 (16 sts).

Purl 1 row.

Next row: K1, ssK, K2, K2tog, K2, ssK, K2, K2tog, K1 (12 sts).

Cast off using three-needle cast-off technique (see page 17).

Head

Using pale pink 5-ply (sportweight) yarn and 3.25mm (UK 10, US 3) knitting needles, cast on 10 sts.

Next row: K1, M1, K to last st, M1, K1 (12 sts).

Next row: P1, M1, P to last st, M1, P1 (14 sts).

Rep last 2 rows once more (18 sts).

Next row: K1, M1, K to last st, M1, K1 (20 sts).

Purl 1 row.

Rep last 2 rows once more (22 sts).

Next row: K10, M1, K2, M1, K10 (24 sts).

Next row: P11, M1, P2, M1, P11 (26 sts).

Next row: K12, M1, K2, M1, K12 (28 sts).

Next row: P13, M1, P2, M1, P13 (30 sts).

Next row: K14, M1, K2, M1, K14 (32 sts).

Next row: P15, M1, P2, M1, P15 (34 sts).

Work 6 rows in SS.

Next row: K1, ssK, K11, K2tog, K2, ssK, K11, K2tog, K1 (30 sts).

Purl 1 row.

Next row: K1, ssK, K9, K2tog, K2, ssK, K9, K2tog, K1 (26 sts).

Purl 1 row.

Next row: K1, ssK, K7, K2tog, K2, ssK, K7, K2tog, K1 (22 sts).

Next row: P1, P2tog, P5, P2togtbl, P2, P2tog, P5, P2togtbl, P1 (18 sts).

Cast off using three-needle cast-off technique (see page 17).

Nose

Using black yarn and 2.75mm (UK 12, US 2) knitting needles, cast on 3 sts.

Next row: (K1, M1) twice, K1 (5 sts).

Work 2 rows in SS.

Next row: P2tog, P1, P2tog (3 sts).

Next row: Sl1, K2tog, psso (1 st).

Thread yarn through rem st and fasten, leaving enough yarn to embroider the mouth.

Ears (make two)

Worked in GS.

Using pale pink fluffy 10-ply (aran) yarn and 4.5mm (UK 7, US 7) knitting needles, cast on 5 sts and knit 6 rows.

Next row: K1, M1, K3, M1, K1 (7 sts).

Knit 5 rows.

Next row: K1, M1, K5, M1, K1 (9 sts).

Knit 5 rows.

Next row: K2tog, K to last 2 sts, K2tog (7 sts).

Rep last row once more (5 sts).

Cast off.

Tail

Using pale pink 5-ply (sportweight) yarn and 3.25mm (UK 10, US 3) knitting needles, cast on 8 sts and, starting with a knit row, work 6 rows in SS.

Next row: K2tog, K4, K2tog (6 sts).

Work 6 rows in SS.

Thread yarn through sts and fasten.

Fur cuffs (make two for arms and two for legs)

Using pale pink fluffy 10-ply (aran) yarn and 4.5mm (UK 7, US 7) knitting needles, cast on 4 sts and, starting with a knit row, work in SS until long enough to go around arm/leg.

Cast off.

Pompom for tail

Worked in GS.

Using pale pink fluffy 10-ply (aran) yarn and 4.5mm (UK 7, US 7) knitting needles, cast on 6 sts and knit 1 row.

Next row: Kfb, K to last st, Kfb (8 sts).

Knit 1 row.

Rep last 2 rows once more (10 sts).

Knit 5 rows.

Next row: K2tog, K to last 2 sts, K2tog (8 sts).

Knit 1 row.

Rep last 2 rows once more (6 sts).

Cast off.

Fluffy top of head

Worked in GS.

Using pale pink fluffy 10-ply (aran) yarn and 4.5mm (UK 7, US 7) knitting needles, cast on 4 sts and knit 1 row.

Next row: K1, M1, K to last st, M1, K1 (6 sts).

Work 4 rows in GS.

Next row: K2tog, K to last 2 sts, K2tog (6 sts).

Cast off.

Making up

With the WS on the outside and the cast-off edge at the bottom, sew the body seam, stuffing with toy filling as you go. This seam will be at the back. Sew the bottom seam closed from side to side.

Placing the cast-off edge at the back of the head, sew the seam that will go underneath the head, stuffing with toy filling as you go. Sew the cast-on edges together up to the nose. To finish the head, see page 17 for instructions on how to gather the nose.

Pin the black beads in place as eyes using the photograph as guidance. Sew in place using black sewing cotton. Run a thread from the back of one eye down to the base of the head and pull slightly to secure, then repeat for the second eye. This gives the eyes a much more realistic look. Embroider eyelashes using straight stitches and black sewing cotton.

Pin the fluffy top of the head in place, putting a tiny amount of toy filling inside. Sew in place. Pin the ears in place, using the photograph as guidance, and then sew in place. Sew the nose to the front of the head using black yarn. Using the length of yarn left at the end of the nose, embroider the mouth using straight stitches. Pin the head to the body and sew it firmly in place.

Sew the foot seam, stuffing with toy filling as you go. Sew the side seam of one leg and stuff with toy filling. Sew the stuffed foot to the end of the leg with the leg seam at the back. The cast-off end of the foot should be towards the back. Sew the seam at the top of the leg together from side to side. Work three stitches over the paw to distinguish the separate toes. Repeat for the second leg and foot. Using the photograph for guidance sew the legs to the body.

Fold one arm in half and sew the seam. The cast-off stitches of the arm form the paw. Stuff with toy filling and embroider claws on the paw, using pale pink yarn and straight stitches, and using the photograph as guidance. Repeat for the second arm. The seam will be at the bottom of the arm. Pin the arms on to the side seams of the body and sew in place.

Using pale pink yarn, sew a cuff around each of the wrists and legs of the poodle, using the photographs for guidance.

Sew the tail seam and sew to the back of the body, using the photograph for guidance. The seam is placed underneath. The tail is not stuffed. Using pale pink fluffy yarn, stitch around the pompom and gather, stuffing with toy filling. Sew to the end of the tail.

Outdoors Dog

Outdoors dog just wants to have fun and splash about in some puddles in his cute wellington boots. Do not forget to put his coat on if it is cold outside – it is easy to make with the row-by-row instructions.

Materials

- 45m (49¼yd) of oatmeal 10-ply (aran) yarn
- 20m (22yd) of green 5-ply (sportweight) yarn
- 10m (11yd) of brown 5-ply (sportweight) yarn
- 35m (38¼yd) of cream 5-ply (sportweight) yarn
- Small amount of black 4-ply (fingering) yarn
- Toy filling
- Two 6mm (¼in) black beads
- Black sewing cotton
- Two stitch markers
- Chenille sticks

Tools

- 2.75mm (UK 12, US 2), 3.25mm (UK 10, US 3) and 4mm (UK 8, US 6) knitting needles
- Stitch holder or spare needle

Tension

9–10 sts measured over 5cm (2in) and worked in SS using 4mm (UK 8, US 6) knitting needles and 10-ply (aran) yarn

Size

14cm (5½in) tall to the top of the head

Body and front legs

Start at the bottom edge of the right foot.

Using oatmeal yarn and 4mm (UK 8, US 6) knitting needles, cast on 10 sts.

Next row: K2, (Kfb) three times, K5 (13 sts).

Purl 1 row.

Next row: K2, (K2tog) three times, K5 (10 sts).

Work 7 rows in SS.

Next row: Cast off 5 sts, K to end of row (5 sts).

Next row: Cast off 2 sts, P to end of row (3 sts).

Next row: K1, M1, K to end of row (4 sts).

Next row: Cast on 10 sts, P to last st, M1, P1 (15 sts).

Next row: K to last st M1, K1 (16 sts).

Work 19 rows in SS, placing a stitch marker at either end of row 10.

Next row: K to last 3 sts, K2tog, K1 (15 sts).

Next row: Cast off 10 sts, P to last 3 sts, P2togtbl, P1 (4 sts).

Next row: K1, K2tog, K1 (3 sts).

Next row: Cast on 2 sts, P to end of row (5 sts).

Next row: Cast on 5 sts, K to end of row (10 sts).

Work 7 rows in SS.

Next row: K2, (Kfb) three times, K5 (13 sts).

Purl 1 row.

Next row: K2, (K2tog) three times, K5 (10 sts).

Cast off (WS).

Belly

Using oatmeal yarn and 4mm (UK 8, US 6) knitting needles, cast on 4 sts. Starting with a knit row, work 4 rows in SS.
Next row: K1, M1, K2, M1, K1 (6 sts).
Work 5 rows in SS.
Next row: K1, M1, K4, M1, K1 (8 sts).
Work 21 rows in SS.
Next row: K1, ssK, K2, K2tog, K1 (6 sts).
Work 3 rows in SS.
Next row: K1, ssK, K2tog, K1 (4 sts).
Work 5 rows in SS.
Cast off.

Head

Start at the bottom of the head.
Using oatmeal yarn and 4mm (UK 8, US 6) knitting needles, cast on 10 sts and, starting with a knit row, work 2 rows in SS. Place these sts on a stitch holder or spare needle.
Using oatmeal yarn and 4mm (UK 8, US 6) needles, cast on 10 sts and, starting with a knit row, work 2 rows in SS, making the second section.
Next row: With RS facing, K across 10 sts on needle and then K across 10 sts on holder (20 sts).
Purl 1 row.
Next row: K1, M1, K8, M1, K2, M1, K8, M1, K1 (24 sts).

Next row: P1, M1, P10, M1, P2, M1, P10, M1, P1 (28 sts).
Work 2 rows in SS.
Next row: K11, ssK, K2, K2tog, K11 (26 sts).
Next row: P10, P2tog, P2, P2togtbl, P10 (24 sts).
Next row: K9, ssK, K2, K2tog, K9 (22 sts).
Next row: P8, P2tog, P2, P2togtbl, P8 (20 sts).
Next row: K7, ssK, K2, K2tog, K7 (18 sts).
Purl 1 row.
Next row: K6, ssK, K2, K2tog, K6 (16 sts).
Next row: P1, P2tog, P2, P2tog, P2, P2togtbl, P2, P2togtbl, P1 (12 sts).
Cast off.

Back leg (right)

Using oatmeal yarn and 4mm (UK 8, US 6) knitting needles, cast on 10 sts.
Next row: K2, (Kfb) three times, K5 (13 sts).
Purl 1 row.
Next row: K2, (K2tog) three times, K5 (10 sts).
Work 3 rows in SS.
Next row: K8, w&t.
Next row: P3, w&t.
Next row: K to end of row.
Purl 1 row.
Next row: K1, M1, (K3, M1) twice, K3 (13 sts).
Purl 1 row.

I'm ready to go!

159

Next row: Cast off 9 sts, M1, K3 (5 sts).
Next row: Cast off 2 sts, M1, P1, M1, P1 (5 sts).
*Next row: K1, M1, K to last st, M1, K1 (7 sts).
Next row: P1, M1, P to last st, M1, P1 (9 sts).
Work 4 rows in SS.
Next row: K1, ssK, K to last three sts, K2tog, K1 (7 sts).
Next row: P1, P2tog, P1, P2togtbl, P1 (5 sts).
Cast off.

Back leg (left)

Using oatmeal yarn and 4mm (UK 8, US 6) knitting needles, cast on 10 sts.
Next row: K5, (Kfb) three times, K2 (13 sts).
Purl 1 row.
Next row: K5, (K2tog) three times, K2 (10 sts).
Work 3 rows in SS.
Next row: K5, w&t.
Next row: P3, w&t.
Next row: K to end of row.
Purl 1 row.
Next row: (K3, M1) three times, K1 (13 sts).
Purl 1 row.
Next row: Cast off 2 sts, M1, K to end of row (12 sts).
Next row: Cast off 9 sts, M1, P to last st, M1, P1 (5 sts).
Work as for back leg (right) from * to end.

Ears (make two)

Using oatmeal yarn and 4mm (UK 8, US 6) knitting needles, cast on 6 sts. Starting with a knit row, work 4 rows in SS.
Next row: K1, ssK, K2tog, K1 (4 sts).
Work 3 rows in SS.
Next row: K1, K2tog, K1 (3 sts).
Next row: Sl1, P2tog, psso (1 st).
Thread yarn through rem st to fasten, leaving a length of yarn for making up.

Tail

Using oatmeal yarn and 4mm (UK 8, US 6) knitting needles, cast on 4 sts. Work 4 rows in SS.
Next row: K1, M1, K to last st, M1, K1 (6 sts).
Purl 1 row.
Next row: K4, w&t.
Next row: P2, w&t.
Next row: K to end of row.
Work 3 rows in SS.
Cast off.

Nose

Using black yarn and 2.75mm (UK 12, US 2) knitting needles, cast on 3 sts.

Next row: (K1, M1) twice, K1 (5 sts).

Work 3 rows in SS.

Next row: ssK, K1, K2tog (3 sts).

Next row: Sl1, P2tog, psso (1 st).

Thread yarn through rem st to fasten, leaving a length of yarn long enough to embroider the mouth.

Making up

Starting with one of the front legs, thread a length of oatmeal yarn through the bottom edge of the foot and gather to form the bottom of the foot. Sew up the side seam and stuff firmly with toy filling, placing a chenille stick inside the toy filling. Repeat for the second front leg.

Matching the middle of the cast-off edge of the belly to the stitch marker at the back of the body, and the middle of the cast-on edge of the belly to the stitch marker at the front of the body, pin the belly in place. Stuff the body firmly with toy filling and sew the seams of the belly in place. Sew the cast-off edge of the top of each front leg to the belly, using the photograph on the right for guidance.

Sew up both of the back legs in the same way as the front legs. Pin the top of the back leg to the body as shown in the photograph, stuff gently with toy filling and sew in place, sewing the cast-off edge of the top of the leg to the belly.

Fold the cast-off edge of the head in half and sew the stitches together. Sew the head seam that will be at the bottom of the head, stuffing with toy filling. Taking the length of yarn from the last decreased stitch of the ear, use a darning needle to run the yarn down the edge stitches on one side of the ear and pull slightly to make the ear bend over. Repeat for the second ear but pull the yarn tighter to make the ear fold over more (see photograph). Pin the ears in place using the photograph for guidance, then sew them firmly in place. Using black sewing cotton, sew the two beads in place for eyes. Sew the black nose to the front of the head, placing the cast-on edge at the top, then use the length of yarn left at the end of the nose to embroider the mouth in place using straight stitches. Sew the head firmly to the front of the body.

Fold the tail in half and sew the seam. Sew it in place using the photograph for guidance and placing the seam on the top.

Boots (make four)

Using brown yarn and 3.25mm (UK 10, US 3) knitting needles, cast on 4 sts and knit 2 rows.

Next row: K1, M1, K2, M1, K1 (6 sts).

Knit 4 rows.

Next row: K1, (K2tog) twice, K1 (4 sts).

Knit 4 rows.

Cast on 8 sts at the beginning of the next 2 rows (knitting both rows) (20 sts).

Next row (RS): Change to green yarn and, starting with a knit row, work 2 rows in SS.

Next row: K7, ssK, K2, K2tog, K7 (18 sts).

Next row: P6, P2tog, P2, P2togtbl, P6 (16 sts).

Next row: K5, ssK, K2, K2tog, K5 (14 sts).

Work 4 rows in SS.

Knit 2 rows.

Cast off loosely and evenly.

Making up

Sew up the back seam of the first boot. Sew the sole into place along the brown edge of the boot. Place a small amount of toy filling in the toe of the boot, then place the boot on the dog's leg. Repeat for the other three boots.

Coat

When working the cable section of the coat, please see the abbreviations on page 192.

Using cream yarn and 3.25mm (UK 10, US 3) knitting needles, cast on 20 sts and work as follows:

Row 1: (P2, K4) three times, P2.

Row 2: (K2, P4) three times, K2.

Row 3: Cast on 6 sts at the beginning of the row, P2, K4, (P2, C4F) three times, P2 (26 sts).

Row 4: Cast on 6 sts at the beginning of the row, (K2, P4) five times, K2 (32 sts).

Row 5: (P2, K4) five times, P2.

Row 6: (K2, P4) five times, K2.

Row 7: (P2, C4F) five times, P2.

Row 8: As row 6.

Repeat rows 5–8 twice more.

Row 17: (P2, K4), twice, P1, cast off 6 sts, (K4, P2) twice (leaving you with two sets of 13 sts).

Row 18: Turn work and continue over first set of 13 sts. (K2, P4) twice, K1.

Row 19: Cast off 2 sts, K2, P2, C4f, P2 (11 sts).

Row 20: K2, P4, K2, P3.

Row 21: Cast off 1 st, K1, P2, K4, P2 (10 sts).

Row 22: K2, P4, K2, P2.

Row 23: K2, P2, C4F, P2.

Row 24: As row 22.

Row 25: K2, P2, K4, P2.

Row 26: As row 22.

Row 27: As row 23.

Row 28: As row 22.

Repeat rows 25–28 once more.

Cast off.

With WS facing, rejoin yarn to rem 13 sts.

Row 18: K1, P4, K2, P4, K2.

Row 19: P2, C4F, P2, K4, P1.

Row 20: Cast off 2 sts, P2, K2, P4, K2 (11 sts).

Row 21: P2, K4, P2, K3.

Row 22: Cast off 1 st, P1, K2, P4, K2 (10 sts).

Row 23: P2, C4F, P2, K2.

Row 24: P2, K2, P4, K2.

Row 25: P2, K4, P2, K2.

Row 26: As row 24.

Row 27: As row 23.

Row 28: As row 24.

Repeat rows 25–28 once more.

Cast off.

Making up

With RS facing, pick up and knit 72 sts around the outside edge of the coat. Work 4 rows in K2, P2, rib. Cast off.

With RS facing pick up and knit 32 sts around the neck edge of the coat. Work 8 rows in K2, P2 rib. Cast off.

Sew the front seam of the coat together, from the top of the neck rib to the bottom of the edging rib. Place the coat on the dog and fold the collar over.

Christmas Dog

Get into the Christmas spirit with Christmas Dog and his fun sweater, which is knitted using the Fair Isle technique (see page 14), and finished off with a little embroidery. His antlers really help to get him into the party spirit!

Materials

100m (109⅜yd) of brown 10-ply (aran) yarn
Small amount of black 4-ply (fingering) yarn
Black sewing thread
Toy filling
Two 8mm (⅜in) black shanked buttons

Needles

4mm (UK 8, US 6) and 2.75mm (UK 12, US 2) knitting needles

Tension

9–10 sts measured over 5cm (2in) and worked in SS using 4mm (UK 8, US 6) knitting needles and 10-ply (aran) yarn

Size

26cm (10¼in) from top of head to bottom of feet

Body (front)

Using brown yarn and 4mm (UK 8, US 6) knitting needles, cast on 12 sts and, starting with a knit row, work 2 rows in SS.
Next row: K1, M1, K to last st, M1, K1 (14 sts).
Work 3 rows in SS.
Next row: K1, M1, K5, M1, K2, M1, K5, M1, K1 (18 sts).
Work 3 rows in SS.
Next row: K1, M1, K7, M1, K2, M1, K7, M1, K1 (22 sts).
Work 3 rows in SS.
Next row: K1, M1, K9, M1, K2, M1, K9, M1, K1 (26 sts).
Purl 1 row.
Next row: K1, M1, K11, M1, K2, M1, K11, M1, K1 (30 sts).
Work 13 rows in SS.
Next row: K1, ssK, K9, K2tog, K2, ssK, K9, K2tog, K1 (26 sts).
Purl 1 row.

Next row: K1, ssK, K7, K2tog, K2, ssK, K7, K2tog, K1 (22 sts).
Purl 1 row.
Next row: K1, ssK, K5, K2tog, K2, ssK, K5, K2tog, K1 (18 sts).
Next row: P1, P2tog, P3, P2togtbl, P2, P2tog, P3, P2togtbl, P1 (14 sts).
Next row: K1, ssK, K1, K2tog, K2, ssK, K1, K2tog, K1 (10 sts).
Next row: P1, (P2tog, P2togtbl) twice, P1 (6 sts).
Cast off.

Body (back)

Using brown yarn and 4mm (UK 8, US 6) knitting needles, cast on 10 sts and, starting with a knit row, work 2 rows in SS.
Next row: K1, M1, K to last st, M1, K1 (12 sts).
Work 3 rows in SS.
Rep last 4 rows once more (14 sts).
Next row: K1, M1, K5, M1, K2, M1, K5, M1, K1 (18 sts).
Work 3 rows in SS.
Next row: K1, M1, K7, M1, K2, M1, K7, M1, K1 (22 sts).
Work 3 rows in SS.
Next row: K1, M1, K9, M1, K2, M1, K9, M1, K1 (26 sts).
Work 7 rows in SS.
Next row: K1, ssK, K7, K2tog, K2, ssK, K7, K2tog, K1 (22 sts).
Purl 1 row.
Next row: K1, ssK, K5, K2tog, K2, ssK, K5, K2tog, K1 (18 sts).
Purl 1 row.
Next row: K1, ssK, K3, K2tog, K2, ssK, K3, K2tog, K1 (14 sts).
Purl 1 row.
Next row: K1, ssK, K1, K2tog, K2, ssK, K1, K2tog, K1 (10 sts).
Next row: P1, (P2tog, P2togtbl) twice, P1 (6 sts).
Cast off.

Legs (make two)

Using brown yarn and 4mm (UK 8, US 6) knitting needles, cast on 14 sts and, starting with a knit row, work 12 rows in SS.

Next row: K6, M1, K2, M1, K6 (16 sts).

Next row: P7, M1, P2, M1, P7 (18 sts).

Next row: K8, M1, K2, M1, K8 (20 sts).

Next row: P9, M1, P2, M1, P9 (22 sts).

Next row: K10, M1, K2, M1, K10 (24 sts).

Next row: P11, M1, P2, M1, P11 (26 sts).

Work 4 rows in SS.

Next row: K1, ssK, K7, K2tog, K2, ssK, K7, K2tog, K1 (22 sts).

Cast off rem 22 sts using the three-needle cast-off technique (see page 17).

Arms (make two)

Using brown yarn and 4mm (UK 8, US 6) knitting needles, cast on 12 sts and, starting with a knit row, work 12 rows in SS.

Next row: K1, M1, K4, M1, K2, M1, K4, M1, K1 (16 sts).

Purl 1 row.

Next row: K1, M1, K6, M1, K2, M1, K6, M1, K1 (20 sts).

Work 3 rows in SS.

Next row: K1, ssK, K4, K2tog, K2, ssK, K4, K2tog, K1 (16 sts).

Purl 1 row.

Cast off using the three-needle cast-off technique (see page 17).

Head

Using brown yarn and 4mm (UK 8, US 6) knitting needles, cast on 14 sts and purl 1 row.

Next row: K1, M1, K to last st, M1, K1 (16 sts).

Next row: P1, M1, P to last st, M1, P1 (18 sts).

Rep last 2 rows once more (22 sts).

Next row: K1, M1, K to last st, M1, K1 (24 sts).

Purl 1 row.

Rep last 2 rows once more (26 sts).

Next row: K12, M1, K2, M1, K12 (28 sts).

Next row: P13, M1, P2, M1, P13 (30 sts).

Next row: K14, M1, K2, M1, K14 (32 sts).

Next row: P15, M1, P2, M1, P15 (34 sts).

Next row: K16, M1, K2, M1, K16 (36 sts).

Next row: P17, M1, P2, M1, P17 (38 sts).

Work 8 rows in SS.

Next row: K1, ssK, K13, K2tog, K2, ssK, K13, K2tog, K1 (34 sts).

Purl 1 row.

Next row: K1, ssK, K11, K2tog, K2, ssK, K11, K2tog, K1 (30 sts).

Purl 1 row.

Next row: K1, ssK, K9, K2tog, K2, ssK, K9, K2tog, K1 (26 sts).

Next row: P1, P2tog, P7, P2togtbl, P2, P2tog, P7, P2togtbl, P1 (22 sts).

Next row: K1, ssK, K5, K2tog, K2, ssK, K5, K2tog, K1 (18 sts).

Cast off rem 18 sts using three-needle cast-off technique (see page 17).

Ears (make two)

Using brown yarn and 4mm (UK 8, US 6) knitting needles, cast on 7 sts and, starting with a knit row, work 6 rows in SS.

Next row: ssK, K to last 2 sts, K2tog (5 sts).

Purl 1 row.

Rep last 2 rows once more (3 sts).

Next row: Sl1, K2tog, psso (1 st).

Next row: Kfbf (3 sts).

Purl 1 row.

Next row: K1, M1, K to last st, M1, K1 (5 sts).

Purl 1 row.

Rep last 2 rows once more (7 sts).

Work 6 rows in SS.

Cast off.

Nose

Using black yarn and 2.75mm (UK 12, US 2) knitting needles, cast on 7 sts and, starting with a knit row, work 2 rows in SS.

Next row: K1, ssK, K1, K2tog, K1 (5 sts).

Purl 1 row.

Next row: ssK, K1, K2tog (3 sts).

Next row: Sl1, P2tog, psso (1 st).

Fasten off rem st, leaving a length of yarn long enough to embroider the mouth.

Tail

Using brown yarn and 4mm (UK 8, US 6) knitting needles, cast on 8 sts and, starting with a knit row, work 2 rows in SS.

Next row: K6, w&t.

Next row: P4, w&t.

Next row: K to end of row.

Purl 1 row.*

Rep from * to * once more.

Next row: ssK, K to last 2 sts, K2tog (6 sts).

Purl 1 row.

Rep last 2 rows once more (4 sts).

Thread yarn through rem sts and fasten.

Making up

Pin the side seams of the body pieces together with the cast-off edge at the bottom. Stuff with toy filling and sew up the seams.

To make up the head, place the cast-off edge at the back of the head, sew up the seam that will go underneath the head, stuffing with toy filling as you go. Sew the cast-on edges together up to the nose. To finish the head see page 17 for instructions on how to gather the nose. Using black sewing thread, sew the black shanked buttons in place as eyes, using the photograph as guidance. Run a thread from the back of one eye down to the base of the head and pull slightly to secure. Repeat for the second eye. This gives the eyes a much more realistic look.

With WS together, fold one ear in half and carefully sew the side seams. Repeat for the second ear. Pin the ears in place on the top of the head, then sew both in place, curving them slightly and using the photograph for guidance.

Sew the nose to the front of the face and embroider the mouth using the length of yarn left at the end of the nose and straight stitches.

Sew the head to the body matching the seam under the head with the centre of the body.

Fold one arm in half and sew the seam. Stuff with toy filling, then embroider claws on the paw using brown yarn and straight stitches, using the photograph for guidance. Repeat for the second arm. Pin the arms on to the side seams of the body and sew, placing the seam underneath the arm.

Sew the back seam of one leg, stuffing with toy filling. Repeat for the second leg and pin both legs in place on to the bottom seam of the body. Use the photograph for guidance when placing the legs.

Sew the seam of the tail (this will be at the top when it is sewn on to the body) and place a small amount of toy filling inside. Sew in place at the bottom of the body.

Antlers

Materials

- Small amount of dark brown 4-ply (fingering) yarn (used double)
- Small amount of red 4-ply (fingering) yarn
- Chenille stick

Needles

4mm (UK 8, US 6) and 2.75mm (UK 12, US 2) knitting needles

Long antler pieces (make two)

Using a double strand of dark brown yarn and 4mm (UK 8, US 6) knitting needles, cast on 6 sts and work in SS until work measures 6cm (2⅜in).
Cast off.

Short antler pieces (make four)

Using a double strand of dark brown yarn and 4mm (UK 8, US 6) knitting needles, cast on 6 sts and work in SS until work measures 2cm (¾in).
Cast off.

Headband

Using red yarn and 2.75mm (UK 12, US 2) knitting needles, cast on 10 sts and work in SS until work measures 10cm (4in).
Cast off.

Making up

To make one antler, sew the side seam of a long piece, sewing a stitch in from the edge and using mattress stitch (see page 14) to make the antler stand up better. Sew two small pieces in the same way and sew one to each side of the long piece using the photograph as guidance. Repeat for the second antler.

Fold the headband and sew the side seam, inserting a double length of chenille stick as you go. Finish sewing the seam. Sew each antler on to the headband placing them in the centre approximately 1cm (½in) apart, using the photograph for guidance.

Bend the headband slightly, so that it fits comfortably on the dog's head.

Christmas sweater

Materials

- 80m (87½yd) of royal blue 4-ply (fingering) yarn
- 10m (11yd) of brown 4-ply (fingering) yarn
- 3m (3¼yd) of dark brown 4-ply (fingering) yarn
- Small amount of red 4-ply (fingering) yarn
- Small amount of sparkly white 4-ply (fingering) yarn

Needles

3mm (UK 11, US 2/3) knitting needles

Tension

Approximately 7 sts measured over 2.5cm (1in) and worked in SS using 3mm (UK 11, US 2/3) knitting needles and 4-ply (fingering) yarn

Front

Using royal blue yarn and 3mm (UK 11, US 2/3) knitting needles, cast on 40 sts and work 4 rows in K2, P2 rib.

Starting with a knit row, continue in SS following the reindeer chart (top left on opposite page), using the Fair Isle technique (see page 14).

Continue following the chart and work the armholes as follows:

Cast off 2 sts at the beginning of the next two rows (36 sts).

Row 1: K1, ssK, K to last 3 sts, K2tog, K1 (34 sts).

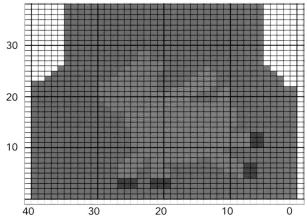

Chart for the Christmas sweater

Row 2: P1, P2tog, P to last 3 sts, P2togtbl, P1 (32 sts).
Rep row 1 once more (30 sts).*
Work 11 rows in SS.
Shape neckline as follows:
Next row: K11, cast off 8 sts, K10.
Working over the first set of 11 sts, P 1 row.
Next row: Cast off 2 sts at the beginning of the row (9 sts).
Purl 1 row.
Rep last 2 rows once more (7 sts).
Next row: K1, ssK, K4 (6 sts).
Purl 1 row.
Cast off.
With WS facing rejoin yarn to rem 11 sts.
Cast off 2 sts at the beginning of the row (9 sts).
Knit 1 row.
Rep last 2 rows once more (7 sts).
Purl 1 row.
Next row: K4, K2tog, K1 (6 sts).
Purl 1 row.
Cast off.

Back

Using royal blue yarn and 3mm (UK 11, US 2/3)
knitting needles, cast on 40 sts and work as for
front to the end of the armhole shaping (marked
with *).
Starting with a purl row, work 15 rows in SS.
Next row: K10, cast off 10 sts, K9.
Working over the first set of 10 sts, purl 1 row.
Next row: Cast off 4 sts, K5 (6 sts).
Purl 1 row.
Cast off. With WS facing, rejoin yarn to rem 10 sts.
Cast off 4 sts, P5 (6 sts).
Work 2 rows in SS.
Cast off.

Sleeves (make two)

Using royal blue yarn and 3mm (UK 11, US 2/3) knitting
needles, cast on 28 sts and work 4 rows in K2, P2 rib.
Starting with a knit row, work 2 rows in SS.
Next row: K1, M1, K to last st, M1, K1 (30 sts).
Work 3 rows in SS.
Rep last 4 rows once more (32 sts).
Work 2 rows in SS.
Cast off 2 sts at the beginning of the next 2 rows
(28 sts).
Next row: K1, ssK, K to last 3 sts, K2tog, K1 (26 sts).
Purl 1 row.
Rep last 2 rows once more (24 sts).
Cast off.

Making up

Join right shoulder seam. Using royal blue yarn and with
RS facing, pick up and knit 24 sts around the front neckline
and 20 sts around the back neck shaping (44 sts).

Work 4 rows in K2, P2 rib and cast off in rib. Join the
left shoulder seam. Sew the sleeves in place and sew the
side seams and underarm seams.

Embroider details on to the reindeer, using the
photograph below for guidance.

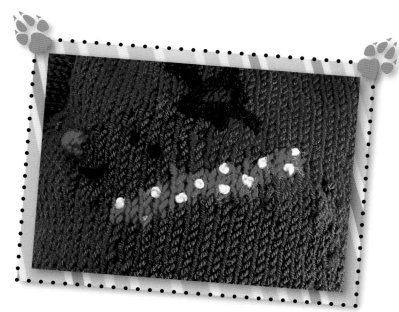

Danger Dog

Look! Up in the sky! Danger Dog is here! This tiny superhero is ready for action in his hat, cape and legwarmers. The lightning strike on his cape is knitted using the Fair Isle technique (see page 14).

Materials
57m (62⅜yd) of grey 5-ply (sportweight) yarn
Small amount of black 4-ply (fingering) yarn
Two 6mm (¼in) black beads
Toy filling
Black sewing cotton
Chenille sticks

Tools
3.25mm (UK 10, US 3) and 2.75mm (UK 12, US 2) knitting needles
Stitch markers

Tension
25 sts measured over 10cm (4in) and worked in SS using 3.25mm (UK 10, US 3) knitting needles and 5-ply (sportweight) yarn

Size
14cm (5½in) from nose to tail

Body and front legs
Start at the bottom edge of right foot.
Using grey yarn and 3.25mm (UK 10, US 3) knitting needles, cast on 10 sts.
*Next row: K5, turn.
Next row: P3, turn.
Next row: K3, turn.
Next row: P3, turn.
Next row: Knit to end of row.
Next row: P5, P3B, P2.*
Work 12 rows in SS.
Next row: Cast off 5 sts, K to end of row (5 sts).
Next row: Cast off 2 sts, P to end of row (3 sts).
Next row: K1, M1, K to end of row (4 sts).
Next row: Cast on 14 sts, P to last st, M1, P1 (19 sts).
Knit 1 row.

Next row: Cast on 2 sts and P to end of row (21 sts).
Work 27 rows in SS, placing a stitch marker at either end of row 13.
Next row: Cast off 2 sts, P to end of row (19 sts).
Knit 1 row.
Next row: Cast off 14 sts, P to last 3 sts, P2togtbl, P1 (4 sts).
Next row: K1, K2tog, K1 (3 sts).
Next row: Cast on 2 sts, P to end of row (5 sts).
Next row: Cast on 5 sts, K to end of row (10 sts).
Work 13 rows in SS.
Work from * to *.
Cast off.

Belly
Using grey yarn and 3.25mm (UK 10, US 3) knitting needles, cast on 5 sts. Starting with a knit row, work 4 rows in SS.
Next row: K1, M1, K3, M1, K1 (7 sts).
Work 5 rows in SS.
Next row: K1, M1, K5, M1, K1 (9 sts).
Work 15 rows in SS.
Next row: K1, ssK, K3, K2tog, K1 (7 sts).
Work 17 rows in SS.
Next row: K1, ssK, K1, K2tog, K1 (5 sts).
Work 5 rows in SS.
Cast off.

Back leg (right)
Using grey yarn and 3.25mm (UK 10, US 3) knitting needles, cast on 10 sts.
Next row: K5, turn.
Next row: P3, turn.
Next row: K3, turn.
Next row: P3, turn.
Next row: K to end of row.
Next row: P5, P3B, P2.
Work 12 rows in SS.

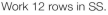

Next row: Cast off 5 sts, K to end of row (5 sts).

Next row: Cast off 1 st, P to end of row (4 sts).

**Next row: K1, M1, K to last st, M1, K1 (6 sts).

Next row: P1, M1, P to last st, M1, P1 (8 sts).

Rep last two rows once more (12 sts).

Work 6 rows in SS.

Next row: K1, ssK, K to last three sts, K2tog, K1 (10 sts).

Next row: P1, P2tog, P to last 3 sts, P2togtbl, P1 (8 sts).

Next row: K1, ssK, K to last three sts, K2tog, K1 (6 sts).

Cast off.**

Back leg (left)

Using grey yarn and 3.25mm (UK 10, US 3) knitting needles, cast on 10 sts.

Next row: K8, turn.

Next row: P3, turn.

Next row: K3, turn.

Next row: P3, turn.

Next row: K to end of row.

Next row: P2, P3B, P5.

Work 12 rows in SS.

Next row: Cast off 1 st, K to end of row (9 sts).

Next row: Cast off 5 sts, P to end of row (4 sts).

Work as for back leg (right) from ** to **.

Head

Using grey yarn and 3.25mm (UK 10, US 3) knitting needles, cast on 10 sts.

Next row: K1, M1, K to last st, M1, K1 (12 sts).

Next row: P1, M1, P to last st, M1, P1 (14 sts).

Rep last 2 rows once more (18 sts).

Next row: K1, M1, K to last st, M1, K1 (20 sts).

Purl 1 row.

Rep last 2 rows once more (22 sts).

Next row: K10, M1, K2, M1, K10 (24 sts).

Next row: P11, M1, P2, M1, P11 (26 sts).

Next row: K12, M1, K2, M1, K12 (28 sts).

Next row: P13, M1, P2, M1, P13 (30 sts).

Next row: K14, M1, K2, M1, K14 (32 sts).

Next row: P15, M1, P2, M1, P15 (34 sts).

Work 6 rows in SS.

Next row: K1, ssK, K11, K2tog, K2, ssK, K11, K2tog, K1 (30 sts).

Purl 1 row.

Next row: K1, ssK, K9, K2tog, K2, ssK, K9, K2tog, K1 (26 sts).

Purl 1 row.

Next row: K1, ssK, K7, K2tog, K2, ssK, K7, K2tog, K1 (22 sts).

Next row: P1, P2tog, P5, P2togtbl, P2, P2tog, P5, P2togtbl, P1 (18 sts).

Cast off using the three-needle cast-off technique (see page 17).

Nose

Using black yarn and 2.75mm (UK 12, US 2) knitting needles, cast on 3 sts.

Next row: (K1, M1) twice, K1 (5 sts).

Work 2 rows in SS.

Next row: P2tog, P1, P2tog (3 sts).

Next row: Sl1, K2tog, psso (1 st).

Thread yarn through rem st and fasten, leaving a length of yarn long enough to embroider the mouth.

Ears (make four)

Using grey yarn and 3.25mm (UK 10, US 3) knitting needles, cast on 6 sts and, starting with a knit row, work 4 rows in SS.

Next row: K2tog, K2, K2tog (4 sts).

Purl 1 row.

Next row: K2tog twice (2 sts).

Next row: P2tog (1 st).

Thread yarn through rem st and fasten.

Tail

Using grey yarn and 3.25mm (UK 10, US 3) knitting needles cast on 7 sts and, starting with a knit row, work 6 rows in SS.

Next row: K1, K2tog, K1, K2tog, K1 (5 sts).

Work 7 rows in SS.

Thread yarn through sts and fasten.

Making up

Starting with one of the front legs, thread a length of yarn through the bottom edge of the foot and gather to form the bottom of the foot. Sew the side seam and stuff with toy filling, placing a chenille stick inside the toy filling. Repeat for the second front leg.

Matching the middle of the cast-off edge of the belly to the stitch marker at the back of the body and the middle of the cast-on edge of the belly to the stitch marker at the front of the body, pin the belly in place. Stuff the body firmly with toy filling, sewing the side seams of the belly in place. Sew the cast-off edge of the top of each front leg to the belly, pushing the end of the chenille stick inside the body.

Sew each back leg in the same way as the front legs. Pin the top of the back leg to the body as shown in the photograph, stuff gently with toy filling and sew in place, sewing the cast-off edge of the top of the leg to the belly.

To make up the head, place the cast-off edge at the back of the head, sew the seam that will go underneath the head, stuffing with toy filling as you go. Sew the cast-on edges together up to the nose. To finish the head, gather the nose using the instructions on page 17.

Using black sewing thread, sew the black beads in place as eyes, using the photograph as guidance. Run a thread from the back of one eye down to the base of the head and pull slightly, secure. Repeat for the second eye. This gives the eyes a much more realistic look.

With WS together, sew two ear pieces together. Repeat for the second ear. Pin the ears in place, leaving a 2cm (¾in) gap between them and using the photograph as guidance. Sew them in place.

Sew the black nose to the front of the head using black yarn and embroider the mouth using the length of yarn left at the end of the nose and straight stitches.

Pin the head to the body, using the photograph as guidance and sew firmly in place. Sew the tail seam and insert a chenille stick. Place a small amount of toy filling in the base of the tail. Poke the end of the chenille stick into the body to secure it and sew the tail in place.

Danger Dog outfit

Materials

- 35m (38¼yd) of blue 5-ply (sportweight) yarn
- 15m (16½yd) of lime 5-ply (sportweight) yarn
- Small star button

Needles

3.25mm (UK 10, US 3) knitting needles

Cape

Using blue yarn and 3.25mm (UK 10, US 3) knitting needles, cast on 28 sts and work 4 rows in GS.

Continue working as follows and at the same time work the lightning flash chart over the centre 8 sts and the next 20 rows.

Next row: Knit all sts.

Next row: K3, P to last 3 sts, K3.

Next row: K2, ssK, K to last 4 sts, K2tog, K2 (26 sts).

Next row: K3, P to last 3 sts, K3.

Rep last two rows a further six times (14 sts).

Next row: K2, ssK, K to last 4 sts, K2tog, K2 (12 sts).

Next row: K3, P to last 3 sts, K3.

Next row: Cast on 6 sts, K9, ssK, K2, K2tog, K3 (16 sts).

Next row: Cast on 6 sts, K to end of row (22 sts).

Next row: K to last 4 sts, K2tog, yo, K2 (this forms a buttonhole).

Knit 1 row.

Cast off.

Leggings (make four)

Using blue yarn and 3.25mm (UK 10, US 3) knitting needles, cast on 12 sts and knit 1 row.

Starting with a knit row, work 8 rows in SS.

Purl 1 row.

Cast off.

Lightning points (make four)

Using lime yarn and 3.25mm (UK 10, US 3) knitting needles, cast on 4 sts.

*Work 2 rows in GS.

Next row: K2tog, K2 (3 sts).

Next row: K1, K2tog (2 sts).

Next row: K2tog (1 st).

Next row: K1.*

Cast on 3 sts at the beginning of the next row, K to end of row (4 sts).

Rep from * to * once more.

Cast off rem 1 st.

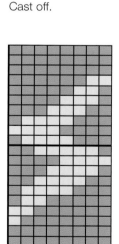

Chart for Danger Dog's cape

Hat (make two)

Using blue yarn and 3.25mm (UK 10, US 3) knitting needles, cast on 22 sts and, starting with a knit row, work 2 rows in SS.

Next row: K17, w&t.

Next row: P4, P2tog, P2togtbl, P4, w&t.

Next row: K3, ssK, K2tog, K2, w&t.

Next row: P1, P2tog, P2togtbl, P1, w&t.

Knit to end of row.

Knit 1 row.

Change to lime yarn.

Cast off loosely and evenly.

Sew the cast-on edges of the two hat pieces together, leaving two holes for ears to go through, 2cm (¾in) apart.

Using lime yarn and 3.25mm (UK 10, US 3) knitting needles and with RS facing, pick up and knit 8 sts along one side edge to make a chin strap.

Starting with a WS row, purl 1 row.

Next row: K1, ssK, K to last 3 sts, K2tog, K1 (6 sts).

Purl 1 row.

Rep last two rows once more (4 sts).

Work 6 rows in SS.

Thread yarn though sts and fasten.

Rep these instructions to make a chin strap on the other side of the hat.

Spikes (make three)

Using lime yarn and 3.25mm (UK 10, US 3) knitting needles, cast on 5 sts and knit 2 rows.

Next row: K2tog, K to end of row (4 sts).

Next row: K to last 2 sts, K2tog (3 sts).

Rep last two rows once more (1 st).

Thread yarn through rem st and fasten.

Making up

Sew all the ends in and lightly press the cape. Sew the star button on to the cape neckband on the opposite side to the buttonhole.

Sew the spikes to the centre top of the hat, using the photograph for guidance. Sew the two chinstrap ends together and place the hat on the head, pulling the ears through the holes.

Sew the side seam of the leggings; this seam will be at the back. Sew the three lightning points along the back seam of the leggings, using the photograph for guidance. Slide a legging on to each of Danger Dog's legs.

Best in Show

This scruffy little pup has won the judges' hearts with his appealing expression and scooped the Best in Show prize and a giant bone! Scruffy pup is knitted in a textured yarn, which makes him very cuddly.

Materials
- 80m (87½yd) of fluffy light brown 10-ply (aran) yarn
- Small amounts of red and black 4-ply (fingering) yarn
- Toy filling
- Two 10mm (⅜in) black shanked buttons
- Black sewing cotton
- Small piece of cardboard

Needles
4.5mm (UK 7, US 7) and 2.75mm (UK 12, US 2) knitting needles

Tension
15 sts measured over 10cm (4in) and worked in SS using 4.5mm (UK 7, US 7) knitting needles and 10-ply (aran) yarn

Size
21cm (8¼in) high when sitting (see opposite)

Note: All pieces of the dog, except for the ears, are knitted in SS. When sewing together, the WS is on the outside as this side is more fluffy.

Body and base
Using light brown yarn and 4.5mm (UK 7, US 7) knitting needles, cast on 20 sts and, starting with a knit row, work 2 rows in SS.
Next row: K1, M1, K8, M1, K2, M1, K8, M1, K1 (24 sts).
Purl 1 row.
Next row: K11, (Kfb) twice, K11 (26 sts).
Purl 1 row.
Next row: K12, (Kfb) twice, K12 (28 sts).
Purl 1 row.
Next row: K13, (Kfb) twice, K13 (30 sts).
Purl 1 row.

Next row: K14, (Kfb) twice, K14 (32 sts).
Purl 1 row.
Next row: K15, (Kfb) twice, K15 (34 sts).
Purl 1 row.
Next row: K16, (Kfb) twice, K16 (36 sts).
Work 9 rows in SS.
Cast off 14 sts at the beginning of the next 2 rows (8 sts).
Work 2 rows in SS.
Next row: K1, M1, K to last st, M1, K1 (10 sts).
Work 7 rows in SS.
Next row: K1, K2tog, K to last 3 sts, K2tog, K1 (8 sts).
Purl 1 row.
Rep last 2 rows once more (6 sts).
Cast off.

Front legs (make two)
Using light brown yarn and 4.5mm (UK 7, US 7) knitting needles, cast on 9 sts.
Next row: K6, turn.
Next row: P3, turn.
Next row: K3, turn.
Next row: P3, turn.
Next row: K to end of row.
Purl 1 row.
Work 14 rows in SS.
Cast off 1 st at the beg of the next 2 rows (7 sts).
Cast off 2 sts at the beg of the next 2 rows (3 sts).
Cast off.

Back legs (make two)
Using light brown yarn and 4.5mm (UK 7, US 7) knitting needles cast on 9 sts.
Next row: K6, turn.
Next row: P3, turn.
Next row: K3, turn.
Next row: P3, turn.
Next row: K to end of row.
Purl 1 row.
Work 8 rows in SS.
Cast off.

Head

Using light brown yarn and 4.5mm (UK 7, US 7) knitting needles, cast on 10 sts and purl 1 row.

Next row: K1, M1, K to last st, M1, K1 (12 sts).

Next row: P1, M1, P to last st, M1, P1 (14 sts).

Rep last 2 rows once more (18 sts).

Work 2 rows in SS.

Next row: K8, M1, K2, M1, K8 (20 sts).

Next row: P9, M1, P2, M1, P9 (22 sts).

Next row: K10, M1, K2, M1, K10 (24 sts).

Next row: P11, M1, P2, M1, P11 (26 sts).

Next row: K12, M1, K2, M1, K12 (28 sts).

Next row: P13, M1, P2, M1, P13 (30 sts).

Work 6 rows in SS.

Next row: K1, ssK, K9, K2tog, K2, ssK, K9, K2tog, K1 (26 sts).

Purl 1 row.

Next row: K1, ssK, K7, K2tog, K2, ssK, K7, K2tog, K1 (22 sts).

Next row: P1, P2tog, P5, P2togtbl, P2, P2tog, P5, P2togtbl, P1 (18 sts).

Next row: K1, ssK, K3, K2tog, K2, ssK, K3, K2tog, K1 (14 sts).

Cast off using the three-needle cast-off technique (see page 17).

Ears (make two)

Using light brown yarn and 4.5mm (UK 7, US 7) knitting needles, cast on 7 sts and work 8 rows in GS.

Next row: K1, ssK, K1, K2tog, K1 (5 sts).

Knit 1 row.

Next row: ssK, K1, K2tog (3 sts).

Next row: Sl1, K2tog, psso (1 st).

Fasten off rem st.

Nose

Using black yarn and 2.75mm (UK 12, US 2) knitting needles, cast on 6 sts and, starting with a knit row, work 4 rows in SS.

Next row: K2tog, K2, K2tog (4 sts).

Next row: (P2tog) twice (2 sts).

Next row: K2tog.

Thread yarn through rem st and fasten, leaving a length of yarn long enough to embroider the mouth.

Tail

Using light brown yarn and 4.5mm (UK 7, US 7) knitting needles, cast on 8 sts and, starting with a knit row, work 6 rows in SS.

Next row: K5, w&t.

Next row: P3, w&t.

Next row: K to end of row.

Purl 1 row.*

Rep from * to * once more.

Next row: K1, K2tog, K2, K2tog, K1 (6 sts).

Thread yarn through rem sts and fasten.

Rosette

Centre

Using red yarn and 2.75mm (UK 12, US 2) knitting needles, cast on 5 sts.

***Purl 1 row.

Next row: K1, M1, K to last st, M1, K1 (7 sts).

Purl 1 row.

Rep last 2 rows once more (9 sts).

Work 4 rows in SS.

Next row: K1, ssK, K to last 3 sts, K2tog, K1 (7 sts).

Purl 1 row.

Rep last 2 rows once more (5 sts).***

Purl 1 row. (On the RS, this creates a fold line).

Rep from ** to ** once more and then cast off rem 5 sts.

Frill

Using red yarn and 2.75mm (UK 12, US 2) knitting needles, cast on 7 sts.

Work the following 20 row pattern and rep 5 more times, then cast off.

Row 1: Knit.

Row 2: Purl.

Row 3: K4, w&t.

Row 4: Purl to end of row.

Row 5: K5, w&t.

Row 6: Purl to end of row.

Row 7: K4, w&t.

Row 8: Purl to end of row.

Row 9: Knit.

Row 10: Purl.

Row 11: Purl.

Row 12: Knit.

Row 13: P4, w&t.

Row 14: Knit to end of row.

Row 15: P5, w&t.

Row 16: Knit to end of row.

Row 17: P4, w&t.

Row 18: Knit to end of row.

Row 19: Purl.

Row 20: Knit.

Ribbons (make two)

Using red yarn and 2.75mm (UK 12, US 2) knitting needles, cast on 2 sts and knit 1 row.

Next row: K1, M1, K to end of row (3 sts).

Next row: Knit.

Rep last 2 rows until there are 7 sts.

Continue working in GS until work measures 5cm (2in). Cast off.

Making up

All pieces of this dog are sewn together with the WS on the outside.

With the WS on the outside, sew up the seam of the body. This will be at the front of the dog. The cast-on edge is at the top. Stuff with toy filling. Fold the base up and pin in place. Sew the base to the body.

With the head shaping forming the top of the head and the cast-off edge forming the back of the head, sew the seam along the bottom of the head and up the front, stuffing it with toy filling as you go.

Next, sew the black-shanked buttons in place as eyes using black sewing cotton. Run the thread from the back of the first eye down to the base of the head and pull slightly, before securing it in place and repeating the process for the second eye. This gives the eyes a more realistic look.

Pin the ears in place on the top of the head and then sew them in place. Use black yarn to sew the nose to the front of the head; then, using the length of yarn left at the end of the nose, embroider the mouth using straight stitches. Sew the head to the body using the photographs for guidance on placement.

Sew up the back seam of one front leg and then stuff with toy filling. Repeat for the second leg and pin the legs in place at the front of the body so that the feet touch the floor. Sew up the back seam of the back leg and sew across the cast-off edge, ensuring the back seam is in the middle of the top seam. Repeat for the second back leg. Using the photograph for guidance, pin the legs in place just underneath the body towards the back before sewing them in place.

Sew up the side seam of the tail and sew it to the back of the body, placing the seam on top.

Cut a small circle of card to go in the centre of the rosette. Fold the centre of the rosette in half over the card and sew around the edge. Sew the cast-on and cast-off edges of the frill carefully together and pin in place around the centre. Sew the frill to the centre piece. Sew the cast-on and cast-off edges of the frill carefully together and pin in place around the centre. Sew the frill to the centre piece. Fold one ribbon in half along the top edge and sew it to the bottom edge of the centre behind the frill. Repeat for the second ribbon, using the photograph as guidance. Using black yarn, embroider the number 1 on the front of the rosette using straight stitch.

Sweetheart

Sweetheart just wants to be loved. He can be knitted up quickly in garter stitch (just knit), which makes him a great project for new knitters wanting to learn some additional skills. He is only tiny, so he will make a great keyring or bag charm.

Materials
- 35m (38¼yd) of biscuit 10-ply (aran) yarn
- Small amount of dark brown 4-ply (fingering) yarn
- Toy filling
- Two 6mm (¼in) black beads
- Black sewing thread
- Small heart-shaped button
- Keyring clasp (optional)

Needles
- 4mm (UK 8, US 6) and 2.75mm (UK 12, US 2) knitting needles

Tension
- Approximately 16 sts measured over 10cm (4in) and worked in GS using 4mm (UK 8, US 6) knitting needles and 10-ply (aran) yarn

Size
- 9cm (3½in) when sitting (see opposite)

Body
Worked sideways in GS.
Using biscuit yarn and 4mm (UK 8, US 6) knitting needles, cast on 10 sts and knit 6 rows (GS).
Next row: K6, w&t.
Next row: Knit to end of row.
Work 6 rows in GS.
Next row: K7, w&t.
Next row: K5, w&t.
Next row: K6, w&t.
Next row: K6, w&t.
Next row: K5, w&t.
Next row: Knit to end of row.
Work 6 rows in GS.
Next row: K5, w&t.
Next row: Knit to end of row.
Work 6 rows in GS.
Cast off.

Base
Using biscuit yarn and 4mm (UK 8, US 6) knitting needles, cast on 6 sts and knit 8 rows (GS).
Next row: K1, (K2tog) twice, K1 (4 sts).
Knit 1 row.
Cast off.
Thread yarn through rem sts and fasten.

Head

Using biscuit yarn and 4mm (UK 8, US 6) knitting needles, cast on 14 sts and knit 8 rows (GS).

Next row: K5, (Kfb) four times, K5 (18 sts).

Knit 1 row.

Next row: K5, (Kfb) eight times, K5 (26 sts).

Knit 5 rows.

Next row: K5, (K2tog) eight times, K5 (18 sts).

Knit 1 row.

Next row: K5, (K2tog) four times, K5 (14 sts).

Knit 1 row.

Cast off.

Legs (make two)

Using biscuit yarn and 4mm (UK 8, US 6) knitting needles, cast on 7 sts and knit 8 rows (GS).

Next row: K3, M1, K1, M1, K3 (9 sts).

Next row: K4, M1, K1, M1, K4 (11 sts).

Next row: K5, M1, K1, M1, K5 (13 sts).

Next row: K6, M1, K1, M1, K6 (15 sts).

Knit 2 rows.

Cast off.

Arms (make two)

Using biscuit yarn and 4mm (UK 8, US 6) knitting needles cast on 6 sts and knit 8 rows (GS).

Next row: K1, M1, K to last st, M1, K1 (8 sts).

Knit 3 rows.

Next row: (K2tog) four times (4 sts).

Thread yarn through rem sts and fasten.

Ears (make two)

Using biscuit yarn and 4mm (UK 8, US 6) knitting needles, cast on 4 sts and knit 12 rows (GS).

Next row: K1, K2tog, K1 (3 sts).

Cast off.

Tail

Using biscuit yarn and 4mm (UK 8, US 6) knitting needles, cast on 5 sts and knit 6 rows (GS).

Thread yarn through sts and fasten.

Nose

Worked in SS.

Using dark brown yarn and 2.75mm (UK 12, US 2) knitting needles, cast on 5 sts and purl 1 row.

Next row: K1, M1, K3, M1, K1 (7 sts).

Work 2 rows in SS.

Next row: P1, P2tog, P1, P2togtbl, P1 (5 sts).

Next row: ssK, K1, K2tog (3 sts).

Cast off.

Making up

Sew the cast-on and cast-off edges of the body together. This forms the back seam. Stuff the body gently with toy filling and sew the base in place with the cast-on edge at the front.

Run a length of yarn through the cast-on edge of the head and gather to form the front of the face. Sew halfway along the seam at the bottom of the head from front to back. When you are halfway, gather the remaining sts to make the back of the head rounder.

Pin the ears to the top of the head and sew them in place. Pin the nose to the front of the head using the photograph for guidance and sew it in place.

Use black sewing cotton and a sewing needle to sew the black beads in place for eyes at the start of the head shaping.

Pin the head on to the body, matching the back seam of the head to the back seam of the body. Sew in place, using the photograph for guidance.

Sew up the back seam of the first leg, stuffing it gently with toy filling as you go. Sew the seam along the base of the foot. Repeat for the second leg, then pin them both in place, using the photograph for guidance, before sewing them in place.

Sew up the seam of the arm, stuffing gently with toy filling as you go. Repeat for the second arm, then pin them both in place, using the photograph for guidance, and placing the seam towards the bottom. Sew the arms in place.

Fold the tail in half lengthways and sew it together. Sew it in place at the back of the dog using the photograph for guidance.

Sew the heart-shaped button to the front of the dog using biscuit yarn to finish.

You might like to use biscuit yarn to sew a keyring clasp to the back of the dog, just below the head, as shown below.

Labrador

You might like to give this little labrador away as a gift – he is bound to be loved wherever he goes. Of course, if you can't bear to be parted from this chubby, cuddly chap, keep him for yourself! A big bow made from ribbon sets him off nicely.

Materials
115m (126yd) of mustard 10-ply (aran) yarn
Small amount of black 4-ply (fingering) yarn
Two 8mm (⅜in) black shanked buttons
Toy filling
Black sewing thread
Red ribbon, 60cm (23½in)

Needles
4mm (UK 8, US 6) and 2.75mm (UK 12, US 2) knitting needles

Tension
4–5 sts measured over 2.5cm (1in) and worked in SS using 4mm (UK 8, US 6) knitting needles and 10-ply (aran) yarn

Size
21cm (8¼in) from nose to tail, and 18cm (7in) from top of head to bottom of feet

Body
Using mustard yarn and 4mm (UK 8, US 6) knitting needles, cast on 14 sts and purl 1 row.
Next row: K1, (Kfb, K1, Kfb) to last st, K1.
Next row: Purl 1 row (22 sts).
Next row: K1, (Kfb, K3, Kfb) to last st, K1.
Next row: Purl 1 row (30 sts).
Next row: K1, (Kfb, K5, Kfb) to last st, K1.
Next row: Purl 1 row (38 sts).
Next row: K1, (Kfb, K7, Kfb) to last st, K1.
Next row: Purl 1 row (46 sts).
Work 26 rows in SS.
Next row: K1, ssK, K17, K2tog, K2, ssK, K17, K2tog, K1 (42 sts).
Purl 1 row.

Next row: K1, ssK, K15, K2tog, K2, ssK, K15, K2tog, K1 (38 sts).
Next row: P1, P2tog, P13, P2togtbl, P2, P2tog, P13, P2togtbl, P1 (34 sts).
Next row: K1, ssK, K11, K2tog, K2, ssK, K11, K2tog, K1 (30 sts).
Next row: P1, P2tog, P9, P2togtbl, P2, P2tog, P9, P2togtbl, P1 (26 sts).
Next row: K1, ssK, K7, K2tog, K2, ssK, K7, K2tog, K1 (22 sts).
Cast off using three-needle cast-off technique (see page 17).

Head
Using mustard yarn and 4mm (UK 8, US 6) knitting needles, cast on 14 sts and purl 1 row.
Next row: K1, M1, K to last st, M1, K1 (16 sts).
Next row: P1, M1, P to last st, M1, P1 (18 sts).
Rep last 2 rows twice more (26 sts).
Next row: K1, M1, K to last st, M1, K1 (28 sts).
Purl 1 row.
Next row: K13, M1, K2, M1, K13 (30 sts).
Next row: P14, M1, P2, M1, P14 (32 sts).
Next row: K15, M1, K2, M1, K15 (34 sts).
Next row: P16, M1, P2, M1, P16 (36 sts).
Next row: K17, M1, K2, M1, K17 (38 sts).
Next row: P18, M1, P2, M1, P18 (40 sts).
Next row: K19, M1, K2, M1, K19 (42 sts).
Work 7 rows in SS.
Next row: K1, ssK, K15, K2tog, K2, ssK, K15, K2tog, K1 (38 sts).
Purl 1 row.
Next row: K1, ssK, K13, K2tog, K2, ssK, K13, K2tog, K1 (34 sts).
Next row: P1, P2tog, P11, P2togtbl, P2, P2tog, P11, P2togtbl, P1 (30 sts).

Next row: K1, ssK, K9, K2tog, K2, ssK, K9, K2tog, K1 (26 sts).

Next row: P1, P2tog, P7, P2togtbl, P2, P2tog, P7, P2togtbl, P1 (22 sts).

Next row: K1, ssK, K5, K2tog, K2, ssK, K5, K2tog, K1 (18 sts).

Cast off using the three-needle cast-off technique (see page 17).

Left legs (make two)

Using mustard yarn and 4mm (UK 8, US 6) knitting needles, cast on 6 sts and purl 1 row.

Continuing in SS, cast on 2 sts at the beginning of the next 4 rows (14 sts).

Work 2 rows in SS.

Next row: K1, M1, K to last st, M1, K1 (16 sts).

Work 5 rows in SS.

Next row: K2, (Kfb) five times, K9 (21 sts).

Work 4 rows in SS.

Next row: P9, (P2tog) five times, P2 (16 sts).

Next row: (K2tog) eight times (8 sts).

Purl 1 row.

Next row: (K2tog) four times (4 sts).

Thread yarn through remaining sts and fasten.

Right legs (make two)

Using mustard yarn and 4mm (UK 8, US 6) knitting needles, cast on 6 sts and purl 1 row.

Continuing in SS, cast on 2 sts at the beginning of the next 4 rows (14 sts).

Work 2 rows in SS.

Next row: K1, M1, K to last st, M1, K1 (16 sts).

Work 5 rows in SS.

Next row: K9, (Kfb) five times, K2 (21 sts).

Work 4 rows in SS.

Next row: P2, (P2tog) five times, P9 (16 sts).

Next row: (K2tog) eight times (8 sts).

Purl 1 row.

Next row: (K2tog) four times (4 sts).

Thread yarn through remaining sts and fasten.

Nose

Using black yarn and 2.75mm (UK 12, US 2) knitting needles, cast on 7 sts and, starting with a knit row, work 5 rows in SS.

Next row: P2tog, P to last 2 sts, P2tog (5 sts).

Next row: K2tog, K1, K2tog (3 sts).

Next row: Sl1, P2tog, psso (1 st).

Fasten off rem st, leaving a length of yarn long enough to embroider the mouth.

Ears (make four)

Using mustard yarn and 4mm (UK 8, US 6) knitting needles, cast on 8 sts and, starting with a knit row, work 6 rows in SS.

Next row: K1, M1, K to last st, M1, K1 (10 sts).

Work 5 rows in SS.

Next row: K1, M1, K to last st, M1, K1 (12 sts).

Work 3 rows in SS.

Next row: K1, ssK, K to last 3 sts, K2tog, K1 (10 sts).

Next row: P1, P2tog, P to last 3 sts, P2togtbl, P1 (8 sts).

Cast off.

Tail

Using mustard yarn and 4mm (UK 8, US 6) knitting needles, cast on 12 sts and, starting with a knit row, work 8 rows in SS.

Next row: K1, ssK, K to last 3 sts, K2tog, K1 (10 sts).

Purl 1 row.

Rep last 2 rows three more times (4 sts).

Thread yarn through rem sts and fasten, leaving a length of yarn long enough to sew the side seam of the tail.

Making up

Starting at the cast-off end of the body, sew the seam and stuff with toy filling. Gather the cast-on edge and fasten. Sew the head together in the same way, up to the nose. To finish the head, gather the nose following the instructions on page 17.

Place two ear pieces with WS together and sew around the edges to make one ear. Repeat for the second ear. Pin the ears in place on either side of the centre four stitches on the top of the head. Sew in place.

Using black sewing thread, sew black-shanked buttons in place as eyes and run a length of yarn from the back of each eye to the bottom of the head, pulling the yarn and securing. This gives the face a realistic look. Sew the nose in place using black yarn and embroider the mouth using

straight stitches and the length of yarn left at the end of the nose. Place the head at the cast-off end of the body, using the photograph for guidance, and sew in place.

Gather the yarn at the bottom of the foot and sew the base of one foot and the side seam of the leg. Stuff with toy filling, then repeat for other three legs. Pin the legs in place on the body, using the photograph as guidance. The legs are shaped to fit on the curved sides of the body so take care to make sure they are on the correct side.

Sew the side seam of the tail. Stuff with toy filling. Pin the tail in place with the seam facing towards the top of the dog, then sew it in place.

Tie a ribbon into a bow around the dog's neck.

Cuddle Pup

Cuddle Pup is super-easy to knit and makes great use of the variegated yarn available. He has his arms out for a cuddle and would be a great project for a new knitter – just remember to give him his quirky embroidered smile for the perfect finishing touch.

Materials
- 140m (153yd) of variegated 12-ply (chunky) yarn
- Small amount of brown 10-ply (aran) yarn
- Small amount of black 4-ply (fingering) yarn
- Toy filling
- Two 8mm (⅜in) black shanked buttons
- Black sewing thread

Needles
- 2.75mm (UK 12, US 2) knitting needles
- 4.5mm (UK 7, US 7) knitting needles
- 5.5mm (UK 5, US 9) knitting needles

Tension
13 sts measured over 10cm (4in) and worked in SS using 5.5mm (UK 5, US 9) knitting needles and 12-ply (chunky) yarn

Size
24cm (9½in) from top of head to bottom

Body (make two)
Using variegated yarn and 5.5mm (UK 5, US 9) knitting needles, cast on 26 sts and, starting with a knit row, work 2 rows in SS.

Next row: K1, M1, K to last st, M1, K1 (28 sts).

Purl 1 row.

Rep last 2 rows twice more (32 sts).

Work 22 rows in SS.

Next row: K1, ssK, K to last 3 sts, K2tog, K1 (30 sts).

Work 3 rows in SS.

Rep last 4 rows twice more (26 sts).

Next row: K1, ssK, K to last 3 sts, K2tog, K1 (24 sts).

Purl 1 row.

Rep last 2 rows three times more (18 sts).

Next row: K1, ssK, K to last 3 sts, K2tog, K1 (16 sts).

Next row: P1, P2tog, P to last 3 sts, P2togtbl, P1 (14 sts).

Next row: K1, ssK, K to last 3 sts, K2tog, K1 (12 sts).

Cast off.

Base
Using variegated yarn and 5.5mm (UK 5, US 9) knitting needles, cast on 10 sts and purl 1 row.

Next row: K1, M1, K to last st, M1, K1 (12 sts).

Next row: P1, M1, P to last st, M1, P1 (14 sts).

Rep last 2 rows twice more (22 sts).

Work 4 rows in SS.

Next row: K1, ssK, K to last 3 sts, K2tog, K1 (20 sts).

Next row: P1, P2tog, P to last 3 sts, P2togtbl, P1 (18 sts).

Rep last 2 rows twice more (10 sts).

Knit 1 row.

Cast off.

Snout

Using variegated yarn and 5.5mm (UK 5, US 9) knitting needles, cast on 20 sts and purl 1 row.

Next row: K1, ssK, K to last 3 sts, K2tog, K1 (18 sts).

Next row: P1, P2tog, P to last 3 sts, P2togtbl, P1 (16 sts).

Rep last 2 rows once more (12 sts).

Rep first row once more (10 sts).

Cast off.

Ears (make two)

Using variegated yarn and 5.5mm (UK 5, US 9) knitting needles, cast on 8 sts and, starting with a knit row, work 4 rows in SS.

Next row: K1, M1, K to last st, M1, K1 (10 sts).

Work 9 rows in SS.

Next row: K1, ssK, K to last 3 sts, K2tog, K1 (8 sts).

Next row: P1, P2tog, P to last 3 sts, P2togtbl, P1 (6 sts).

Cast off.

Ear linings (make two)

Using brown yarn and 4.5mm (UK 7, US 7) knitting needles, cast on 8 sts and, starting with a knit row, work 6 rows in SS.

Next row: K1, M1, K to last st, M1, K1 (10 sts).

Work 7 rows in SS.

Next row: K1, ssK, K to last 3 sts, K2tog, K1 (8 sts).

Purl 1 row.

Rep last 2 rows once more (6 sts).

Cast off.

Nose

Using black yarn and 2.75mm (UK 12, US 2) knitting needles, cast on 3 sts and purl 1 row.

Next row: K1, M1, K to last st, M1, K1 (5 sts).

Purl 1 row.

Rep last 2 rows once more (7 sts).

Work 2 rows in SS.

Next row: K1, ssK, K1, K2tog, K1 (5 sts).

Cast off.

Arms (make two)

Using variegated yarn and 5.5mm (UK 5, US 9) knitting needles, cast on 14 sts and, starting with a knit row, work 12 rows in SS.

Next row: K1, ssK, K1, K2tog, K2, ssK, K1, K2tog, K1 (10 sts).

Purl 1 row.

Cast off.

Feet (make two)

Using variegated yarn and 5.5mm (UK 5, US 9) knitting needles, cast on 16 sts and, starting with a knit row, work 6 rows in SS.

Next row: K1, ssK, K2, K2tog, K2, ssK, K2, K2tog, K1 (12 sts).

Purl 1 row.

Cast off.

Tail

Using variegated yarn and 5.5mm (UK 5, US 9) knitting needles, cast on 10 sts and, starting with a knit row, work 10 rows in SS.

Next row: (K2tog) five times (5 sts).

Thread yarn through rem sts and fasten.

Making up

Sew the body pieces together and stuff them gently with toy filling. The cast-on edges are at the bottom. Pin and sew the base in place. Fold the cast-off edge of the snout in half and sew the cast-off stitches together. Sew up the shaped seam, then pin it in place on the body with the seam underneath, using the photograph for guidance. Stuff gently with toy filling and sew in place.

Fold the arm in half and sew up the side seam. Stuff gently with toy filling and sew the cast-on edges together. Repeat for the second arm. Pin the arms in place on the body at a slight angle and sew in place using the photograph for guidance and placing the seams towards the bottom.

Fold the foot in half and sew up the side seam. Stuff gently with toy filling and sew the cast-on edges together. Repeat for the second foot. Pin the feet in place along the bottom seam of the body and base, then sew them in place.

Fold the tail in half and sew up the side seam. Stuff it with a small amount of toy filling. Sew the tail in place approximately 3cm (1¼in) up from the bottom of the back.

With WS together, pin and sew the ear lining to the ear, then repeat for the second ear. Pin the ears in place at a slight angle at the top of the head using the photograph as guidance, then sew them in place.

Sew the nose to the front of the snout with the cast-off edge at the top and embroider the mouth using straight stitches and black yarn, using the photograph for guidance. Using black sewing cotton, sew the black shanked buttons in place for the eyes above the snout, approximately four stitches apart as shown opposite.

Abbreviations

beg	beginning
CC	contrast colour
cm	centimetre(s)
C4F	slip the next two stitches on to a cable needle and hold at the front of the work. Knit the following two stitches and then knit the two stitches from the cable needle
DK	double knitting (8-ply) yarn
foll	following
GS	garter stitch
in	inch(es)
inc	increase
K	knit
K2tog	knit 2 stitches together
K2togtbl	knit 2 stitches together through back loop
K3B	pass next stitch to RH needle, pick up stitch 3 rows below and knit together with this stitch. Repeat for next two stitches. This creates a 'fold' in the knitting
Kfb	knit into front and back of stitch (increasing one stitch)
Kfbf	knit into the front, back and front of the stitch (increasing two stitches)
M	marker
MC	main colour
mm	millimetre(s)
M1	make a backwards loop on your needle by twisting the yarn towards you and slipping the resulting loop on to the right-hand needle. On the following row, knit or purl through the back of the stitch

P	purl
P2tog	purl 2 stitches together
P2togtbl	purl 2 stitches together through back loop
P3B	pass next stitch to RH needle, pick up stitch 3 rows below and purl together with this stitch. Repeat for next two stitches
PM	place marker
psso	pass slipped stitch over
rem	remaining
rep	repeat
rev	reverse
RH	right hand
RS	right side(s)
sl	slip a stitch
SM	slip marker from left to right needle
SS	stocking stitch
ssK	slip 2 stitches knitwise one at a time, pass the 2 slipped stitches back to the left needle, knit both together through the back of the loop
ssP	slip 2 stitches knitwise one at a time, pass the two slipped sts back to the left needle, purl 2 slipped stitches together from the back, left to right
st(s)	stitch(es)
tbl	through the back of the loop
tog	together
w&t	wrap and turn (see techniques, page 14)
WS	wrong side(s)
yo	yarn over needle